American Lives | Series editor: Tobias Wolff

American Lives

A Reader

EDITED BY ALICIA CHRISTENSEN

INTRODUCTION BY TOBIAS WOLFF

University of Nebraska Press | *Lincoln & London*

© 2010 by the Board of Regents of the University of
Nebraska. Introduction © 2010 by Tobias Wolff. Acknowl-
edgments for the use of copyrighted material appear on
pages 301–2, which constitute an extension of the
copyright page. All rights reserved. Manufactured in the
United States of America. ∞

Library of Congress Cataloging-in-Publication Data

American lives : a reader / edited by Alicia Christensen;
introduction by Tobias Wolff. p. cm. — (American
lives series)
ISBN 978-0-8032-2805-4 (pbk. : alk. paper)
1. Autobiographies—United States. 2. United States—
Biography. I. Christensen, Alicia, 1978–
CT211.A478 2010   920.02—dc22   2009030480

Set in Minion by Bob Reitz. Designed by A. Shahan.

CONTENTS

ALICIA CHRISTENSEN

Preface

It was my great fortune to work as Ladette Randolph's assistant when I first joined the University of Nebraska Press. Not only was I able to learn from this talented and highly regarded editor who conceptualized and developed the press's American Lives Series, it was part of my job to read memoirs such as those excerpted here. Though I have moved on from my assistant position and Ladette has moved across the country, I still await the newest addition to the series with eager anticipation. Each volume supplies a lovely reminder of what all good books should do: influence the reader to consider the world in a new way.

Though the life stories and perspectives presented herein are remarkably varied, familiar human emotions run through them all. Fan Shen, Peggy Shumaker, Laurie Alberts, and Charles Barber must all come to grips with unexpected deaths. Shen, just a youth when Chairman Mao officially launched the Cultural Revolution, describes in "Long Live the Red Terror!" how his thrill at the pageantry and excitement of the new movement quickly turned to sickened fear as the more sinister aspects of the revolution emerged. In "Moving Water, Tucson," Shumaker relives an exhilarating and horrible flash flood from her childhood. Alberts, haunted by the death of her ex-boyfriend, attempts to understand the destructive life he lived with and without her in "Winter 1997." "The Weight of Spoons" is Barber's account of how, after his friend's suicide, he found solace in contemplating small, tangible objects, such as an eggshell, and in performing everyday actions, one of which involves the purchase of a purple shirt.

For John Skoyles's uncle, a particular piece of clothing—a "Hard Luck Suit"—imparts misfortune. After purchasing it, he loses at the track, and the offending suit is immediately incinerated. Skoyles is in awe of his street-wise uncle in much the same way Brenda Serotte is filled with wonder and admiration for her Turkish grandmother. "Fortuna" describes Nona, a cook, medicine woman, healer, and fortune-teller who makes her living reading palms, interpreting cups, and prescribing poultices for the community. Marvin Arnett's father requires no mystical powers to foresee the consequences of the actions of the "Boys of Summer," who hawk a rainbow of sweaters around the Detroit neighborhood where Arnett grew up, and though the seasons contrast, Ted Kooser peppers his lyrical ruminations on the cold months in Nebraska with episodes from his own childhood in "Winter."

Dinty Moore, Eli Hastings, Dinah Lenney, and Natalia Singer all spend considerable time contemplating father-child relationships. In "Son of Mr. Green Jeans," Moore considers the concept of fatherhood in an entirely unexpected way: he delineates and links his personal attitudes and anxieties about fatherhood with TV dads, the position of the father in pop culture, the various roles fathers play in the animal kingdom, and his relationship with his own father. Hastings, who also presents the good and the bad of fatherhood, focuses on his relationship with his dad in eight vignettes in "Good, Alright, Fine." Lenney receives earth-shattering news about her missing father in "Acting," while Singer juxtaposes the shocking *Challenger* and Chernobyl explosions with unsettling, but not unexpected, news about her dad.

Mothers and motherhood are the focus of the excerpts by Aaron Raz Link and Hilda Raz, Janet Sternburg, Mary Felstiner, and Jonathan Johnson. Link and Raz write about their discomfort and confusion with neat and precise labels for human identity.

"Not Coming Out" details the problems of our societal reliance on clear-cut definitions for complicated individuals. Sternburg's *Phantom Limb* illustrates the challenges of providing for an elderly mother. In this excerpt she muses on the number of details one must handle as a child caring for a parent and evokes the stark frustration and fear felt by a multitude of grown children who have been placed in such situations. Felstiner and her husband contemplate the consequences of expanding their family in "Alternatives, 1979" as Felstiner's rheumatoid arthritis goes into remission for a brief period, while Johnson and his wife endure an emotionally harrowing event described in an excerpt from "The Second Trimester." "A Measure of Acceptance" details the barrage of mental and physical tests that Floyd Skloot must undergo to prove to his insurance company that his illness is not faked and that he is still in need of disability payments.

In "The New Kitchen," Mimi Schwartz discovers that remodeling projects are a common undertaking among long-married couples and muses on the desire for the bright, shiny, and new. Marriage is also the center of Lee Martin's "One I Love, Two I Love." Martin intersperses the story of how he wooed his wife with the tale of his own great-grandparents' courtship. Like Lee, Sonya Huber reconstructs her family history and speculates on the difficult position in which her grandfather found himself following the German revolution of 1918. "The Promise of Power" draws a connection between Huber and her grandfather, who both make momentous decisions that ultimately disappoint their parents.

Ultimately, the excerpts presented here vary greatly in subject and style—and that is just what one would expect from a series that portrays American lives. This series has been and continues to be a gigantic umbrella for the diverse and tremendously talented American writers whose stories deserve to be told. Far from the slew of scandalous tell-alls and ghost-written celebrity memoirs published over the past few decades, this exemplary series brings together beautiful and compelling personal stories by authors who are as meticulous and thoughtful about their craft as they are in their introspection.

TOBIAS WOLFF

Introduction

Several years ago, in his *Harper's* essay "Autobiography in the Age of Narcissism," William H. Gass came to this judgment: "He who writes his autobiography is already a monster." I admit I laughed out loud when I struck this line, partly no doubt from discomfort—I had recently finished the second (and last, I promise!) of my own memoirs—but mostly at its bald, unsparing wit. I was even willing to acknowledge a certain amount of truth in Gass's proposition, knowing that in order to write about my own life I had necessarily exposed the lives of others to public view and told their stories as well as my own, mostly without their permission. Of course I'd devised excuses for these breaches of privacy. Had I not examined my own deeds and character with at least as stern a gaze as I turned on others? Was I to be held hostage by the squeamishness of those unwilling to have their pictures taken, and put on exhibit? Finally (I knew this response was unfair even as it came to me), if they didn't like the way I wrote about them, about the way our lives intersected, why didn't they write their own damned memoirs?

But this wasn't really Gass's complaint, this question of privacy. His problem with the memoir is that, in his view, it cannot by its nature be done honestly—that in writing about ourselves we inevitably prettify our self-portraits at the expense of truth. He disparages autobiography as a bastard branch of history, pretending to history's authenticity but without its neutral, impersonal, objective view of the past.

And here he lost me, and loses me still, because his vision of

xi

the discipline of history is either risibly naïve or deliberately en-
nobled for the sake of argument, which would make him even
worse than the monstrous autobiographer, who at least, by Gass's
account, is helpless in his misrepresentations. The historian, as
much as the memoirist, is subject to preconceptions, bigotries,
professional resentments and ambitions, predispositions and
blindnesses of which he can be only partly aware. Objectivity
is an ideal that the historian must by honor pursue, and must
by nature fail to achieve. Why else would we have such different
accounts of, say, the causes of World War I, given that historians
are working from essentially the same archival resources? The
Marxist historian sees things through the Marxist lens, already
screwed deeply into his eye socket before he's read the first dis-
patch from Sarajevo. History is not simply a recitation of facts, it
is an ordering of facts to produce a narrative; and facts, being in-
finite, are infinitely susceptible to manipulation. Every historian
is hostage to the distortions and limitations of subjectivity—the
vantage point of all human vision.

Indeed, it seems to me that autobiography strikes at least as
fair a bargain with its reader as history, precisely because it ac-
knowledges its subjectivity. And we allow for that—we are always
aware, in reading a memoir, that we are getting just one side of
a complicated story, a certainly partial, perhaps self-serving account, and possibly one that is not true at all. Of course we can
sometimes be fooled by novels masquerading as memoirs, as
we can be fooled by novels masquerading as histories. There is
really no way to tell, in the absence of incontrovertible evidence,
if a memoirist is lying to you, but part of the pleasure of reading
this form is in measuring the tale against your judgment of the
teller, gradually taking shape as you make your way through the
narrative. Even before their serial falsities were exposed, I grew
very skeptical of Lillian Hellman's autobiographies because of
their relentlessly self-promoting nature and tone. She was always

the principled person in the room, the smart one, the brave one, the one who kept her head when all those around her were losing theirs. I accept that heroic people exist—I have known a few. But they have this in common: they do not see themselves as heroic. They do what they do because they think it is right, and wouldn't dream of boasting about *not* having done something that was wrong.

In short, it is as hard for us to see ourselves clearly as it is for the historian to see the past clearly. But I have to say that the memoirs I admire show little evidence of any impulse toward self-flattery. Rather the opposite. I have noticed a tendency toward diffidence and even a certain embarrassment in the self-representations of memoirists, in some cases rising (or sinking) to the level of mockery and condemnation. This too can be a form of untruth, even, paradoxically, of self-inflation: see what a good person I am, to show how bad I used to be. But in the best memoirs, which are the only ones that should concern us (we don't dismiss poetry altogether because some poems—even most poems—aren't very good), I see revealed a particular but recognizable human character, and am made to feel the way life acts on that character for good and ill. As we enter more deeply into a memoir we naturally begin to test the narrator's tone, his tale, his very self-conception, against our own experience and knowledge of life. When an entire story seems designed to paint its narrator as a walking book of virtues or Byronic, bourgeois-defying vices, we are free to disbelieve. When the memoirist tells us, on no evidence but her own word, that she wandered into the forest as an orphaned toddler in World War II and was rescued and raised by a pack of wolves, we are allowed, indeed *compelled*, to laugh at her gall, and to look elsewhere for the thrilling moment of human recognition and even complicity that this form can so richly provide.

There are many such moments in this anthology, a sampler

gleaned from the American Lives Series of the University of Nebraska Press. Here's just one example of what I'm talking about. In *Gang of One*, Fan Shen's account of growing up in China during the Cultural Revolution, we are made witness to the joys of skipping school and taking to the streets in the name of revolution, of chanting dire threats at fearful citizens, and humiliating figures of authority—the more elevated and powerful the better. One poor soul, a famous general weighted with decorations, died of a heart attack in front of his baying captors, an event whose immediate aftermath Shen recalls as follows: "The rally went on with even greater fervor for another hour, and I, along with all the Red Guards, shouted slogans at the dead body on the chair, denouncing the general's treacherous final act of escaping the revolution prematurely."

Just so. This grotesque scene, imbued with both tragedy and ghastly humor, is one we would like to view as distant from our own experience and tendencies, in social terms an exotic event, freakish as the eruption of a volcano. Yet there aren't many of us who, upon reading this and reflecting honestly upon their own youthful characters, could declare that they would have been sure to resist the temptations of anarchy and a self-righteous settling of scores with one's elders. Our narrator was neither hero nor villain, but in his individual story of ecstatic surrender to the tidal pull of the mob, we can read outward and into the nature of the mass movements that have so disfigured our history; indeed, through just such modest personal accounts those terrors of history are made intelligible. Here we find no pretense of superiority, of skepticism or even compassion—not in the moment, anyway; the compassion is all in the telling, in the very act of remembering.

You will see that quality of recognizable humanity glittering throughout the memoirs from which this book was drawn: in Floyd Skloot's classic account of trying to rebuild his life, indeed his very self, after suffering a viral brain disorder—a wry, exqui-sitely detailed story of a hard journey not yet accomplished, and with no heroic feats, except for the book you hold in your hand; in John Skoyles's funny, touching hymn to the New York City of his boyhood and the raffish uncle who undertook to school him in its dark arts; in Laurie Alberts's halting attempts to un-derstand the suicide of a friend, and to assess the degree of her own failure to prevent it, as if she had that power, which she did not; in Dinty Moore's witty, original, interestingly formed "Son of Mr. Green Jeans"; in Mary Felstiner's struggle to be at home again in a body made strange to her by crippling arthritis—not in the end the story of a pathology, but of a family, as at bottom most of these stories are.

These fine selections will, I hope, whet your appetite for the books themselves. Though necessarily personal, their gaze seems mostly to be directed outward rather than inward, however dif-ficult and turbulent the lives they describe. While acknowledging that they occupy a particular place in the world, and must view the world from that place rather than from a godlike distance, these writers are intensely interested in what lies beyond them—how the world at large acts, and acts on them, and, finally, hesi-tantly, how they themselves have acted upon the world. This is, after all, history—history from the inside out.

American Lives

FAN SHEN

"Long Live the Red Terror!"

Gang of One: Memoirs of a Red Guard

C hairman Mao, the Great Leader, officially launched the Cultural Revolution in his May 17 proclamation in the *People's Daily*, calling for the masses to smash the five-thousand-year-old Chinese culture and to rid the country of any foreign influence, in order to build a brand new communist culture. "Power to the Red Guards!" said the Great Leader. "Expose and destroy the hidden enemies who have been sleeping among your ranks!" ordered the Great Leader. Overnight, people young and old all rose at the summons of the Great Leader. After the giant bonfire, the fire of the Revolution spread fast and wide throughout the Big Courtyard.

No one could have imagined that such chaos was possible in the Big Courtyard, whose buildings were most stern-looking and whose life, for adults and children alike, was highly regulated. Situated at the west end of the long and wide Eternal Peace Boulevard that runs from east to west through the whole city of Beijing, the Big Courtyard is an enclosed compound with high, solemn gray walls that housed the headquarters of the People's Liberation Army. A square park with short pine trees divides the Big Courtyard evenly into two parts: the residential area on the south and the business area on the north. The south side is a self-sufficient and orderly community, with sixteen identical four-story apartment buildings neatly arranged in four blocks, a hospital, a shopping complex, a huge public dining hall where all my friends and I bought our meals with food coupons since we were in first grade, and the Flying Wing School, which I attended since I was three. This is the whole sphere of my childhood and I never knew any freedom growing up in such an orderly place. Every minute of my life, from the moment I was awakened in the morning to the moment I was put to bed, was carefully planned by my parents and teachers. I was not allowed to go outside of the gray wall that encircled the Big Courtyard and I never played with children outside. Nor was I allowed to go beyond the little park lined with trimmed pine trees to the north side, which is called the "Little Forbidden City" and is guarded by soldiers. The north side always seemed to me like a ghost city with clean and quiet and empty streets leading to the three cheerless, dark-green office buildings on the right, and to several smaller brown buildings known as generals' quarters on the left.

But in just a few days, the call of the Great Leader turned the quiet and orderly Big Courtyard into a big boiling cauldron, and the normal life that I had been living was shattered. The adults in the Big Courtyard and the senior students at our school formed various Red Guard teams and began writing big-letter posters and holding all kinds of rallies around the clock. My school was closed the day after we burned the books, and we were told to join the revolution. I was overjoyed. No school and a revolution! Nothing could be better! I especially enjoyed the freedom that I suddenly gained from my parents: they became so busy attending meetings that they were hardly home during the day and were forced to allow me more freedom to come and go, as long as I went out to read revolutionary posters and did not forget to take my sister to the public dining hall to eat.

Having been brought up in a very strict family, I took full advantage of my newfound freedom and went out every day to read posters or to simply get away from the apartment. No more torturous afternoon naps! For many days, I roamed the Big Courtyard with my friends and stood among adults reading the innumerable sensational and entertaining posters. At the outset of the revolution, the posters were hung in neat rows in my school's classrooms and auditorium, but soon they spread out onto any space available. The larger ones were posted on the walls and windows of residential buildings or hung from long ropes strung among the pine trees in the park, and the smaller ones on lampposts and tree trunks. At first, most posters were serious debates among various Red Guard "fighting teams," all of which bore impressive names like "Red Iron-Fist Corps," "The Crimson-Terror Battalion," and "The Scarlet-Blood Regiment." It was a totally confusing war of words for a twelve-year-old like me. For all I could make out, all the Red Guard teams claimed to be fighting for the Great Leader, but they could not agree on who were the hidden enemies that the Great Leader wanted them to expose. Oddly, they seemed to find the hidden enemies in other Red Guard teams, and they seemed to hate each other so much that they called each other "guards of capitalist dogs" and wanted to chop their opponents with "ten thousand knives" as if they were worse than Japanese Devils. It is truly amazing, when I think back on those posters, that the Red Guards used so much paper and ink to fight each other when they were all comrades under the Great Leader. But in those days, nobody saw the ridiculousness of the fight among Red Guard factions.

I certainly did not. For quite a few days, I racked my young brain reading the confusing posters and trying to detect who the real enemy was. But the more I read, the more confused I was and, finally, I lost interest in the debate and turned my attention to more entertaining posters, which started to appear more often. These were amusing exposés of the dirty pasts and corrupt lifestyles of members of the opposing factions. One such poster gave a graphic account of a young school nurse's affair with an older officer; another detailed the collection of fine clothes and furs that our school superintendent had; and a third exposed a math teacher who had a taste for imported beer and cigarettes. All of these would be silly and insignificant charges today, but were considered grave bourgeois offenses in those days. The poster which drew the largest crowd exposed a shocking incident about the former chairman, Liu Shaoqi. When he visited Indonesia, the poster said, he was invited by Sukarno, the president of Indonesia, to watch naked women bathe in a specially designed pool with secret observation windows. To this day I don't know if these stories were true or not, but in those days, I believed everything in the posters.

The first few weeks of the revolution went breathtakingly quickly and except for a few hours of sleep each night, I was hardly home, not wanting to miss any exciting event of the revolution. During the day, with all the seriousness of a little revolutionary, I entertained myself by reading sensational stories that grew more bizarre each day. Since the big-letter posters had made all the buildings open for inspection, my friends and I were allowed into the formerly tightly guarded "Little Forbidden City" and into those dark-green office buildings to read posters. But the real fun was at night. I wolfed down my dinner at the dining hall as quickly as I could and ran out with my friends to see "struggle rallies" at my school where "capitalists and their running dogs" were paraded and humiliated. Night after night, my friends and I sat in the front row and took in the drama: our old math teacher, with dignified white hair, crying and begging for mercy; the superintendent of my school, a middle-aged woman, getting her face painted black by Red Guards; and a senior student wearing a Red Guard armband collapsing and falling off the stage after tearfully shouting revolutionary slogans.

Not long after the Great Leader's proclamation, the sultry summer temperatures rose exponentially in Beijing, and so did the intensity of the revolution. The attendance at the nightly "struggle rallies" swelled quickly from a few dozen to several thousand. In late June I attended three massive "ten-thousand-man" rallies, which brought Red Guards from all over Beijing to the Big Courtyard. A gigantic open stage was hastily constructed on the soccer field just for these rallies.

The first mass rally was against General Luo, the former Chief of Staff of the People's Liberation Army, who the Red Guards said was a hidden traitor. As usual, before the rally began, my friends Baby Dragon and Snivel and I worked our way through the legs of adults and found a perfect spot directly in front of the stage. Sitting in a sea of red—red flags, red armbands, red banners with slogans—I was very excited and was very eager to do my part to fight the enemy who had been hiding in the army for so many years. When the rally started in the early evening, the general was brought onto the stage by two Red Guards amid a deafening roar of revolutionary slogans. He wore white casts on both his legs and could not stand on his own. "He tried to jump out of a second-floor window, pretending to commit suicide," a nearby member of the Red Guard told us.

The general was planted in a chair on the stage, but the guards had scarcely released their grip and turned their backs when the old man collapsed and slumped to the ground. In the sharp bluish floodlight, his face had turned ghastly white, like a piece of tofu.

"He is playing dead!" Baby Dragon shouted.

"Pull him up! Pull him up!" Snivel and I shouted.

"Pretending to be dead won't save your skin!" the man who just gave us the information on the general yelled at his white, lifeless face.

A soldier with a red armband strutted over and splashed a glass of cold water on the ashen face on the ground, but the general barely moved. The soldier bent down and pulled the general's head up by the hair. We clapped our hands and laughed at the distorted, ugly face. The old man moaned and his jaws flapped mechanically as if he were drowning, gasping for air.

"He knows how to put on a show," our informant said to us and we all laughed.

"Don't try to fool us," I shouted to the old man. "Stand up and face the people!"

The soldier propped him up on the chair again. From where we stood, we could almost touch the general's blanched face. His face was so haunting in its pallor that many nights after the rally I could still vividly see the sunken eye sockets, the bluish lips, the chalky skin wrapped around a skeleton, the sweat-soaked dusty green uniform, the half-torn insignia, and the trembling hands. Of course, as I gazed at the ghastly figure, I felt no pity.

Now that the target of the rally had been stabilized, the meeting began. As with all such rallies, it began with thunderous slogans bellowed from loudspeakers. Like a row of gigantic black toads, the loudspeakers formed a semicircle around the edge of the stage, barely three yards from our faces. The sound from them was so powerful that I could feel each syllable strike my face.

"CONFESSION OR DEATH!"

"LONG LIVE THE RED TERROR!"

"LONG LIVE THE GREAT CULTURAL REVOLUTION!"

We raised our fists and shouted with the loudspeakers. The shouting served its purpose. It got our blood boiling and we got more and more angry at the enemy sitting before us. One after another, people read indictment papers and we shouted more slogans after each one. We were halfway through the rally when the old general again slipped off the chair and slumped to the ground.

"He's playing dead again!" My friends and I shouted. "Get him up! Get him up!"

A soldier walked over and tried to pull him back onto the chair. He then frowned and checked the old general's pulse.

"He's dead!" he shouted to the people in front of the stage. "He's really dead!"

We did not believe him. Several people went on stage and checked again. But it was true. The man was dead—probably from a heart attack.

We did not feel sorry for him, though. Revolutionaries, as we were taught since childhood, should feel no mercy for enemies. In fact, we became angrier at him for dying so soon. The rally went on with even greater fervor for another hour, and I, along with all the Red Guards, shouted slogans at the dead body on the chair, denouncing the general's treacherous final act of escaping the revolution prematurely. It was the first time that I saw a dead man, but I did not feel the terror of death, for the fervor of the revolutionary fire around me had temporarily removed the possibility of fear.

The target of the second "ten-thousand-man" rally was the mayor of Beijing, Peng Zhen, and this rally was more fun than the first. When the mayor was brought on stage, he wore a cream-colored Western suit splashed with red paint and a paper stove-pipe hat that was as long as his body. His wife, a fat, nondescript woman, was wearing a ridiculously tight red dress. The dress was slit up the side to expose her red underwear, and through the tear we could see her plump white thighs. She was also wearing high-heeled shoes which were obviously too small for her feet. During the rally, several Red Guards shaved half of her head in a "yin-yang" fashion and made her walk about the stage like a prostitute. As she staggered on the high heels and wagged her half-shaved head this way and that, she looked monstrously comical. We roared with laughter. The mayor and his wife were smart people and they did everything they were asked to. Both of them knelt down before us and knocked their heads loudly on the ground, like grandchildren kowtow to their grandparents during Chinese New Year. The audience was amused by their obedience and satisfied that they bowed down before the people. As a result of their complete submission to the will of the people, the mayor and his wife survived the rally without much bodily harm. Strangely, the rally ended with everybody in a jocular mood.

The target of the third massive rally was General Hei, deputy commander of the army. This was a much more serious rally and had none of the comic atmosphere of the previous rally. From the very beginning of the rally, we found that we were faced with a hardcore enemy who refused to submit to the will of the revolutionary people. As soon as he was brought onstage, General Hei refused to bow down before the people. He was a large and powerful man and when two Red Guards tried to press his head down, he struggled fiercely to keep his head up. Finally, amid deafening slogans from the loudspeakers, an angry Red Guard member leaped onto the stage, slapped the general, tore off his red insignia, and stripped him to his underwear. We all cheered and applauded.

"That's right!" Snivel shouted. "Teach him a lesson!"

"DEATH TO THOSE WHO REFUSE TO BOW DOWN BEFORE THE PEOPLE!"

"DOWN WITH THE HARDENED ENEMY GENERAL HEI!"

The two announcers shouted angrily over the loudspeakers, and we all raised our fists and shouted with them. Blood dripped from the old man's mouth. The general was shocked by the blows and by the thunderous shouting of thousands of voices. He ceased to struggle and let his head be pressed down, but people were not satisfied. "Give him an airplane ride!" someone shouted in the audience. "Yes, an airplane ride! An airplane ride!" we all shouted in chorus. Following popular demand, the three Red Guards on stage twisted his arms back like the wings of an airplane and forced him to bend over until his face almost touched the ground. In just a few minutes, his face became a giant purple raspberry, and a long strand of saliva extended from his mouth onto the stage floor. Despite the airplane ride, General Hei was tough and did not beg for mercy, and he got more for his stubbornness. After the rally, he was paraded around the Big Courtyard in his underwear. A Red Guard tied a rope around his neck and led him around like a dog. We followed him all the way and prodded his sides with sticks whenever he slowed down. I felt no guilt at all when I thrust my stick into the man's bruised legs and arms to get him going. I was a good revolutionary then.

In addition to these grievous and dramatic "struggle rallies," there were massive jocular rallies, where we sang and danced around bonfires and soldiers fired small rockets and firecrackers to celebrate the Great Leader's latest decrees. Worship of the Great Leader reached a fever pitch at those rallies. One rally, for example, which took place right after the rally against General Hei, was to celebrate the occasion of Chairman Mao's sending a case of mangos, a gift he received from the tropical province of Hainan, to the Red Guards of Beijing. The mangos, people proclaimed, were symbols of the Great Leader's love of and trust in the Red Guards. Some people immediately made wax replicas of the mangos and sent them to cities across China, where they were enshrined. Thousands of people shed tears visiting and bowing to them. Even then, it seemed kind of comical to see people bow down before the wax mangos installed in the lobby of my school, but I did not dare to say anything. I do not know what happened to the real mangos and have often wondered about them. No one dared to eat them, that is for sure. Were they permanently preserved in some way? Were they put in large glass jars filled with Formalin preservative? I had seen roundworms preserved in such jars in the nurse's office in my school. Or did the mangos eventually rot? When they rotted, did people dare to throw them away? Would that be considered disrespectful to the Great Leader? I knew, of course, even at the age of twelve, that these were childish questions that should never be asked.

One afternoon, however, the thus far joyful revolution took a sudden turn for me when I saw my first bloody body. This was the first time that I sensed the terrible dark side of the revolution and began to experience a fear of its brutal force.

It was another of those humid afternoons, after the workers had sprayed the poplar trees with lime-water for the third time in as many months in a vain attempt to eradicate the cicadas. Baby Dragon, Snivel, and I had just sat down in the public dining hall to eat lunch when we heard a commotion outside and saw many people running in the direction of the "Little Forbidden City." I threw down my chopsticks and ran outside.

"What happened?" I asked, after flagging down a young boy who trailed a group of older boys.

"A body, a dead man. Someone . . . jumped off . . . a building," stammered the boy, quite out of breath.

I went back in and shouted to my friends: "Let's go. A man jumped off a building."

The front of the dark-green office building was packed with people by the time the three of us arrived. Most of the crowd was youngsters our own age. Despite the crowd, there was not a sound to be heard. Everybody was still and was staring at a twisted lump lying motionless on the concrete. The man must have landed on his head, for it had half disappeared into his neck. Dark blood soaked his brown uniform. His hands were tied behind his back. Since he was facing down, I could see only the back of his head. His white hair, sticky with blood, stood up like the needles on the back of a porcupine.

"Who is he?" Baby Dragon whispered.

"General Hei," answered a tall, skinny young man who did not bother to turn his face as he spoke. I remembered the old man's agonized demeanor when he was paraded in his underwear a few days before. It was so recent that I could still remember how it felt when my stick struck his thigh.

"No need to pity him," a soldier with a red armband said to break the spell of silence. "He was a hidden enemy of the revolution. This is what he deserved in the first place."

The young boy who had informed us of the event at the dining hall stepped out of the circle and inched up to the body. He had a stick in his hand. Very carefully, he thrust the stick under the chest of the dead man, and using it as a lever, he pried the body up and over. My heart fluttered uncomfortably as one side of the body slowly rose. I averted my eyes when the body flipped over. I heard the people gasp. When I turned my eyes back, I saw the most terrible sight: the dead man's face, smeared in dark purple blood, was completely flat—the nose, the eyes, and the mouth were flattened as if they were slits drawn with crayon on a dark-purple sheet of paper. What made the horrible face more frightening were two white teeth, which stuck out and gave it a sinister grin.

Neither my friends nor I waited to see the body removed. Nor did we return to the dining hall to finish our meal that afternoon. For many days after that, I did not go near the green building. Even from a distance, I seemed to be able to see the dark stain on the ground and to smell the stench of violent death.

I tried to tell myself not to be troubled by the ugly death, though. After all, the Great Leader had said that "Revolution is not a dinner party, not painting or embroidery, and cannot be gentle and polite," and we should not pity the enemies who were beaten or humiliated to death by revolutionary people. Still, the sight of the horrible grinning face left a terrible image in my mind that would not go away. I began to feel afraid, for I knew that I had played a role in the old man's death and that

I would be punished one way or another. I did not admit to my friends that I was afraid of ghosts, but for months after the death of the old general, I always carried a rock in each of my hands whenever I walked in dark places at night, and braced myself for a fight with the general's ghost.

PEGGY SHUMAKER

Moving Water, Tucson

Just Breathe Normally

Thunderclouds gathered every afternoon during the monsoons. Warm rain felt good on faces lifted to lick water from the sky. We played outside, having sense enough to go out and revel in the rain. We savored the first cool hours since summer hit.

The arroyo behind our house trickled with moving water. Kids gathered to see what it might bring. Tumbleweed, spears of ocotillo, creosote, a doll's arm, some kid's fort. Broken bottles, a red sweater. Whatever was nailed down, torn loose.

We stood on edges of sand, waiting for brown walls of water. We could hear it, massive water, not far off. The whole desert might come apart at once, might send horny toads and Gila monsters swirling, wet nightmares clawing both banks of the worst they could imagine and then some.

Under sheet lightning cracking the sky, somebody's teenaged brother decided to ride the flash flood. He stood on wood in the bottom of the ditch, straddling the puny stream. "Get out, it's coming," kids yelled. "GET OUT," we yelled. The kid bent his knees, held out his arms.

Land turned liquid that fast, water yanked our feet, stole our thongs, pulled in the edges of the arroyo, dragged whole trees root wads and all along, battering rams thrust downstream, anything you left there gone, anything you meant to go back and get, history, water so high you couldn't touch bottom, water so fast you couldn't get out of it, water so huge the earth couldn't take it, water. We couldn't step back. We had to be there, to see for ourselves. Water in a place where water's always holy. Water remaking the world.

That kid on plywood, that kid waiting for the flood. He stood and the water lifted him. He stood, his eyes not seeing us. For a moment, we all wanted to be him, to be part of something so wet, so fast, so powerful, so much bigger than ourselves. That kid rode the flash flood inside us, the flash flood outside us. Artist unglued on a scrap of glued wood. For a few drenched seconds, he rode. The water took him, faster than you can believe. He kept his head up. Water you couldn't see through, water half dirt, water whirling hard. Heavy rain weighed down our clothes. We stepped closer to the crumbling shore, saw him downstream smash against the footbridge at the end of the block. Water held him there, rushing on.

LAURIE ALBERTS

Winter 1997

Fault Line

Here in our house in Vermont, Tom ran a wire from a pine tree to our living room window, hung bird feeders. Squirrels were the first to find them. We had to slide the feeders farther along the wire so the squirrels couldn't jump from the tree. One just tried and fell, but then he leaped from the snowy ground and made it, scrabbling onto the tipping feeder. We'll have to hang it higher. I don't really begrudge the squirrels. I enjoy their antics, their twitching tails and the way they traverse the wire suspended upside down, paw over paw, like a kid on a ropes course.

What does this have to do with Kim? Now I am the one taking solace from nature, as Kim once said he did. I with my body chemistry corrected. My husband and child asleep upstairs. Snow, crusted, a crisp hard blanket stretches from tree to tree. That is what the medicine is like, it covers. But I know what's underneath. I know because I've stopped taking the pills and the darkness returns immediately, a presence that travels with me, a haunting that flutters about me like bat wings.

What of Kim's medication? When did that start, and why did it cost so much?

My daughter, not yet four, told me yesterday as she was struggling into her snowsuit that the first kid in her preschool class to get into his or her snow clothes gets to be line leader. *Line leader.* Her world, in which it's thrilling, an honor, to be the first to lead the other three-year-olds out to the play yard. I don't remember that emotion but I recognize in its existence the loss of something, a perspective, a view of the world in which small things matter so greatly. It makes me want to go upstairs and climb in bed beside her and nuzzle my nose up to her little hand or against her small smooth back, to touch her sweetness. My great good fortune. Kim, why did you deny yourself this?

Sunday movies, laundry, a nap with Becky while Tom and our neighbor snowshoe, then before it gets dark Becky and I dress for the cold and go out for a walk. She slides down snow banks and the dogs cavort. I have to half-pull her up our long, steep driveway. Inside, she puts on a red summer dress with a big white collar, then retreats to the world of her troll house while Tom and our neighbor warm themselves with bourbon. I make myself a rum drink.

See, Kim, how companionably we drink here, each having just one, maybe two? The woodstove warms us; a child plays nearby, speaking in low, muted voices to her toys. The dogs groan and shift on their mats in the kitchen. This is winter, this is our life.

What am I trying to say to you? I have this and you don't, didn't, never chose to? Lost the ability to? You said you didn't want kids and I didn't believe you. You loved them. Or is it the drink, that we can do this, have one, set it aside, go on with the evening, and you had to keep returning to that bottle? That bourbon bottle I saw in your freezer when you had apartments, in a cupboard in a motel room near Forty-second Street in New York? Your brother says it went past that, came to gallons of cheap vodka and Gatorade, your special cocktail.

I'm angry, contemptuous. You could have had all this and more. You had parents who loved each other, loved you. Who lived in great normalcy, who offered only simple expectations. So why, then?

It's easy to see myself as the snake in this picture. What grandiosity, a friend says. To think I had that power to ruin a life. It's a disease. Even the AMA admits it. Alcoholism, for all its devastations, is so ordinary, so prosaic. Yet what can be compared with it, a disease that changes the personality, removes one from life long before death? But it wasn't just the booze. Kim's disintegration began prior to his drinking getting out of hand. Disintegration is a good word for it. He stopped being integrated.

On my way home from work—I am teaching at a college in Massachusetts, driving down from Vermont—I took a back road off the highway and pulled into the parking lot of one of Kim's regular haunts, the Stanley Motor Lodge, now the Valley View Motel. I had heard from my mother and Matt that Kim stayed there when his employer, a packager of study skills courses for colleges and prep schools, moved its northern office to Massachusetts. I sat in the lot feeling nauseated, shaky. Interstate 91 roared behind the building. No valley view here. For weeks I had stared at the fading paint on that building as I commuted past on the highway, trying to get the courage to stop in. From the outside, it didn't look that bad. Fresh light-brown paint covered the motel exterior, though a Bud Lite ad displayed next to the vacancy sign didn't bode well. I entered the dark office. Paper peeling from the walls. A large beer and juice cooler with sliding doors by the entry. A short fiftyish Indian or Pakistani woman came to greet me. I launched in: "Did this used to be the Stanley Motor Lodge?"

"Yes."

"Did you own it then?" Her dark eyes questioning now. Did I sound like some tax investigator?

"I'm an old friend of a man who used to stay here. Kim Janik?"

"Oh, yes." She nodded. "A very nice man. He was my regular. Every year in the winter he stayed."

"He died two years ago," I said.

"What happened? He was a very nice man. A very nice man. The last few years he didn't talk to anyone."

"It was the drinking," I said.

"Yes, yes. The drinking. When I cleaned his room, I found

half-gallon vodka bottles. One night, you know, he kicked the walls." She smiled at me, trying to figure out what it is I wanted from her, what I was doing there.

I couldn't—didn't want to—conceive of this Kim, kicking walls, causing damage. "Did he apologize the next day? When he kicked the wall?"

She looked at me uncomprehendingly.

I told her that I hadn't seen him in five years when he died. I lied, it was ten, but I was afraid that ten would make it seem like I didn't have the right to ask about him.

"You were his friend," she said. "Why didn't you help him?"

I gazed about uneasily. "I couldn't be with him. He was in love with me."

"Ah, so that is why. Because you broke off."

"No, no, he drank for a long time before that. I couldn't stand his drinking." An easier truth, a convenient one.

"You are married?"

"Yes."

"You have children?"

"One little girl."

"Ah, of course, you couldn't break your marriage." She nodded knowingly, relieving me from blame. "But he had no one."

"That was one of the things I couldn't stand. He was so isolated."

"Yes, yes. A woman, she must have the social, you know, but not the man. Not the man."

"Oh, my husband is very social. Some men. . . . But Kim, when he kicked the wall, did he . . ." This was important to me—a contrite Kim, apologetic, was preferable, less changed.

She waved me silent. Two grungy women had come in, girls. Prostitutes or junkies, maybe. One wore gray leggings under a waist-length black leather jacket, multiple earrings, heavy makeup. The other was messy, blond, rumpled in flannel.

"Are you staying tonight?" the owner asked these women.

"We don't know. We won't know until we hear from someone."

"Don't you like your room?"

"No." I tried to imagine what this room could be like, that girls such as these didn't like it.

"We can change it. You can be in the other building. There is room now. I will make a call." She lifted the phone.

"We changed our room last night."

"Checkout is eleven," she said. She looked worried.

Finally, the girls negotiated to pay an extra seven dollars to stay in the room until 12:30. It was now close to 11:00. They were waiting for someone to bring them drugs, probably. Is this what Kim lived among? If they turned tricks, did he frequent such women? Or was he beyond that, beyond the lust that plagued him with me?

The girls bought juice and left.

"So," I started again, "did he pay for damages, when he kicked the wall?" Was he still that responsible, did he know what he'd done?

"No damages." She shrugged. "It was his mother's fault. I met her; she came out with his younger brother from Colorado to get him. She was a realtor, you know."

"Yes, a very nice woman," I echoed her wording about Kim. "Very religious. Jesus was everything to her. She thought Jesus would take care of Kim."

"It was her fault," the proprietor insisted. "A mother must find a wife for her son, he must settle down, he must have responsibilities or he has nothing to live for. I have a son, twenty-three. He must marry, have a family, pay bills, you know? So that he doesn't just drift. You must have family. Kim Janik had nothing."

"Nothing to live for," I echoed.

"Family," she said. "You have a husband, a child. These are the boundaries." She put her flattened, upright hand on the counter like a fence. "You know? Women, we live with these boundaries. You, you have a child, a husband, now you must think of them. You must forget the past, forget about Kim Janik, think only of your child or you will make yourself sick."

"Yes," I said, "yes," to please her, to have her think well of me, but of course I couldn't forget. I reached across the counter to grasp her hand. She gripped mine and met my eyes.

"Thank you," I said.

I was sick already. I had made myself sick with Kim's death. He would be aware of the irony of me being drawn to him now. And he, the most private of men, would hate this. So why, then? I need to know what happened, and what part is mine. What would have happened if he'd never met me? Did I come into his life and bend it out of shape, or would he have broken anyway? Was there some fault line running through him? A fault is a weakness, an error, culpability, but also a fracture in the earth's crust accompanied by a displacement of one side with respect to the other. Perhaps it was our fault line, not his alone, and I got to rise as he fell.

"You aren't talking to us," Tom complained that night. I shook myself. "I'm sorry. I didn't realize . . ." I told him about the motel, the woman, and my lie. "I'm going down some long tunnel of sadness," I said.

"As long as you don't get obsessed," Tom said.

That night I woke several times thinking of Kim. What does this mean for Tom, for Becky, I wonder. In the midst of it, I'm only half with them. But am I ever more than half? I love them, and I want to hide. I want to read, to be left alone, alone, alone. I want to lie in a dark room and drift into that half sleep in which the past runs behind my eyes like a movie.

We had dinner at my mother's. She was afraid, she said, that Tom might be jealous of all this attention to Kim's memory. Or maybe it would bother him because of his father's drinking.

"No," Tom said, "that doesn't bother me, but you said you're traveling down some long tunnel of sadness, and if it takes you away from Becky and me I won't like it."

"See," my mother said. When Tom took Becky home to bed, I stayed to help clean up. She brought it up again before I headed home. "Don't talk about it in front of him," she counseled.

As though I could help it. *Who made you the marriage expert?* I wondered. Time had, the way time made Nixon an elder statesman.

"Why do you think he kicked the wall?" I asked Tom that night in bed. It haunted me, the image of Kim alone in that terrible room.

Tom said, "Rage at the world he thought had put him there. At himself."

I try to imagine Kim like the mumbling, raging, incoherent drunks I've known in Alaska, seen in New York. I can't picture him like that. I suppose it's possible that under their spittle, their gin blossoms, their ranting slurred speech, some of them were once as sweet, as clean and hopeful and smooth skinned as Kim used to be.

CHARLES BARBER

The Weight of Spoons

*Songs from the Black Chair: A Memoir
of Mental Interiors*

Eight days later, on a Monday morning, I was reading over the weekend's football scores in the newspaper when the telephone rang.

It was Nick. His voice was different. He was crying.

"Charlie, did you hear?"

"No," I said.

"I just got a call from William Court," he said. "Henry killed himself up at the farm."

"What?" I heard myself say.

"Henry killed himself up at the farm . . . The motherfucker." Nick was sobbing.

"Jesus Christ," I said. I sat down. I felt my grip loosen on the telephone. I felt kicked in the stomach. I felt once again that immediate infusion of acid into the depths of my intestines.

"How?" I said.

"He asphyxiated himself. He suffocated himself somehow in the van . . . with the exhaust. I don't know, I guess he rigged up some hose and rerouted the van's exhaust back into the cabin."

"When did it happen?" I felt foolish asking these practical questions; they didn't matter, all that mattered was that he was dead.

"William found his body yesterday. He might have done it a couple of days ago."

"I can't believe he fucking did it," I said.

"Oh, I can." Nick said, just slightly more composed now. "The poor motherfucker . . ."

I couldn't imagine Henry not being alive. I tried to see him as no longer moving. I couldn't see him that way. Even in his compromised, troubled state he had been talking, drinking, joking—and of course, trying to kiss me—just a week ago.

It hit me . . . Trying to kiss me . . . could that have made a difference? Could I have made a difference?

Nick said, "Do you think he asked us up as a way to say goodbye?"

"I don't know. I don't know," I said, speaking very softly. "How would I know?"

I didn't want to talk anymore.

"Nick, I'll call you later. In an hour."

"Okay."

"Are you okay?" I said.

"No," he said.

I hung up the phone and moved slowly. I recall in those moments moving very slowly in everything I did. I had a feeling of looking at myself from above. I saw myself go to the couch and lie down. I saw myself get up again after a while, go get some blankets, lie down again, and shut my eyes. I saw myself stay there for most of the next couple of days.

Unlike Nick, I didn't cry. I never have cried over Henry's death. (Perhaps if I had, I wouldn't have needed to write a book about it.)

It didn't seem real. But then again, nor was I shocked, really. Of course I was at first, but then everything was just numbness. And then after a long period of numbness, came the feeling, the slow and profound realization, that things had changed. The earth under my feet would never feel as solid; the links between us all could shatter at any time. And then it was numbness again. And then it was upset, and then it was deep and almost unbearable upset and fear. All I wanted to do was go to sleep.

Jesus, Henry, why? Why now? Couldn't you have told us what you were planning? Couldn't you have waited it out a little longer? Did you have to do it?

Slowly, I came to understand that Henry had done something awful. Something that he should not have been allowed to do. A crime against nature and the order of things, defying convention and provoking us all—as Henry was wont to do—disturbing and muddying the waters, indefinitely. So the suicide hadn't been so clean after all. But then at other times I felt he did what he had the perfect right to do, and it made perfect sense given the pain he was in.

Yes, I freaked out there on the couch. I sweated; I had difficulty breathing, alternately breathing hard and then gasping for breath; I didn't want to be awake, or alive. I went through great panics. He had tried to kiss me. I'd rebuffed him. Nick and I had left afterward at the first opportunity. We—I—had let him hang. How did that make him feel? What was it like when he woke up later that day, probably late in the afternoon, hungover, feeling completely abandoned? Was that the moment when he made up his mind? Had I . . . had we . . . contributed to his death? Had I killed him?

Should I have kissed him? Should I have hugged him, had sex with him, given him whatever he wanted? Would that have made a difference? By not kissing him, what did I do? I tried to wrap my mind around these questions, and in anxiety gave up after I couldn't think about them anymore. But I thought about these questions, for weeks, and months. They became my obsessive loops of thought, side by side with all the other OCD material mucking up my brain.

When my parents came home at dinnertime the day Nick called, I tried to act fully composed when I told them about Henry's death. They had already heard the news on campus. They had tried to call me, but I hadn't picked up the phone. My mother and father were shocked and duly sympathetic. They were upset for Henry's parents. My mother said to me, "Your father and I knew someone at Oxford who killed himself. He was also young, and intelligent. It was very sad."

My mother's words were meant to comfort, but they only angered me. It was as if she were saying there was a precedent for what had happened. In my state of confusion, I at least wanted to think that what I was going through was unique—that a suicide had never happened before, at least not one quite like this, in the history of the world. That nobody else had felt what I was feeling. It was as if my mother was saying that Henry's death was somehow respectable, that there was an Old World antecedent for such behavior. But I didn't say any of that. I just nodded.

That night, Nick and I met up and went for a long soggy walk around the campus. It was just like the old days; we walked in circles. We walked in the same circles that we used to walk with Henry. It was pitch-dark. We could have gone somewhere light and dry to talk, but it didn't seem right. There seemed no more fitting tribute to Henry than to walk around the campus in the dark and the rain.

When Nick and I met that evening, we didn't hug, and we didn't say "how awful." Nor did we say "I'm sorry," or "It was his choice and we need to respect it." We didn't say what everybody else said to each other. There was no need to. I don't think we said all that much to each other in the rain.

But we did talk about why. Actually it was not so much why, but why *now*. Without ever talking about it, we knew that Henry had been ready to pick himself off at any time. Had the weekend been a planned farewell? Had it been as choreographed, in its own way, as the trashings or the placement of *Microbe Hunters* on the dashboard? We talked about the mysterious trip to California and the West. "You know what I think?" Nick said. "I think he realized then that his problems weren't going to go away. When he set out, as the Microbe Hunter, he might have believed that if he went to a different place, his problems would go away. When they didn't, or got worse, that's when he decided to come back East to kill himself."

I didn't disagree. I think we both felt that the whole thing was planned, but we couldn't quite bring ourselves to say it. It still bothers me.

Nick and I speculated about Henry's body. Mr. Court must have had to make the arrangements. I imagined Henry in a morgue somewhere in Massachusetts. A cold, quiet morgue.

❧ ❧

Henry's funeral was on an unusually warm day a month later in the college chapel. It was early December, and it must have been close to sixty degrees. The delay in scheduling the funeral resulted, of course, from everybody's shock but also, I imagine, from the difficulty in finding an appropriate, dignified way to put Henry to rest.

Mrs. Court was from an Irish Catholic family, and in the brief time I'd spent with her, I sensed that she was fitfully religious. But after Henry died, she became fervently Catholic. She enlisted a priest, I'm not sure from where, to preside over the service.

Nick, Sam—who was back from India, where he had lived for a couple of years after high school—and I were the ushers. We met outside the chapel a half hour before the ceremony. Nick wore a pinstripe suit—certainly the first time I had seen him so attired—and I had dug out an old suit of my father's. Sam, still tanned from the years in India, arrived at the event wearing a pink tuxedo. He wore a fuchsia jacket and pink trousers with black stripes, and black sneakers.

"What the hell are you up to?" Nick said, sounding both annoyed and impressed.

Sam smiled. "It's a celebration, man. A celebration of Henry's life."

But it's more than that, I thought. There was an edge to Sam's costume, and to his voice. Sam was pushing back. In his mind, Henry had inflicted an absurd and hurtful act on us all, and Sam was going to wear an absurd costume to acknowledge the sheer meanness of Henry's choice. I understood, but I couldn't muster any anger toward Henry. A few weeks later, at a bar, Sam confirmed his anger toward Henry. "He could have gone on," Sam told me. "He could have survived. He just gave UP!" And what did you ever do to help him, I thought. And then I stopped. For what had I ever done to help him?

I was surprised to see that there were about 150 people in attendance. It was a diverse crowd. The great majority of those attending were colleagues of Henry's parents at the college, who were there only out of a forlorn sense of duty. My parents were there, as were probably half the entire faculty above a certain age. Most of those present, including the priest, had never known Henry. But that was okay—it was clear that, except for the eulogy that Mr. Court was going to deliver, the ceremony was not at all about Henry.

A minority of those paying their respects were various murky friends and associates of Henry's. There were friends of Henry's from the restaurant, a couple of friends of ours from high school, and a few especially disreputable-looking types that I suspected Henry knew from his drug travels. I had never met or seen any of the druggy types. Henry had kept that side of his life separate.

Henry's sister was there. She had returned from I don't know where—I think she may have been living in New Zealand. She was perhaps five years older than Henry, and I hardly knew her. I had pretty much forgotten she existed. She was never around when we were growing up and must have left home at a young age. I didn't recognize her at first; in the great Henry Court tradition she had dyed pink hair and, I think, a nose ring. She looked beautiful, and awful. Nick escorted Mrs. Court into the church and seated her in the front row. I sat my parents in a row somewhere in the middle. Nick said later that he feared that Mrs. Court would go into some epileptic fit precipitated by dread and horror. He was amazed and relieved to have gotten her seated in the pew without incident. Nick and I were aware from the start that Mrs. Court might never fully recover from the blow. For all her oddities, one thing everybody knew about Mrs. Court was that she was passionate about everything she involved herself with, whether it was English literature, alcohol, or her son. This very passion had turned Henry away. But you knew, we all knew, that she would feel his death—this probable rejection of her and everything she believed in—with a passion of the most negative, and possibly most destructive, sort.

Of course, in Catholic tradition suicide is a mortal sin. The priest did not address the reason for Henry's death, but seemed to place great emphasis on the need for "God's forgiveness of sins." He delivered an earnest workmanlike eulogy, and he seemed viscerally relieved when he was done.

"Henry was in a lot of pain for a long, long time." I distinctly remember that's how Mr. Court began his eulogy, or speech, or whatever it was, about Henry. (He wrote me not long ago that was not at all how he began it. Such is memory.) It remained to him to address the nature of Henry's death. He explained that death had always been near Henry, that as a child, he had twice nearly died from serious illnesses. This was news to me; Henry had never spoken about any of it. The speech was, in effect, an explanation of the amount of pain that Henry had been in, and a defense of Henry's unquestioned right to take his life to get rid of that pain. In his recent letter to me, Mr. Court said that he hadn't planned to rationalize Henry's death, but the "priest had pissed me off with all that sin stuff." But what I recall is not so much what he said, but how he said it: Mr. Court was clear-eyed, strong, and unapologetic.

He didn't lose his composure once. I felt very close to him as he spoke. I don't know why exactly. My contacts with him had been quick and somewhat superficial, but there, in the chapel, I responded to his enormous sense of clarity. He was wonderfully, exquisitely clear. He knew what happened. He explained what happened. He explained how he saw it. He was able to stand up in front of everybody. He showed that he was able to function in the midst of it. Sure, it was oddly dry and removed. I suppose it had about it the feel of a textual exegesis. But that was Mr. Court's nature. What did we expect him to do, beat his chest and tear his hair out? I didn't care how he arrived at his stability—the thing was that he got there. He retained, in other words, the ability to function.

A much smaller group assembled for the burial afterward. As Henry's coffin was being placed in the ground in that corner of the graveyard closest to the Dunkin' Donuts, and a group of about thirty of us soberly stood and watched, a great black bird flew across the sky. Nick and I were standing toward the back of the group. "What the fuck is that?" said the man next to us, an English professor who was the world's greatest expert on Laurence Sterne or somebody like that. The three of us watched the unidentifiable great beast—it seemed part crow, part raven, part vulture—fly into the strangely warm afternoon air. After the ceremony, Nick and I went on one of our campus walks. Independently we had both come to the conclusion that the great fucking disturbing bird had been the spirit of Henry, presiding over the ludicrous spectacle.

The night of the funeral I had tea with Sam and his father, Tony, the poet in residence. The Blakes were fun, theatrical people, full of life and humor.

Tony was indignant about the suicide. "I've had bad weeks, even bad months, when life was not particularly pleasant, or even worth living. But suicide? Never. He was young and handsome and clever. I mean, it makes you feel the world is just one big funeral pyre." He shook his body, as if trying to throw off the horror of the day.

"But wasn't Mr. Court's composure during the eulogy remarkable?" I said.

"I couldn't believe it," said Tony, indignantly. "It was perverse. If it had been my bloody son, you can be damn sure that I wouldn't have been so fucking composed."

The Blakes held a flamboyant annual New Year's Eve party. In our circles, it was the social event of the year. All the interesting people in Cold River went, from the manager of the town dump to some of the town's wealthiest families. That year's party, held a few weeks after the funeral, was held in honor of Henry Court. Sam and Tony placed a picture of Henry (how they were able to locate a picture of him, I don't know) on the front door and put a sign up asking that everybody remember his spirit. We all agreed that drinking to oblivion seemed a much more fitting tribute to Henry than any Catholic eulogy by a priest that never knew him.

Some months after the funeral a Letter to the Editor appeared in the Cold River newspaper. The letter addressed American policy toward Cuba and was sympathetic to the Cubans. It was signed by William Court.

"Isn't it funny, that he's writing about this?" I said to my mother. "I mean, who cares about Castro when his son has died?"

My mother said, "It's what he needs to do now. It's a sign that he's getting back to normal."

❦

In the days and nights after the suicide, I began to find some tranquility in unexpected things. Things like objects.

I spent great amounts of time looking at objects. Until that point I had taken very little account of the physical things that exist in the world. I'd never really noticed them. Typically I was always thinking, usually about things of no consequence, but thinking nonetheless. I, and Henry, and my parents, and Henry's parents, and pretty much everyone I knew, lived exclusively in the mental sphere.

But now, in the quiet of my parents' house in the weeks after Henry's death, I contemplated things as they were. I looked at shoes and pears and spoons and tangerines and cardboard. I looked at the shapes of things, the curve of wine bottles and onions and carved wood. I looked at details—the hundreds of miniature dimples on the surface of an eggshell, like on skin, and the hundreds of miniature white spots that you see if you look closely at a Red Delicious apple.

I also spent great amounts of time examining text. Not books or magazines—nothing momentous like that. Mainly I read product labels—the contents of toothpaste and shampoos, the ingredients of brownies. I read classified ads for hours about things for sale, apartments for rent, cats and dogs to adopt. Nothing was more enjoyable—therapeutic, even—than reading the directions on the back of an antacid carton.

To me, no American writer wrote better about mental vulnerability (or "emotional bankruptcy," as he called it) than F. Scott Fitzgerald. In his last broken-down years, when he was saturated with alcohol and scorched from trooping his wife in and out of mental hospitals, Fitzgerald wrote poetically, rapturously even, about his "crack-up," and the crack-ups of others. One of his last short stories was "The Lost Decade," about a former architect who is making a reentry into the world after a disappearance of ten years spent in drunken oblivion. Trimble, the architect, is at lunch at a fine restaurant in midtown Manhattan with a young, enthusiastic magazine editor, Orrison, whose task it is to reorient him to the world. After lunch, Orrison offers to give Trimble a tour of the shining new skyscrapers that have arisen in midtown during Trimble's decade-long disappearance. They stand outside the restaurant:

"From here you get a good candid focus on Rockefeller Center," [Orrison] pointed out with spirit "—and the Chrysler Building and the Armistead Building, the daddy of all the new ones."

"The Armistead Building," Trimble rubber-necked obediently.

"Yes—I designed it."

Orrison shook his head cheerfully—he was used to going out with all kinds of people. . . .

He paused by the brass entablature in the cornerstone of the building. "Erected 1928," it said.

Trimble nodded.

"But I was taken drunk that year—every-which-way drunk. So I never saw it before now."

"Oh." Orrison hesitated. "Like to go in now?"

"I've been in it—lots of times. But I've never seen it. And now it isn't what I want to see. I wouldn't ever be able to see it now. I simply want to see how people walk and what their clothes and shoes and hats are made of. And their eyes and hands. . . .

"What do you want to see most?" Orrison asked. . . .

Trimble considered.

"Well—the backs of people's heads," he suggested. "Their necks—how their heads are joined to their bodies. I'd like to hear what those two little girls are saying to their father. Not exactly what they're saying but whether the words float or submerge. . . ."

"The weight of spoons," said Trimble, "so light. A little bow with a stick attached. The cast in that waiter's eye. I knew him once but he wouldn't remember me." . . .

It was all kind of nutsy, Orrison decided. . . .

That's just the way I felt, that's all I wanted to do, all that I was capable of doing at the time: feel the weight of spoons. Spoons and bowls and melons and the text of the classified section, all these were enormously soothing, affirming. They brought solace. They were neutral—they were not going to self-destruct and disappear.

I was reduced—or elevated perhaps—to feeling the weight of spoons. Yes, elevated. Elevated to feeling the weight of spoons. It felt good to think no more but simply to coexist with the world of objects.

❦ ❦

I resolutely, consciously, told myself that Henry's suicide did not make me suicidal. I had heard about copycat suicides, and I rejected that idea firmly. If Henry died, why should I die? Of course I was thinking the same anguished thoughts, the same loopy thoughts of words repeating and violent urges and crazy ideas that I had since Harvard Yard, and now I had the additional guilt and sense of fragility induced by Henry's death, but I was not going to succumb to them.

Shortly after Henry died, I was driving with a friend on a road I'd driven on hundreds of times. Jim was a friend from another circle of acquaintances; he didn't know Henry or Nick. Randolph Road went down a hill and intersected with a rural highway. At the intersection was a blinking red light.

Instead of stopping at the flashing light, I accelerated.

"What the hell are you doing, Charlie?" shouted Jim.

Before I could react, we had passed through the intersection at sixty miles an hour. If a car or truck had been going along that highway, surely Jim and I would have died.

"What the fuck is wrong with you?" Jim said.

I didn't answer. "I'm sorry," I said, uselessly.

"You could have killed us!" Jim said.

"I'm sorry," I said again.

❦ ❦

Perhaps it all came down to a purple shirt.

A few days after I almost killed Jim on Randolph Road, I was in a clothing store, deciding whether or not to buy a shirt. I was in an odd mood. The store was large and warehouselike, and the piped-in music was loud and unsettling. I picked the shirt off the rack—it was a purple canvas Levi's shirt. The usual considerations ran through my mind—did it fit? could I afford it? did I want to afford it?—when it struck me . . . why buy the shirt at all? There's a good chance you might not be around in a few weeks or months. You may not even be alive to wear it.

Listening to these last thoughts, I was just about to put the shirt back on the rack and walk away, when I thought: you have to decide whether to buy the shirt or not. It's one or the other. You have to take a stand.

Fuck it, I thought, I need to buy the shirt. I don't care if I can't afford it, I don't care if I don't like it, I don't care if it's the ugliest, silliest, most ridiculous looking shirt in the world—I need to buy it.

I need to buy it.

I bought the shirt.

JOHN SKOYLES

Hard Luck Suit

Secret Frequencies:
A New York Education

have a tip on a horse," Fred said on the phone. "Want to get in on it?"

I said I did.

"How much can you get?"

"Money?"

"Of course 'money!'" I could hear him chuckling.

"I have about a hundred and thirty nine," I said. I left off "dollars." I was always halting my sentences with Fred to make them jazzier.

"Bring it, and more if you can." I thought I could scrounge through my junk drawer, where a few stray bills lay crushed among old keys, gum wrappers, whistles, and stubby pencils. I told him I had been listening to Nebel. "Which night? With the guy talking about BHT? To keep stuff on the shelves longer? You know, there is more knowledge on the airwaves alone than in all the colleges in the world. I've gotta run, love to your mother. Oh, one more thing—how about I line up a girl to meet us later, for dinner?" When I paused, he said, "Okay, don't worry. I heard about your talk with Van. It's nothing to be ashamed of. I'll ask Madeline to bring a girl. And this will be another first too, your first job with me. We're a team now, right? See you then." Since we were a team, I thought Fred might give me the key to his place. I wanted to take it out during the week and run its teeth over the tip of my finger. I wanted to throw a party and greet Long John and Florence Psychic at the door. I wanted to show Linda the fancy bed. When an errand brought me anywhere near the Upper East Side, I looked toward Fred's and felt a pang close to homesickness. I mentioned this, and he said, "That's not

homesickness. You don't live there. You've got away-sickness—
you just want to get away."

My sleeplessness continued, and I listened to Long John
interview the man Fred mentioned who claimed an evil race
lived deep in the earth. The Deros, short for Detrimental Ro-
bots, rigged certain elevators in New York, so that if passengers
pressed basement twice, they would travel straight down, three
miles, into the boiling hearth where these monsters made their
home. During one of Long John's endless commercials for a dis-
infectant so strong that one drop could deodorize an airplane
hangar, I worried about the money I risked, Christmas money
saved to buy a Zenith TransOceanic radio. For a long time I'd
wanted to hear overseas broadcasts, which wasn't possible on
my cheap transistor. I started to replay Linda's words about Fred,
and I worried. I worried about the promised girl. Not only about
what would be expected of me, but because of my obsession
with Linda. Of all the women in the city and all the mailroom's
thumbed-through magazines showing overinflated blondes pushing their mouths into succulent shapes while lifting gauzy underwear, nothing excited me more than my prim, officious aunt. I
worried whether any other woman would be able to arouse me.
I looked down at my penis, which had shrunk to the size of a
hazelnut, and I worried.

I met Fred at Rumplemayer's on Saturday morning. It was
mid-July, and the lips of the carriage horses around Central Park
foamed with a frothlike meringue. I looked forward to going to
the track, thinking of the train that sped through the stations
without stopping, leaving commuters in its breeze, the train that
blew straight to Aqueduct, the train marked *S* for *Special*. I arrived early and spun twice through the St. Moritz's revolving
doors just for the luxury of entering and leaving. Rumplemayer's
marble soda fountain stood in the center of an enormous pink
room whose walls were hung with stuffed animals. Fred waved

from a booth. He wore a dark pinstriped suit. As I slid in, I straightened my lapels. He asked where I got my tie.

"Tie City." All ties were ninety-nine cents. "I just bought it, for today."

"Don't go there anymore," he said. "That's a junk shop." I looked down at my chest, at the wildest tie I could find, a tie for the racetrack, a tie of good luck. Horse heads and horseshoes covered the kelly green background, pinned to my shirt by a new tie tack, a horse's backside and long tail.

"I have to go to Whitehouse and Hardy later to pick up a suit. I'll get you one that goes better."

"I thought this would bring good luck," I said.

"And I'm sure it will," he said, "but I want you to look more formal. You know, if you go off to college, you'll never learn how to dress. You'll be a bumpkin forever." Fred glanced at the menu and said, "Did you see Gail's putting game on her blackboard? Weird stuff, mutton, venison—she even has tongue! I'll never eat anything from an animal's mouth." He paused. "Let's have eggs." He ordered eggs Benedict for both of us. He had a habit of snorting when he was excited, and he breathed loudly through his nose. His grin never let up, and he called for more ice water whenever I took a few sips, annoying our waiter, an older man.

"We should talk about Van Forkenberry," he said. "Gail told me about what he said to you."

"It's okay, Uncle Fred," I said. "It wasn't your fault."

"I didn't say it was my fault!" he yelled. "I didn't apologize!" I took another sip. Then he whispered, "Never apologize, remember that. Things are too complicated for any one person to take the blame. Van's fallen a long way since his gigolo years at the Commodore Hotel." He yelled again, "Waiter, more water!" And to me, "I feel sorry for him." He looked down at his plate. "How did you feel?"

"I got mad," I said.

"I know you did, but look at it this way. I mean, if a woman flirted with you, you wouldn't feel mad, would you?" I said I wouldn't.

"Then why feel mad at a man? It's the same thing, isn't it? And like I told you before, drop the 'Uncle.' Just call me Fred, okay?" My glass was three-quarters full, and this time the waiter stopped, looked at Fred, and said, "He still has a full glass."

"Do what I say!" Fred ordered, and the waiter went off, returning a moment later with the pitcher. When he had finished, Fred said, "Now, waiter, he'd like more coffee." My cup was empty, but I had had more than enough. I started to object, but Fred shut me up and the waiter smiled a fake sweetness. Fred was onto another subject, hotels, describing the upstairs rooms in the St. Moritz, when the waiter arrived, carrying the tall silver pot. He filled my cup, lifting the spout, which was shaped like a swan's neck, higher and higher as he poured. Soon the coffee began to stipple onto the table, and the cup was still only a third full. He continued to raise it until the droplets thickened into drops, scattering onto my saucer. Fred talked without noticing, stretching his arms to show the size of a honeymoon suite, telling how he sat in the middle of the enormous bed, leaning against the headboard, and had to crawl a long way just to set his drink on the night table. Drops were hitting the cuff of my sleeve, and I moved my arm to my lap. I nodded to the waiter, who kept smiling, his eyes fixed on the cup, which he had filled to the brim. He turned on his heel as Fred continued. I pressed my sleeve with a napkin. The old waiter stood at attention across the room and, when I caught his eye, he looked left and right, lifted his hand from under the towel draped over his forearm, and gave me the finger.

After breakfast Fred said, "We're partners, right? You'll get a kick out of this errand. Get a few things around town and drop them off later. Simple."

"Before we go to the track?"

"The track? Oh, no," he said. "We don't go to the track. We make the bet in town." I was disappointed, but my disappointment changed quickly into wonder about the job. I remembered Gail's description of Eddie, the runner Fred had fired while grinning. We got in a cab, and Fred asked the driver his name. "Paul, we have some errands to run. It involves a bit of waiting here and there, but I'll make it worth your while." He handed a bill over the seat.

"Fine with me," Paul said, tucking it into his shirt pocket.

Our first stop was a shoeshine stand on Lexington Avenue. Fred said, "Remember Mike? Go tell him you're picking up for Fred. I'll wait here." Mike was buffing the shoes of a huge blond man. When he finished, I said, "Good morning. Fred sent me to pick up something for him." It was just like my job as a messenger. Mike stared; after a few long seconds, he answered, "Good morning." A car horn blew hard, but I couldn't tell if it was Paul. Mike shuffled over and gave me an envelope, holding it by the corner so he wouldn't taint it with shoe polish. When I opened the cab door, Fred yelled, "What the hell took you?"

"He was shining a man's shoes."

Fred smiled, but he was irritated. "Kid, don't *you* wait. I'm waiting out here, Paul's waiting, the meter's running, and we don't have time to wait for you to wait."

"I know, but Mike was shining the shoes of a really big guy, Fred." I thought size would impress him.

"Big, schmig," Fred said.

The next stop was Marino's fish store, where the owner spoke with a heavy Italian accent and tried to get me to invite Fred for lunch. "Tell him I've got fresh calamari. I'll fry it in the back. Little lemon." He made a circular, squeezing motion with his fingers, as if over a plate.

"We're in a hurry," I said, taking his envelope.

The counterman at Nat Sherman's didn't trust me and walked

outside to look in the cab. I thought of buying a cigar for Fred. As I looked at the case, the man said, "Brazilian cheroots, mild and sweet." I paused at the door, over a small barrel that held great, fat cigars I pictured in Fred's mouth. The sign read, "Five Cents." From behind the counter the man called, "Those are strictly five-cent cigars." And he held his nose. I made my way through a coin shop, several newsstands in hotel lobbies, Mr. Ret's, and a liquor store. I looked at my reflection each time I had the chance and smoothed down my hair. Mr. Ret gave me another Toblerone candy bar wrapped in tissue, and his shaking hands held mine as I turned to leave. He pressed more tissue into my palm, saying, "This is for Freddie. Tell Fred that this is for him because I don't know who will be getting my things." His mouth quivered as if he were about to cry.

Fred separated the crumpled paper and shook out a gold ring. "This is nice," he said, using his jeweler's loupe to stare at the stone. "Mr. Ret must be dissolving his estate, not feeling well lately. You hold it. You got it from him. Good work." I shifted in my seat to put the ring into my pocket, a deep pocket, unlike my other pants that tossed change onto cushions around the city. Fred had settled into the cab as if it were his office. He pulled money from each envelope and marked the amounts in a little book. Paul peered through his rearview mirror. The bills expanded like sponge when Fred opened the envelopes; the stacks were thick and filthy. He put a note under the rubber band that circled each pile. He saw me staring and said, "Like this?" holding up the black leather book. "It's a *New Yorker* date book, from the magazine. Ever read *The New Yorker*?" I had spent the summer reading everything on the stands, even the odd papers that news dealers hung from the frame of their shacks like fringe, papers of different sizes, tints, and typefaces. I read Breslin in the *Tribune*, loving Fat Thomas and Marvin the Torch. I read the *Wall Street Journal* and the *Sporting News*. I thumbed through the *Hollywood*

Reporter as well as *Variety*. I scanned *Cue*, but I had skipped *The New Yorker*. I didn't like its looks—its cover seemed drawn by adults trying to draw like children. "Madeline gave it to me. She loves it. You'll meet her tonight. She's a model, went to college, some kooky place upstate. In a funny way she reminds me of you." He continued to fiddle with the envelopes while I watched, disappointed that I reminded him of a woman when I wanted to be a man's man. "Paul," he said, "take us to the west corner of Fifty-sixth and Eighth."

Paul pulled in front a fire hydrant, saying, "How about I idle at this 'drant?"

"Fine, Paul," Fred said, "but I want to talk to my nephew in private." He handed over another bill. "Won't be long." Paul got out and leaned against the car in front of us, looking down the block. It was hot, and sweat showed through Paul's yellow T-shirt that said, "wmca Good Guys" on the back. Fred asked, "Did you bring your money?"

"Yes, but I could only get the one-thirty-nine."

"All right," he said. "The money in these envelopes is going on different horses. If you want to put your money on my horse, I'll add it. You have to remember you could lose. But today, I feel sure we'll win."

"I guess I'll bet," I said, "if you think we'll win." I took the money from my wallet and he added it to his stack. He looked at his watch again. "This is what you have to do now. Very simple. But you have to do it right." He slid the stacks of bills between a folded paper and then into my inside jacket pocket. "Ours is the first stack," he said.

I had to use a bathroom. I had drunk several coffees at Rumplemayer's and countless glasses of water. I tried to concentrate on Fred's words while I shifted in the sticky vinyl seat.

"Bernie's waiting at the end of the block, on Ninth Avenue. You just walk down the block and give him the money."

"What does he look like?"

"A little guy. A twerp. But don't worry, he's waiting for you. I told him you look like Prince Charles. I told him, 'Prince Charles is coming in a blue suit!'" Fred was grinning hard and wide. "There's one thing," he said, "and this is what it all comes down to." He stopped smiling, lifted my hand off my leg and pressed it between his palms as he looked at me in a deadly way. "Take these," he said, showing ten strips of bond held together by a paper clip, each with a number written in big letters. "Put these in your pants pocket, and keep your hand on them as you walk."

"Then what?"

"Listen!" When he said this, he raised his hand to the side of my face as if he were about to hit me. "Somewhere down the street you'll pass a guy. He'll be standing next to a building. There should be a number written in chalk right next to him. If it isn't, wait a minute, tie your shoe, something like that. Then look again."

"Suppose it's not there?"

"It'll be there. This guy is gonna write it. Could be there now."

"What do I do with the number?" I was following Fred's words as I had never followed instructions from anyone in school, at Paramount, at home. I was studying every phrase when Paul's profile jutted through the open window, and I jumped, hitting my head on the high roof. Paul was red, and sweat beaded on his face and neck. Fred exploded at him, instantly as flushed as Paul, screaming, "What the fuck do you think you're doing? I'm paying for this time, you miserable little hack!" Paul opened the front door and reached in.

"Just getting my hat, for Christ's sake. It's broiling out here." He grabbed a Yankees cap and left.

Fred turned to me, totally calm again. "You get the number from the wall. Then you count these papers, which will be in your pocket, right? Till you come to the number he wrote. Take it out, keep it in your fist, and then slip it into your breast pocket, under the rubber band of the stack nearest you."

"Our money?"

"Right! But remember, Bernie will see you coming, so don't make a big deal with moving the number."

"Suppose I get the wrong piece of paper?"

"Can't. Feel the first one." He held it out.

"It's rough."

"Yeah, it's sandpaper. You feel for that and then count. One, two, three. Okay?"

"I think so," I said.

"Don't count the sandpaper, start counting after that, then stick the number into our stack." He grabbed me by the elbow. "You know what to do, right? You'll do fine, I know." I checked the stack and put the papers in my pocket, holding my hand there, not wanting to mess up the order. "Remember not to count the sandpaper," he said. "And remember, there's a nice girl waiting for you at the end of this day. Now, go!"

I opened the door, keeping my hand in my pants pocket at the same time. My full bladder ached. Paul jumped into the cab as I left, and as I passed the window, Fred leaned out and whispered, "Good luck, nephew!" It was a weird, harsh whisper.

The white sidewalk steamed in the sun, and I knew why Paul wanted his hat. I was sweating after a few feet. I thought I saw Bernie at the end of the long block, but then he disappeared. I walked too fast and couldn't get myself to slow down. Fred hadn't told me the pace. No one was on the street, and the windows of the brownstones had a sooty look along their sills. I sneezed and restrained myself from yanking my hand to my face, so that instead I twisted around, my hand in my pocket, my elbow out, like a bird with a hurt wing. I saw Bernie on the corner, walking back and forth along the avenue, facing me once in awhile.

I decided that if no one gave me the number, I'd return to the cab, but then a man walked up from the basement stairs, looked at me, and wrote "6" just below the yellow and black arrow that pointed the way to a fallout shelter. I touched the cardboard and began counting. I pulled the sixth strip free and, pretending to sneeze again, brought it to my mouth. I opened the folded paper in my jacket with my fingertips and eased the number under the rubber band. I walked with longer strides. Bernie was now staring at me and then at some pigeons around a lamppost. As I got closer I saw him clearly: gray fedora, tiny features. His nose, eyes, and mouth so close together they formed a circle on his face. It struck me how sophisticated the man in the doorway had looked, a pencil-thin mustache. I thought I should grow one like it. Bernie lit a cigarette just as I reached him, making me wait. Then he shouted, "Let's have it!" as if I held him up. I slapped the envelope into his palm and he stuffed it into his front pants pocket and stalked off. I wanted to dash to the cab, but I walked slower than I had ever walked in my life despite the heat. When I reached the fallout shelter I felt a great ease and confidence and love of the world. I went down the three stairs and relieved myself in a corner. Fifty-sixth Street teemed with objects I suddenly found fascinating, a plastic tricycle, a cracked slate stoop, a litter basket crowned with heaps of dried-out carrots and heads of lettuce. Paul had the radio on, but not to WMCA. Instead, we listened to Ed and Pegeen Fitzgerald discuss pillows made of hops, which they slept on in Austria. Fred didn't even look at me when I got in, but ordered Paul to Whitehouse and Hardy on Fifth Avenue.

"Everything went fine," I whispered to Fred, who nodded indifferently.

As soon as we got out of the cab, he changed. All smiles again. "You got the number?"

"It was six."

"And Bernie?"

"Yes, he didn't say much."

"What's to say?" he said, cupping his palm on the small of my back and escorting me into the clothing store. Fred held the sleeve of his new light-gray suit so that I could inspect it, and I touched the fine colored threads that ran through the fabric. He asked endless questions about the alterations and took almost as much time choosing a tie for me, wrapping each one around his fingers and holding the improvised knot under my chin. He settled on light blue with yellow stripes. On the way out, he paused at rows of slippers that seemed more like shoes, shiny and hard. "A pair of these would last me ten years," he said with a faraway look. "Know why? Because I'm never home." He fit one onto his hand and held it in front of me so that I could see my face.

At dusk the traffic changed, delivery trucks giving way to limousines and sports cars. Fred swung the suit over his shoulder, humming. We ate hot dogs from a vendor and walked to his apartment. We passed a tiny men's shop, Pink's, and Fred looked in the window. "Someday I'm going to have my shirts made," he said, shaking his head in appreciation of the collars and cuffs. "Know what their slogan is? 'Any color, as long as it's Pink!'" A block later, he said, "You'll meet Madeline tonight. You'll really like her. And of course, she's got that girl for you."

"I didn't need a date, Fred."

"Of course you do. You'll have fun. Don't be nervous."

"I'm not nervous," I snapped, sounding like Fred.

"Don't worry," he said, "Madeline has some nice friends."

"How long have you been going out with her?"

Fred seemed thrown by the question, as if he hadn't asked it of himself. "Since February or so. Sometime in the winter." As soon as we entered the apartment, Fred put on the radio and hummed along. Every so often a voice gave the call letters and said, "The Mellow Sound." He took a can of Dr. Brown's Cel-Ray tonic from the refrigerator and held it high. "This is for you. Can only get it in delicatessens. Delicious." He poured it into a wineglass. The radio gushed a sentimental song dominated by intensely vibrating strings. Fred ran over and spun the dial. "I hate the mandolin," he said. Long John Nebel came on, doing an ad for the world's best shoeshine. He said, "The leather is softened by rubbing it with the tibia of an elk, polished to a high gloss by a lamb's wool buffing bonnet on a power drill." The method was invented by a bootblack in the St. Louis airport, where you had to mail your shoes. Nebel continued, "After an application of Van-Van oil, the shine is baked under Cooper-Hewitt lights."

"I'd like that shine," Fred said, "but I'm not sending my Church's." He sat at one end of the kitchen table making phone calls while I sat at the other, drinking the tonic and paging through papers and magazines Fred had picked up. He pointed dramatically to a stack of old *New Yorkers*, and I picked one to read in preparation for meeting Madeline. When I thought I'd neared the end of a long piece on amphibious cars, it continued for five more pages. I walked out to the terrace, suddenly very tired, and lay down on a lounge chair next to Fred's new acquisition, three identical sculptures of the Venus di Milo. The evening air felt cool, and I reviewed the places I had been. I particularly relished peeling off the number six. Realizing again that I'd done it right, I laughed with relief. I couldn't wait for the results of the race and imagined celebrating if we won. I also wanted to see Fred with a woman. Would he be gracious or gruff? Would he be both a "man's man" and a "ladies man"? I didn't want to see myself with a woman. I wanted to learn how to act first, as I had learned other things, like how a drink or two could change a dull evening. For the first time, I wanted a drink just to see how much better things could get. Fred took a shower and changed into his suit. I knotted my new tie, and he inspected it. "Beautiful," he said, but then he brushed my shoulder and examined my hair.

I thought he would criticize the crooked part I could never get straight, but he said, "You know, you have a piece of dandruff on your head as big as a dime."

I hadn't had anything like that before. "Is it okay if I take a shower too?" I said.

"Sure," he said. I'm going out for a few groceries. Back soon."

I rushed to the bathroom mirror and combed my hair with my fingers, exposing a ruddy scalp. Raw patches on my arms began to itch, and skin flaked on my chest as well. The shower made the hives brighter. My face was spared, but for how long? Skin continued to loosen on my scalp and, in a panic, I searched the apartment for a remedy. I found a vacuum cleaner in the hall closet and removed the attachment. I knelt in my underwear and vacuumed my head with the aluminum pipe, praying that Fred would not walk in. In the bathroom I saw the treatment had pulled my hair into triangular points, as if a dozen tents were pitched around my head. I took a can of Ajax from under the sink and washed my hair again, scrubbing it ruthlessly. I poured Ajax onto a hot washcloth and rubbed my chest and arms. When I wiped the mirror clear, I saw I had found a kind of solution. I had made my entire chest and arms bright red, but a pink aura outlined my forehead and sideburns, like I had worn a helmet for a long time. In the medicine cabinet I found something I had never seen before: flesh-colored talc, and I dusted my hairline. I was grateful Fred did not inspect me when he returned. As he put the groceries into the closet, I sat in a chair away from the light.

"I've been thinking," he said. "You did a good job today."

"Thanks," I said. "It was fun."

"Fun! Yes, it was!" he said, as if he had never thought of it that way. He laughed and said, "Let me have Mr. Ret's ring." I opened the tissue and Fred plucked it out, shaking it in his fist. "I'll give it to Madeline tonight." We got on the elevator and Fred jingled the coins in his pocket, humming again. It was a tune I recognized but couldn't place, a song I knew, one we had heard together. Then it came to me. The jingle from WNEW, the station where Fred heard "The Make Believe Ballroom." As we walked down the street, he said, "I have a wonderful evening planned. We'll meet Madeline and her girlfriend, and then we'll have drinks, dinner, maybe music. She's bringing Shelley, I think it's Shelley. Christ!" he said suddenly, "You'll need to get her something too."

"Like what?"

"Just something. Like I have this ring, you need something, like flowers, but not flowers. Let me think." He walked faster.

"How about a silk scarf?" I said. "They're selling them around the corner."

"A great idea," he said. When we got to the vendor's stand, I lifted up a red square brightened by a silver pattern. Looking closely, I saw they were punctuation marks: rows of exclamation points, asterisks, ampersands. Fred showed no interest and just nodded his head. After he paid, he began going through his pockets, searching his pants and jacket. "Do you have that ring?" he asked.

"No, Fred. I gave it to you." I could hear a whine in my voice.

"Where? In the hall?"

"Kitchen."

We started back to the apartment. Fred did not return Fitz's greeting. After inspecting the counters, sink, and drainer, Fred moved the table and chairs and explored the floor and molding. He emptied the vegetable bins. I combed the thick white wall-to-wall rug of his bathroom on my hands and knees, crawling before his closet doors that formed a wall of mirrors.

"No luck?" he asked, poking his head in.

"No luck," I answered. He stood in the doorway in his tight white undershirt, jockey shorts, and black socks. A few minutes later he bent over the dining-room table, rubbing the heel of his palm over every inch of the suit. "Maybe it fell into the lining," he said.

But it hadn't. Fred put on another suit. Before we left, he opened the refrigerator and took a long swig of Cel-Ray. I stared at his back. When he turned, he looked at me holding the paper bag with the scarf, as if he suddenly remembered I was there. "Leave the scarf," he said. Fred carried the new gray suit over his arm. Instead of getting on the elevator, he walked to the incinerator and stuffed the suit down the shaft. "That's a hard luck suit," he said. "It lost that ring. I don't want a suit that loses things."

I thought he could have given it away. I'd seen how much Fred had paid and, as we left the building, I couldn't help saying, "Maybe we should have dropped it off at the Salvation Army— you know, for the poor."

Fred kept up his brisk walk and looked over at me, puzzled. "Why? Give away bad luck? To the poor? So they can lose what little they already have?"

He was adamant about hard luck, and I became even more quiet, remembering the words, "You're through, Eddie." I also felt fortunate I hadn't lost the ring myself. I had gotten attached to my blue suit.

BRENDA SEROTTE

Fortuna

The Fortune Teller's Kiss

Mas vale fortuna en tierra ke bonacha en la mar. Good luck
on the ground is worth more than sailing on a clear sea.

➥ LADINO PROVERB

When my father was a very young child, acutely ill
with spinal meningitis, his own mother saved his
life. To cure him she performed a "secret ceremony" that involved heating a lump of lead in a special
bowl, uttering holy prayers known only to her, and enclosing the
nearly dead boy under a sheeted tent.

"She melted the *kourshoum*, lead, in a bronze bowl," my father
said. "The lead hissed and popped; pieces shot up to the ceiling.
The whole place filled with smoke."

His fever raged for three days, but Nona refused to call an
ambulance. Like many immigrants, the elders in my family were
terrified of the "hospital men" who regularly came roaring down
Suffolk, Orchard, Ludlow, or Rivington streets to take sick children away. Many times their mothers never saw them again.

According to other family members who remembered this,
the ritual could be performed only on the day of the new moon,
according to the lunar calendar. When they told the story, my
aunts argued about how many healers were actually present.
Some said four women, some said only two plus Behora. Tantes
Sultana and Allegre didn't do these kinds of rituals, which were
in the realm of healers and medicine women of a certain higher
caliber. My paternal grandmother, obviously, was the real thing,
and when she held sessions like these, superstitious neighbors
who got wind of what was going on fled the building.

Even with her magic, my father got worse. On the fourth day of his enclosure ritual, Nona resorted to a drastic measure: she changed her son's name. Born Samuel, she changed my father's name to Victor, recited the Evil Eye incantation for a "new" boy, and Dad miraculously recovered. Most people had no idea he had once been Samuel.

Behora's mother and grandmother had also been healers in Celebria, near Istanbul, where she was born—if that's really where she came from. It could have been Izmir; in her case, history was fuzzy. I learned to not expect accurate details because stories changed every day. We do know that the province was filled with clairvoyants, and no one doubted her gifts.

Instinct told me that she was different from other grandmas. She scared me more than a little, not like Mother scared me, with unexpected bouts of rage, but in a subtle way. Like when you turn to talk to someone who's vanished. There was something simple about my friends' grandmas that Nona Behora wasn't.

To visit her apartment was a treat I looked forward to. She had curios and trinkets from Turkey: spangled head coverings many Turkish women wore, called *yemeni*, hookah pipes, long- and short-handled gold Turkish coffee pots, a battered, hand-carved oud that had belonged to my grandfather, and an opaque "wishing" ball, her version of a crystal ball. I was allowed to touch and look at everything but was extremely careful when I did. At Nona Behora's I caused no mischief.

Although she practiced all manner of fortune-telling, Nona's main business was reading, with astounding accuracy, the black-patterned mud, or grounds, left over from a cup of Turkish coffee. In this she saw your past, your future, and your soul and also if your soul had been cursed. In that case she was an expert at "soul retrieval"; you'd have to pay more, naturally, but she could lift the curse and remove the ink, dark as coffee grounds, that was staining your essence.

If you held out your hand, she'd read your palm and tell you something intimate about yourself that she couldn't possibly have known. She read tarot cards, which she kept in an old shoebox, triangle-wrapped in a black cloth, and she read runes, hieroglyphic alphabet stones engraved with cryptic symbols, which she wore pinned to her slip in a blue felt bag. They jiggled as she moved.

She used her healing gifts combined with *mumya* powder to solve mysterious maladies of the skin or a bad case of measles. It was rumored that she actually reversed measles-induced blindness once in an eight-year-old girl. This embittered Mother, the fact that her *brúsha*, witch mother-in-law, had died before she could heal my illness: "She would have done magic on you before you ever *saw* the inside of a hospital. I know it." It made me long all the more for my grandma.

On Sundays Mother slept late. Dad liked to spirit me out of the house early to go downtown. I barely had time to stuff an arm in my coat before being whirled, dervish-like, down the stairs. He'd adjust the brim of his hat in the lobby's gilt-framed mirror, and we were off. Usually, it was still dark out; even the garbage trucks hadn't yet rumbled down the block. He walked fast, faster than anyone, even his brothers, and no one matched his stride. I struggled to keep up, my little hand snug and warm inside his huge one, skipping along with the wind gusts that carried the swirling leaves and scraps of paper.

My father was a champion walker. Everybody walked in those days—few people we knew owned cars—but Dad *really* walked. He was always putting on his hat, grabbing his coat, and "going for cigarettes" or "getting the paper" or "getting some air" or "going out to see what's going on." The truth was, he just couldn't stay in one place. Mother said that was why we never moved to the suburbs like "normal" people.

"How would your father have played his numbers or fixed his horses if there were no corner candy stores?"

When I got tired of dragging along, he'd lift me onto his shoulders like he did at the Macy's Thanksgiving Day Parade. I never had to beg him. Silent and majestic in the half-dawn, the Grand Concourse emptied of cars and people was a more interesting street at that time of morning. Across the wide boulevard yellow, white, and red brick art deco buildings, some built with mock facades to look like the Empire State Building, lit up as soon as sunlight spilled over their arched windows and geometric-patterned roofs. Dad pointed them out to me: "Look at that!" I thought it wondrous, too. For a long time I believed that the sun fell from the sky onto the buildings of the Grand Concourse before it touched any other street in the city.

We boarded the practically empty D train at 170th Street and changed at 42nd Street for the forty-minute ride to Delancy. Dad read the paper, and I always had a book, just recently discovering how to read. It never seemed like a long trip. Magically, it was full morning when we emerged from underground. But we never immediately went to Grandma's; first, we strolled all around the Lower East Side. We explored whichever stores were open on Delancy, Grand, Houston, and Orchard. All the Jewish-owned businesses opened Sundays, and although we rarely bought anything, Dad would point to things in the windows and say, "I'm gonna *buy* you this . . . and this—" and that was enough.

Near Grandma's building, at the corner of Suffolk Street, I knew what was coming. He liked to tell me the truck story, how, during the war, he maneuvered an amazingly skillful turn down that very same narrow block, driving a U.S. Army transport truck full of ammunition. My father was to drive one of a caravan of trucks to Florida from the army base at Fort Dix, New Jersey, when he was struck by this incredible longing to see his mother. Impulsively, he turned the truck around after crossing the George

Washington Bridge, detoured to Suffolk Street, and went to his mother's for breakfast.

The stunt naturally earned him an AWOL. When he finally caught up to the transport in Georgia, his excuse to the sergeant was the truth: "I had to have Mama's breakfast. I needed it!" I was convinced that my father could charm the whole U.S. Army and every officer in it.

I would conjure up the details of those Sundays for many months, even for years to come, particularly in hospitals or when I was forced to endure painful procedures on my legs. Often nurses left me alone to cry; you had to be brave, they told us, or else "How will you get *well*?" So I'd close my eyes and fantasize that I was sitting on top of my father's shoulders as he walked downtown to Nona's. That turned off the hysteria that starts in the groin and climbs slowly up to your neck and makes a lump there. I discovered a hidden roadway far enough inside me that I escaped to, and there, often, I smelled lamb cooking, or fresh-baked *boyos*, the Sephardic version of challah bread.

The first time I willed myself inside one of those Sundays was during the two weeks I spent in isolation. They said I was very brave, but what child has the choice? Throughout my months, years, of hospital visits, I never met one cowardly child. We were all "brave." Bravery is easy when you haven't figured out how sick you really are nor the enormity of that sickness in relation to the rest of your life.

Healers of different ethnicities existed all over the city in the 1950s, but few were authentic diviners: "Your grandmother was notorious, the real thing," Mother said, "and much in demand. How do you think she survived?" Nona was widowed at forty-seven. Grandpa Chelebón, "Charles," whom all the brothers' sons on my dad's side were named after, died long before I was born. He had worked in a Christmas lights factory along with his eight brothers, and there was talk about branching out, adding colored lights as ornaments. But it wasn't to be. On the night of my grandparents' twenty-fifth wedding anniversary, while the family assembled in Nona's apartment for a party, my grandfather had a massive heart attack at the factory, and they found him the next morning, buried under a pile of tiny lights and tangled wires.

"My father *knew* Christmas lights would one day be a big business in this country," Dad said, sighing. It was the family curse: all nine uncles would *almost* get rich, *almost* invent something useful.

Suddenly alone and penniless, his young widow had no choice but to practice her art. Thus, Nona Behora became a famous Lower East Side fortune teller. Lines formed on her stoop day after day, queuing up into the narrow, smelly stairwell. The stairs were steep, hard for me to climb as a little girl, and I marveled at how she did it on those lumpy, swollen legs. It was amazing, in fact, that she even fit in the narrow stairwell, she was so huge.

Nona Behora was obese, fatter than any other person I'd ever seen then and even now. She was six times bigger than my friends' grandmothers, and so she hated having her picture taken. Every picture of her shows her clutching a big black pocketbook to her belly in a vain attempt to hide her ruptured stomach. It was the size of her babies that caused her belly to rupture in three places, they said, and that was what eventually killed her. Of course, they told me a lie about her death. The crazy story I got was that "she caught a *really* bad cold, and it didn't get better." Thereafter, whenever I caught one, I was sure I'd die.

All her boys were hefty at birth, but the last one, my uncle Albert, weighed a gigantic sixteen pounds. Some family members said fourteen, but no matter. Mother said the hospital took a mother-and-baby picture and sent it to one of the daily newspapers. My fears alternated between catching a really bad cold and giving birth to a monster baby.

She had a lovely face, though. Atop that wide neck and mis-shapen body sat a doll's head with chiseled features, smooth and unblemished. Her olive skin and silky black hair was a replica of the graceful flamenco dancer whose face we had on a postcard from Spain. Nona never complained, that I remember, but her obese body must have suffered. At her death, a cousin swore, she weighed four hundred pounds and was too huge to be carried down the narrow stairwell. Carpenters were called to remove the large front window frame in order to get her out.

"They hoisted her down, poor thing, while the whole block watched."

Nona's regular customers would wait as long as it took for one of her famous readings, often long enough to finish the *Mirror, Daily News, Jewish Daily Forward,* or *La Vara,* a Sephardic newspaper in print until the late 1940s that was written entirely in Ladino with Hebrew characters. She charged three bucks for a reading—two if you were short of cash.

All the Turks read cups or pretended to. In Middle Eastern homes it was a mark of hospitality to serve Turkish coffee the minute company arrived. You were not a *benedám,* a decent human being, if you didn't and were talked about as having the "manners of a horse." To be asked: "Kieres un kavesiko?" Would you care for a little Turkish coffee? Was a formality. You never refused, and you *never* asked for a second cup, or you'd lose face and not be invited back. Either the host or a girl of marriageable age brought out the tray with the good demitasse cups, glasses of water, Jordan almonds, Turkish Delights candies, or a rare delicious treat: a white-jelly fondant called *sharope.*

Behora always had a large crowd and neighborhood women to assist her, and once in a while this helping neighbor got into trouble. Grandma had a hard rule about how the *libríks,* those tall gold coffee pots, should be washed. In order to preserve the coffee's special flavor, you were to wash them in cold water only.

An incident occurred when the woman tried to do it her own way, by scrubbing the pot with steel wool and then soaking it in hot water. She was ejected from the apartment.

"Out the window, Nona?" I asked, excited. I knew well their obsession with throwing things out of windows. She laughed.

"Yes, *mi kookoovaya!*" She called me her "little owl" because she thought I was very smart.

Of the many stories concerning my Grandma Behora, this out-of-the-window stuff, which my dad inherited, was among the strangest. I never figured it out. *Echelo por la ventana*: throw it out the window, became a catchphrase for anything that displeased them. An in-law legend in the family had to do with the time Nona met her son Kelly's betrothed. The girl's parents came with a cake, but apparently they failed to make a favorable impression on my grandmother. There was an argument; the future in-laws walked out in a huff, Behora marched to the window, and, just as they passed underneath it, she dumped the remainder of the chocolate cake out the window.

"My brother and his *novia*, bride, nearly stepped in it!" my dad howled. "It just missed her shoes!"

The Recipe for Destiny began with three heaping teaspoons of the fine, pulverized grind to each small cup of water. I've seen my uncles come to fisticuffs over this recipe, whether or not to use equal amounts of sugar to coffee before boiling. All agreed that it had to be boiled three times—taken off and then put back on the flame. Why three? "It just has to be," Dad said. Individual cups were then heated with boiling water, and some of the coffee foam was spooned into each one before filling.

It was bitter tasting, even watered down and sugared, but you got used to it. Guests either loved *kave Turko* or pretended to, scared not to drink it. After the proper amount of time and conversation, the remaining liquid in your cup was swished around, the cup turned upside down, and your hands placed crisscross on top of it, so that the cup could leech your "spirit," one of the first steps in retrieving a damaged soul. Then, when the fortune teller was ready, she announced: "Kaves d'alegria!" a prayer for "happy news."

Then, with the seriousness of a doctor's examination, Nona diagnosed your fate.

I learned some useful information by listening, stuff I'd one day use at parties to become, what else, the center of attention: Numbers were always about time. A large number meant years in a person's life; smaller numbers meant days or hours. Palm trees signified good luck, but other trees, like oaks or maples, meant prepare for a catastrophe. Airplanes—Grandma always made out their wings, no one else ever saw them—meant travel, of course, as did boats, but a boat usually foretold a romantic end. Also, boats could mean a desire to escape something. These shapes Grandma easily discerned: "See *Chika*?" She'd point, showing me here and here and there, and I'd pretend to see what she saw.

Every so often, money made a cameo appearance. Those times guests became ecstatic. Round shapes were coins, small moneys; rectangles were the larger, dollar amounts. Grandma usually saw rectangles, not coins. Or, in the middle of a reading, she'd see a bizarre picture. Once she saw a horse's head in my father's cup. "How apropos!" Mother said, rolling her eyes. And she almost always saw a boat in his cup, declaring out loud that her son had a desire to escape his life:

"Ah . . . Victor, Victor . . . he wants to travel . . . he'll leave on a long journey." It infuriated Mother.

"It's all *crap*! His mother reads whatever she damn well pleases in those cups!" But even Mother admitted that, if she was one thing, Grandma was smart. She kept her mouth shut and didn't *ask* questions; she let people give *her* the questions they wanted answered, so that they blabbed all their own information. "All the professionals work that way," Mother said.

For large family readings on weekends, my grandmother sometimes ventured out of her own neighborhood. A visit to the Bronx was rare, but occasionally she did it. Those times, I'm sad to say, I was ashamed of her because of her size and tried not to acknowledge her as my relative. If I spotted her dark head emerging from the 170th Street subway stop, I ran into the building before she saw me. I always seemed to be outside when she came. Once she saw me, I had to walk to her and help her carry her things, and endure snickers and giggles from all the kids. I baked in shame as her elephantine figure approached.

Some kids were mean enough to point; they laughed as she trudged snail-like up the Concourse. This in itself was a remarkable feat, given her size and condition. I was so torn. One part of me wanted to run to her, open my arms as wide as possible, like I did when I entered her house, and hug her. The other side of me wished she had stayed home. She seemed out of place on the wide, sunny street, dressed, even on the warmest days, in that tremendous black overcoat. I didn't always understand that it was meant to cover up her body. She dragged two loaded shopping bags, one in each hand, so heavy with foodstuffs and clothing that they scraped the sidewalk.

"Look at the fatso!" kids shouted. Some told me, "Your grandma's *fat* and *ugly*! She looks like a *man*!" That was because of the faint but noticeable mustache on her upper lip. No matter that the bags were filled with gifts for me and my brother—flannel pajamas, shirts, blouses, and the sweet delicacies we loved that were found only on the Lower East Side—I still cringed.

If I didn't make it into the lobby before she saw me, where I could hide, I was forced to watch her climb. I held my breath as she struggled up the outer stoop of four steep steps, often teeter-tottering backward. The shopping bags had a seesaw effect; they pulled her one hand forward, while the other side fell back. But it prevented a fall. Then she climbed the inner stoop, which was a longer flight of marble steps—all this without ever holding the banister—and, finally, she made it into the lobby. We lived in the rear of the building, so her journey wasn't through; now she had to make it across the lobby and up two more flights of stairs to our apartment. My mother would be waiting at the door most times with a glass of water.

When all the uncles and their wives and kids got together, someone was bound to play a joke on the fortune teller. When she got up to go to the bathroom, they switched coffee cups. When Nona came back she continued the reading, amazingly making sense, predicting something fitting to the person, even if his cup had been switched. It was uncanny.

"Nobody fooled Mama," Dad said. "Nobody."

For twenty dollars, which was a lot of money for most folks, Nona performed a believable table séance, where she communicated with *los muertos*, dead loved ones. Even hearing about it gave me nightmares. This communication involved some preparation. The drapes were pulled shut, so that it was dark even on the sunniest day. She'd put on a dreamy Turkish record of slow, instrumental oud music, and one of her card-playing Sephardi cohorts was paid a couple of dollars to thump the wall in the adjoining room from time to time, for further atmosphere. The same person would also watch that the record didn't skip.

"Trouble always happened," Dad said. Dead people's relatives started out excited but soon became agitated and frightened. "It was more than they bargained for." Some screamed; some wept uncontrollably. In general it caused a commotion, and neighbors called the cops. Grandma got arrested, for the fifth or sixth time, for "engaging in gypsy practices." A couple of hours later one of her sons bailed her out, and in a few days she was back in business, with many of the same Irish cops who had arrested her as new clients.

I asked her once if she could truly speak to the dead and if she had ever talked to her husband, Grandpa Chelebón, about me. She winked, smiling mysteriously: "He knows you, *si*."

"What did he say about me?"

"He knows you don't like your brother. He said it's okay!"

It was a relief to know that Grandpa in heaven forgave me for hating the baby. I was under the childish impression that no one knew I wished he'd never been born. Everyone adored the baby. It was a brand-new experience for me; up until five I was the *kadún* of the harem for a long while, and then there was a sultan-in-training usurping me. When no one was around, I uncovered my brother in his crib and stared at his naked pink body, wondering why, when I thought him so ugly, they thought him so special. I was beginning to get an idea of how important it was to be a *boy*.

A few times I had the privilege of watching my grandmother work. I was six when she died, so I had her three more years and knew her much better than I knew my mother's mother, Benvenuta. I felt a bond with Nona Behora, and it's a good thing I paid attention to her words because soon, for my own survival, I would employ the same, innate perception skills when I needed to "read" people. Her intelligence concerning human nature was vast. Although Mother called her a "professional," which really meant she was a fake, I believe she knew quite a lot.

For one thing she could tell what was going on with people on the inside. She read faces and body language, while allowing for discretion, and could turn on a dime if she thought a prediction she was about to give might upset a client, especially to the point of nonpayment. Then she'd switch it and make up different "good" news.

"Remember," she told me, "tell good news." Even Mother concurred that only amateurs told the bad stuff. "Your grandmother knows better. Or else they blame the clairvoyant for *all* their troubles." I wondered why my mother didn't realize that she, too, blamed Nona for all her troubles.

No poker-faced player could have better concealed visions of illness or marital strife than my grandmother. After the client left, she'd tell me the real story about them. When she read, if she raised just one eyebrow or if her mouth twisted to one side, the future was dim. Similarly, if she pursed lips, it meant that she was figuring out what to say, stalling for time. When she bit her lower lip, real trouble: usually health. Money problems? She'd nod once. I got to know the code after a few times, and later, in the hospital, I became an expert in figuring out the doctors.

When they made their rounds, they put on certain faces. Almost never did they tell the truth, certainly not to kids. When they examined me they gave themselves away by biting or pursing their lips or by lifting an eyebrow. I got to know how a tilted head at a certain angle meant they were surprised by something—not necessarily bad. That's when I knew I wasn't going to die, too. When doctors conferred with parents, their faces *and* their coloring changed entirely, especially when delivering bad news. They'd step back, turn pale, and bite their lip.

Kind nurses blinked a lot. The mean ones didn't look at me at all, kept their heads rigid, had perennially furrowed brows, and their lips were always "skinny." The meaner the nurse, the taller and straighter they held themselves. Good nurses always slumped a bit. This is what Nona taught me.

I had no doubt that Nona was brilliant. She spoke Arabic, Turkish, French, and Spanish fluently but could neither read nor write English, though she spoke it well enough to attract a few Irish-American and Italian customers. Yiddish she steadfastly refused to learn, but she understood enough to know when her Ashkenazi clients talked behind her back. Those times they'd get a reading they wished they hadn't.

"She had a way about her that, when she read, the whole room got quiet," Mother said. In any language she could restore your health or curse you mightily and was equally fond of doing both.

There were many family stories concerning her uncanny powers and just as many about her fractured relationships with people in and outside the family: "If my mother cursed a person, gave them a *maldisyón*," my father said, "it meant doom." And when she could think of nothing to say, she was so good at making things up. One thing she told everybody was that soon they'd receive a letter, an *important* letter. Why? "Because *everyone* gets a letter!"

Mothers would bring her their daughters' bras to study. The bra clung to the body and was therefore a good indicator of a girl's sexual appeal; that's how you knew when she'd marry. Eyes closed, Nona felt the fabric, "listened" to what it told her. Here, too, she acted professionally. She had to be careful of what she said at all times, as it was against Jewish law to stop a wedding ceremony, even if she predicted that the guy was no good. This was touchy, and often she had to keep it to herself. Worse than that kind of trouble was spinsterhood, God forbid. Yet even that had a remedy.

Like many fortune tellers, Grandma doubled as a marriage broker. For a few dollars more she'd tactfully offer her services in the hunt for a suitable man. Tack another dollar on, and she'd read the mother's cup, too, to discern whether or not in-law trouble was in store. Her readings were never boring.

It happened on one of these special Sundays that Behora told my fate. That day we let ourselves in as quietly as possible when we saw she was "in session," deep into reading someone's cup. When she was like that, Dad said, we had to be invisible. Across from her sat the client, a small woman, scrunched down into her chair, who seemed to shrivel up even smaller as the reading continued. I spied on them from Nona's half-open bedroom door.

At one point, close to the end of the reading, the woman wiped her eyes with a tissue, obviously moved by something Grandma had told her. A second after that she laughed, attesting to Nona's brilliant skill for turning things around. Finally, the reading was over. I watched as the lady counted out some dollars and left them on the table. Nona's custom was to not touch money until after the client departed. "Thank you! Thank you!" she said, sounding grateful, and left. I knew my grandmother would be in a very good mood, as the session had ended well. She knew, of course, I had been spying.

"Welcome namesake!" she called out, without turning around. This was my usual greeting, plus a crushing, smothering hug. Her belly was grotesquely lopsided from that unrepaired hernia, the knob of which pushed into my ribs when she held me close. Then she would put me at arm's distance and study my face. She loved it that I looked like her, had her eyes and nose, but I think she wished my hair wasn't red like Mother's. I wondered, and was a little scared about it, if one day I would become as hugely fat as she was. According to my father, I certainly would, but he said it laughing, and I know he loved teasing me.

She was not overly affectionate or demonstrative toward me, certainly not like Tante Alice, and she rarely smiled because she had poor teeth, but for me she managed a turned-up corner of her mouth, a half-smile. It's a habit I copy to this day. That day she was happier than usual to see us. She wasn't one to talk or interact with kids—in fact, you hardly heard her voice unless she was reading fortunes—but I knew she loved me by other things she did, like taking my head in her hands and moving it from side to side. She did that, then she patted the chair next to her.

My love of books amused her, especially that I couldn't yet read them. The books I had were all well-worn, hard-covered classic editions passed down from older cousins, which I looked forward to one day reading. I loved even the *feel* of a book, of turning it over, opening it, smelling the binding. I would spend hours trying to decipher a single sentence.

That day Nona examined the Nancy Drew mystery I carried

and, gratefully, put it down. Once or twice in the past she had done the window thing: taken a book I left on the table, opened it as if to see if she approved of the subject matter, though she couldn't read any better than I, then tossed it. It seemed weird, but she didn't do it angrily. Normally, I would have *screamed*; with Nona Behora, though, I didn't dare. There was something about her that I instinctively didn't want to disturb. *Glenda of Oz* went this way, as did a picture book of exotic tropical fish, which I managed to retrieve from the gutter on our way home.

She asked me that day if I wanted a little cup of Turkish coffee. I didn't but said yes anyway. It seemed that she wanted to read my fortune right away, although she usually served the coffee after breakfast. My father carried in a demitasse cup filled with just a bit of milk, to which she added some coffee. Mother really disapproved of this habit of reading children's cups—she said because they needed to *live* their lives, not have it told to them. Then she'd bite her forefinger and repeat the prayer for protection.

I drank the little cup as fast as I could without choking, turned it upside down, waited a couple of minutes, and then sat back as she read my grounds.

Nona envisioned two things happening to me but told me of only one: that I was going to get lost, probably in the summertime. What she didn't tell me but told my father was that I was going to get sick with an illness I might die from. The premonition, or whatever it was, devastated my father then and my mother later. It changed everything in all our lives for all time, primarily because many Turks believed that she was powerful enough to have stopped it. This was the second time Nona foresaw that her son's firstborn child would be sick.

She studied my cup for so long that morning that I became impatient. "What does it say, Grandma? What does it *say*?" All I could see was mud. She squinted, concentrating harder. It was always fun to have your fortune told—so far. Many times she had told her grandchildren whether or not they'd be getting a new dress for a party or a doll for Chanukah. But that day I sensed her tension and unease, and it transferred to me and made me a little scared. When she finally looked up, she stared past me at a fixed point in the distance. I turned around to look, too; of course, nothing was there. During all this Dad had been looking out the window, smoking, lost in thought. He didn't see his mother place her right hand on top of my head and lift my chin until I found her eyes.

"De tu kaza no te mankes!" May you never be missing from your home! she said.

At that moment my father turned to stare at us. I didn't recognize the look on his face. What she had given me was a standard Ladino blessing for children, one I'd heard many times before. They'd say it if you went to the hospital to get your tonsils out or if you were going on a trip. This insured that you'd come home. It was Nona's tone that made the difference. She spoke so low I could barely hear her, and she started to breathe heavily, too.

The apartment became so quiet for those few seconds that I clearly heard the tick-tocking of the table clock from the next room. Then she leaned forward and tenderly kissed my forehead.

"Don't worry, *Chika*," she said, in her choppy English, "they find you fast!"

It wasn't these strange, out-of-character actions I feared as much as my father's openmouthed face. He took a step toward us then stopped. Finally, the moment ended, she slapped her knees, said "*Venga!*" Come! and we followed her to the table.

I couldn't wait to run into what passed for a kitchen to see what goodies she had prepared for us that morning. The misshapen, "holy" bronze bowl used for the lead-popping ceremonies was stored underneath the sink, where no grandchild dared touch it. Amazing to me was the fact that her kitchen also contained a bathtub and a toilet bowl. It was so narrow a space that a couple of times a year her dress caught fire on the burners, and we'd get a frantic call in the Bronx to come quick, she had scorched her stomach again.

Out of that unbelievably cramped, claustrophobic space came the most wonderful meals, and out of her mouth the best stories. These tales were different than the ones Tantes Sultana and Allegre told. Nona Downtown, as we grandchildren called her, told Turkish ghost stories from the old country, stories about curses that had come true for evil people and predictions that *endivinas* had made that came to pass.

If any of her grandchildren became too wide-eyed or fearful, even better. She seemed to love scaring us; she'd show us an empty cup and ask, "See? See what's in there?" Of course, we were too scared to look. This made her laugh and slap her thighs. All of them, on both sides of the family, were fond of scaring and teasing kids, especially before meals.

Her breakfasts were legendary; Nona Downtown began the day with a feast. My other grandma had been too sickly to ever prepare a meal, let alone a lavish Turkish one, and Mother hated to cook. Even her sisters didn't cook like Nona. She had risen extra early that day to get things ready. The table had been set with a fine, white, flower-embroidered linen cloth from Istanbul. Three plates of oblong, phyllo dough pastries called *borekas*, filled either with cheese or spinach, were already waiting. Next she brought out the large bread rings, the *boyos*, and there was enough for fifteen.

She had cooked us *yaprakes*, stuffed grape leaves, that morning, with hard-boiled brown eggs, from an ancient Sephardic recipe, where the eggs cook in a slow oven for many hours before being braised with onionskins and coffee grounds to give them their brown color. As always, there was a wide assortment of favorite cheeses: feta; goat; the delicious, yellowy *kashkaval*; and a sharp "white cheese" that I refused to taste. My one problem: How would I fit in dessert?

Oh, the sweets! I taste them still. I managed to eat to Downtown Nona's satisfaction—you wouldn't *dare* not to—and I always had room for the best part, her homemade, hard cookie *biscochos*, marble halvah, delectable airy-white meringue balls, miniature Greek baklavas, and the remarkable *mustachudos*—not as delicious as Tante Sultana's walnut balls but remarkable nonetheless. And, of course, Turkish Delights gelatin candy, sesame-crunch candies, and chocolate-covered jelly bars. By the time we were up to the *pepitas*, roasted sunflower seeds that Dad and his brothers ate by the pound, I was pretty nauseous. So Nona packed up everything in case I got hungry on the subway home.

Food hasn't tasted as good since. It may have been too much at one time, but I learned to love food too well after a two-year hiatus for illness, when I refused to eat at all. Our entire clan loved to eat those famous breakfasts with the master. How could my young cousins and I know that one day we'd all have the infamous "Nona hips"? You simply *had* to eat—and praise the food as well.

"Look at the size of this pastry!" my father said. "What perfect eggs! Where did you find them so big? The chicken must have weighed twenty pounds, Mama! *Ke pransa!* What a banquet! Mama, you're my life, my star!"

My father and grandmother shared a special camaraderie of secrets and private jokes. He could always make her laugh by mimicking a relative's walk or odd speech, and she'd slap her big leg and roar. But her moods were mercurial; without changing facial expressions, she'd go from belly laughter to fist pounding, suddenly yelling out a curse for a customer who might have tried to cheat her or a cousin who had possibly offended her: "Low-luck fiend!" she'd shout in Turkish, making me jump. Then the mask lifted, and she was herself, laughing and eating.

Her shifting moods, according to my mother, were the very thing that caused our own bad luck. "She got carried away one day and forgot that she was cursing her own son!" I don't know if Mother truly believed that her mother-in-law was that evil, but I know that I was torn between believing my mother and siding with my dad. I favored Dad, of course, but, still, there was something strange about this huge, dark person . . . I saw Mother's point.

A formal procession was made of serving each dish. Like most Turkish women, Nona deferred to her sons, waiting on them, catering to their needs, and not allowing them to help. I carried what I could, but it was Grandma who brought the heavy *platas* laden with goodies from the kitchen to the front room, making at least ten trips. When the table was crammed full so that not another spoon fit, she finally plopped down into the nearest chair, cursing her bad legs for their slowness, gasping in pain. That's how I remember seeing her the last two or three times we visited—in agony.

We buried ourselves in the work of eating for a long while. Then, as if prearranged, the moment came when both of them dropped their forks, leapt up from their seats—as fast as someone her size could leap—and flew into each other's arms, kissing and hugging. Sometimes she cried or my dad cried; often they both did. I thought that no one could love a mother the way my father loved his. My terrible secret was that I often felt that I didn't love my mother at all. She yelled at me for no good reason or when I spilled something, and I overheard her telling people that I had a "bad disposition." When I asked Dad what that meant, he said he didn't know. "Don't pay attention," he said.

"Why?"

"Because *Y* is a crooked letter."

Nona Downtown knew my secret, I'm sure. She'd pat my braids and examine my scalp when I came, as if she'd seen Mother yanking my hair from its roots that morning as she brushed it. I hated her for that, of course, but not as much as I did for being obsessed with my one-year-old brother. Her whole *face* changed when she picked him up out of his crib. She stopped scowling. It wasn't just me; Dad was jealous of Charlie, too. When *she* stopped scowling, *he* scowled, and it was always when Mother was feeding, holding, playing with, or talking to the baby.

"Oh, you're both such babies!" she liked to say. "Worse than this little guy, aren't they?" Then she'd coo and cluck and say disgustingly loving things to my brother. But I knew I was right. She never took *my* face in her hands and made sounds like that. "But you're not a baby anymore!" she'd say. After mentioning that I hated my mother a couple of times and getting slapped by Sultana for saying it, I kept my mouth shut.

Nona and my father had a fierce attachment like that, too. They dwelled in a theater of gluttony and raw emotion. I tried to find a place to fit into and couldn't, even though my dad made me feel special. When I was in Tante Allegre's house, I came close—until her own family came home.

❦ ❧

When Grandma lay on her deathbed, a woman named Tia Awahdeesh came to see her. Years ago this lady had been elected by the Turkish community to mediate the dispute between Nona and the superstitious parents of girls her sons wanted to date. They were afraid to let their daughters go out with the boys because of their mother's reputation for cursing those she didn't like—which was just about anyone they dated.

"They had to find a very strong woman to face down your grandmother," Mother said. "One like Tia Awahdeesh, who herself had borne only sons."

Apparently, this Tia Awahdeesh lady did her job because all

four of Behora's sons eventually married. People came in throngs, curious to see a legend. By then she, too, was respectfully referred to as "honored Aunt" and was given the title Tia Behoroocha. Privately, though, many still called her the Turkish Witch or the Suffolk Street Sorceress or Spanish Gypsy and, certainly, *La Gorda*: The Fat One.

Some came to give *bezemano*, the practice of kissing the hand of an esteemed elder; some to ask forgiveness for any wrongs they might have knowingly or unknowingly committed. "Most came," Mother said, "so she'd put in a good word for them on the other side."

I don't know at which point I knew that Nona did not read from a script that she had scotch-taped to the bottom of each flowered porcelain cup. I thought this originally because, for everyone, she told variations on the same fortune theme. But I came to know that people's lives weren't all that different. Unattractive women had a harder time finding a man to marry; beautiful women had "many men interested in you" but were often unhappy as well. And everyone got letters. Some people would know sadness early, some later on. Occasionally, there was a terrible prediction and great grief, but, usually, a lucky happenstance, not to worry, was right around life's corner.

The clients created their own futures as they sat through their readings. When Grandma shouted, "Oh, my God!" it didn't necessarily mean that she had seen something awful; invariably, though, the person would jump up or cry out: "I knew it! I *knew* it!" What did they know? They had chosen to believe that a fortune teller knew something, when, in fact, she had foretold nothing. Nothing at all. Even I recognized that this was silly but was careful not to laugh, especially when Grandma winked at me.

Her séances and late-night sessions unearthed the darker side of fortune-telling. I couldn't fathom paying money to be frightened, nor did I understand why anyone would want to contact a ghost or a dead spirit. Yet even the terrified believers returned again and again. I put it together when I got older. It all had to do with Possibility, the hope that a clairvoyant, by saying something, could change something, alter your life significantly or even just a little.

No matter what Mother said about her being "crooked" and "vindictive," words I loved hearing and saying almost as much as *spinster* and its Ladino counterpart, *soltéra*, I was fiercely attached to my exotic, Janus-faced grandmother. Half of us believed in her powers, the other half in her moneymaking skills.

The last time I saw her was the day she told me I'd get lost. As we were about to leave, she whispered to Dad, "Take good care of her!" And he promised he would. He tried, too. But no one stops Fate. Because my father was a man who could never keep his mouth shut, he blabbed about the vision to my mother, who became so incensed with the prediction I would get lost that she smacked me for it in advance and then berated Dad.

"You dope! *Azno!* Donkey's ass! Son of a *witch!*"

She was frightened and furious at the same time. They fought bitterly until he finally slammed out, probably to the Turkish baths. Right away, Mother interpreted Nona's prediction as a curse, and, sadly, she allowed a fortune teller's vision to govern the rest of her life. She chose to believe that the very person who had foreseen it, if only she hadn't said it, could have diverted her *mazál preto*, black luck.

When we left 117 Suffolk Street that day, I looked up as I always did to wave good-bye. Nona was seated by the large front window mechanically shuffling cards, and from where I stood she looked very much the gypsy, her yellow-and-red spangled *yemeni* wrapped around her head. The wooden fortune teller behind glass at the boardwalk penny arcade was dressed almost identically. I always wondered who wrote those fortunes, the ones that fell out of the slot.

I kept looking at her long after she stopped waving to me. She was already lost in thought, probably thinking of an entertaining little *konsejika*, a story, to tell a client. I believed in stories, had already come to the point of needing to hear them.

MARVIN V. ARNETT

The Boys of Summer

Pieces from Life's Crazy Quilt

Т hey came in April, the boys of summer. Resplendent in pastel-colored gabardine suits, wearing faded winter tans, they were the first wave of a two-part pilgrimage that took place yearly, as my father would say, "come hell or high water." They were the true harbingers of spring.

The first wave drove their brightly colored convertibles with the tops up. The second wave, which usually arrived late in May, drove with the tops down, flaunting the butter-soft tan, brown, or black leather upholstery tailor-made for their customized cars. Every time Father saw them, his facial expression would harden into that of an angry old man. He said that although they called themselves survey takers, they were actually con men who did their job well. After the first year, they did not survey our house.

When my father first opened the door to them, he took their measure in full. They were in the neighborhood to take a survey, or so they said, and could he spare a few minutes to answer some questions for a young man working his way through college? Father did not answer but kept his eyes trained on the bright pink Chevrolet convertible visible through the open door.

The questions asked seemed strange to me, but Father appeared to understand them completely. What are your favorite radio programs? Name as many as you can think of.

He smiled and replied, "Kraft Music Hall, Hallmark Hall of Fame, Texaco Theater, the six o'clock news, and, oh yes, Saturday afternoon broadcasts from the Metropolitan Opera."

Suddenly, the atmosphere changed. The young men slammed their folders shut, snapped out "thank you," and rushed downstairs to the Davis apartment. I thought I heard the one with dark hair mumble, "Smart ass nigger," as he trailed the others down the steps. My father just laughed and shut the door. Winking at Mother, he said, "They'll find what they're looking for down there."

All that day they flitted from door to door, asking questions, teasing the ladies of the house, and promising to return the next month to take anyone who wanted to go for a ride in their glistening convertibles. After they left, there was much laughing and comparing of notes between the ladies of the neighborhood. Why, there hadn't been this much excitement since Joe Louis paid his aunt a surprise visit.

It wasn't until church services on Sunday that Mother learned what all the excitement was about. It seemed that the young men had taken much more than a survey. They had also taken orders for sweaters—soft angora sweaters—in rainbow colors of pink, baby blue, canary yellow, lime green, vibrant red, chalk white, and ebony black. For the more adventurous, there were shades of fuchsia, turquoise, wine, and magenta. The mind boggled at the range of styles and colors. To think they were all available for only fifty cents down and twenty-five cents a week. Some of the ladies said they felt a little guilty taking advantage of such nice young men. When Father heard this, he snorted and said, "Taking advantage! Fifty cents down and twenty-five cents a week for the rest of their lives."

He could have saved his breath. For the first time in memory, the neighborhood neither sought nor accepted my father's counsel. The ladies' only concern was for the safe arrival of the sweaters they had ordered. Mother, always loath to admit that she did not understand something, finally broke down and asked Father the question that had been churning around in her head. "William, what does a survey have to do with selling sweaters?"

Father answered, "That's just their way of determining if the people in the neighborhood are dumb enough to be taken in by their scam. If they listen to silly programs, they are probably silly people. That's why my answers to their questions angered them so. They knew I understood the name of the game they were playing."

Mother nodded her head and then said, "Now why didn't I think of that? You always said they were thinking while we were sleeping."

True to their word, the young men were back in less than a month, laden with boxes of ladies' sweaters in assorted colors. A holiday atmosphere invaded the neighborhood. The ladies followed the salesmen from house to house as they delivered orders. A spirit of competition soon set in. Those who had ordered only one or two sweaters asked for more as they witnessed five and six sweaters being delivered to their neighbors. The salesmen had wisely brought along extra sweaters and were able to fill their requests.

When the smoke cleared, many ladies had overextended themselves but were too proud to admit it. They would pull a salesman to the side and ask for additional credit, promising to pay the fifty-cent deposit the following week as well as double the twenty-five-cent weekly fee. The salesman graciously accepted their offer but warned that, since he would be making up the deposits out of his own pocket, he would have to charge interest. The ladies agreed to his terms—after all, it was only interest on fifty cents. As a bonus, the salesmen gave each customer a set of angora socks. It was late afternoon before the salesmen finished their deliveries and drove off, horns blowing. Amid the excitement, Father sat on our porch reading the evening newspaper.

The next Sunday, and for several Sundays to follow, the Church of the True Believers resembled a flower garden far more than the home of a saved and sanctified congregation. The seats of the sanctuary were filled with ladies of every age and description decked out in a rainbow of brightly colored angora sweaters. Although Reverend Elder admonished the congregation not to be taken in by the "garish things of this world," the number of members wearing sweaters increased week by week.

Gradually, the sweater craze reached a climax, and the number of ladies wearing them slipped significantly, then dropped to almost zero. Only a few diehards among the young folk persisted in wearing them long after they had become the worse for wear. Mrs. Robinson, who had purchased four, confessed to my mother, "No matter how carefully I wash them, they just fall apart."

Suddenly, the door was opened. One by one, purchasers of sweaters began to complain about their quality. If they did not fall apart, they faded or lost their shape. In only a few short weeks, most were unwearable. The nadir of discontent came when several ladies began to use their sweaters as dust clothes—it was said they made wonderful dust catchers.

While the sweaters gradually disappeared, the salesmen did not. Every Saturday, regular as clockwork, they would arrive to collect their weekly fees and update the customers' payment booklets. My father was right. It seemed that the ladies would be paying for those sweaters for the rest of their lives. Even the customers who made payments on a regular basis were never completely paid up. Those who missed several payments fell hopelessly behind. Customers who balked at making further payments, citing the shoddiness of the merchandise, were threatened with legal action. The threat alone was enough to whip them back in line. All during the turmoil, Father sat on our porch reading the evening newspaper.

The Fourth of July came and went, and still the boys of summer made their collections every Saturday. The payment booklets were so haphazardly annotated that even the most vigilant customers soon gave up in despair and accepted whatever balance they were given. It was not until just before Christmas that the last balance due was paid off. When my mother relayed the news to my father, he sighed and said, "I hope they've finally learned their lesson."

During the week between Christmas and New Year, my father worked many overtime hours helping out at the Detroit Sheraton Hotel. In the year 1939, the poor were getting poorer, but the rich were getting richer. The downtown hotels were booked solid for dinners, banquets, and luncheons. Theaters and clubs offered the very best acts in the entertainment world. Downtown Detroit was awash with bright lights, glittering decorations, and beautiful people. The crowds in front of the Hudson's Department Store Christmas displays were at least three rows deep. There was something for everyone. When Uncle Smitty said, "Bill, you need to slow down, it's a wonder you don't fall asleep on the bus ride home and miss your stop," my father replied, "I'll rest later, I have to take advantage of the overtime while it's available."

It was on such a night that my father, while leaning against the front window of Sam's Cut Rate Department Store, glanced up and saw an enormous display of ladies' angora sweaters. The display lights had been left on, and the sweaters sparkled like jewels in the tinted lights. Across the top of the display was a banner pronouncing SALE! SALE! SALE! YOUR CHOICE, ONLY $1.69 EA OR 2 FOR $3.00.

Father went door to door on Herbert Street telling everyone about the angora sweaters available at Sam's Cut Rate Department Store. He had talked with a salesman and discovered they could be put in layaway with no additional charge. Since he passed the store every day on his way to and from work, he offered to act as a go-between—buying or making payments on sweaters for anyone who might be interested. He explained that this way the ladies could purchase sweaters practically pain free. Of the thirty, or more, families who lived on Herbert Street, only five accepted his offer. Although he had hoped for more takers, Father was not discouraged. Mother said, "At least it's a step in the right direction. When they see the superior quality of these sweaters, more people will want them."

Mother was right. More people did order the sweaters. While not the most expensive sweaters in the world, their quality far exceeded that of the sweaters sold by the boys of summer. Long after the holiday season was over, the sweaters graced many members of my mother's church.

Gradually, the days warmed as the calendar moved toward spring and the Easter renewal. Although winter was not quite over, the occasional unseasonably warm day held promise for the future. Front doors were left slightly ajar, and windows were raised in an attempt to air out the houses and chase away the winter doldrums. Clotheslines were put up, and sheets were seen flapping in the wind—often frozen solid. No matter, we had survived another winter, and that was a miracle in itself.

They came in April. The boys of summer. They went from house to house renewing old acquaintances while apologizing for the misunderstandings of the previous year. They spoke of how disappointed they had been with the quality of the merchandise provided by their supplier. They felt cheated, and they knew their customers must have felt cheated too. In fact, they felt so badly about the situation that this year they would reduce the down payment per sweater to twenty-five cents, with weekly payments of only twenty cents.

Their former customers were deeply moved. Mrs. Robinson said, "Gracie, I really feel sorry for them. You know the way that supplier took advantage of them is a sin and a shame. I told them not to worry. That no good comes out of evil!"

The salesmen took orders at a rapid rate. Most of those who had ordered the previous year reordered, along with several recent arrivals in the neighborhood. Mother exclaimed in amazement, "William, I wouldn't be surprised if they got twice as many orders as they did last year." Father did not respond. He seemed not to hear her.

All day they flitted from door to door, asking questions, teasing the lady of the house, and promising to return the next month to take anyone who wanted to go for a ride in their glistening new convertibles. After they left, there was much laughing and comparing of notes between the ladies of the neighborhood. Amid the excitement, Father sat unnoticed on our front porch reading the evening newspaper.

TED KOOSER

Excerpt from "Winter"

Local Wonders: Seasons in the Bohemian Alps

Walking our gravel road early in the morning, the sun so slow to rise into the silence, slow to ignite the pure fuel of the air. This is a morning like a roadmap, pink and blue, the destinations only lightly penciled.

Suddenly a crow shakes loose from a tree and flaps away cawing, five slow croaks like a frozen starter motor. Coarse frosty pastures, gray as coyote skins. A magpie, far east of its range, rises and falls with each deep wing beat—a black stone skipped across water.

A maple, bare now but which all summer bent heavily over its leafy shadow, can scarcely hold itself back from human happiness under the least touch of the breeze.

A dozen sparrows burst from a bush by the road, like somebody's name remembered after fifty years.

There's a starling walking the road, scolding himself in a scratchy kvetching voice. He seems out of place in the country, wearing an iridescent navy suit with spots of mud from a passing car, a purple silk neck scarf, and far too much oil in his hair. I have seen him before, walking the concourse at O'Hare in Chicago, dragging a cart of sample cases locked with silver chains.

From its nest in a conical heap of frosty stalks and sticks, a muskrat hears me stopping and sends a ripple of wariness across the pond and into the reeds beyond it. The hollow floods with watchful silence, as if it were part of one great eye. The muskrat waits. I turn a loud heel in the gravel and go on my way.

Along the western horizon, where the night has gone, there's a long white cloud like an opera glove—tiny pearl buttons all the way up to the elbow. And some neighbor came in the night in a hurry to borrow the moon and jerked it so hard from its nail that he left its thin wire, new-moon handle hanging in the west.

❧ ❧

As winter approaches, I begin to get ready for the worst. You never know. I start up my gas-powered generator to see if it runs; I grease and oil my 1947 Farmall Cub tractor with its blade for moving snow; I put a box of kindling near the stove in my library by the pond. I check the pressure tank in the well. I put the glass inserts in the storm doors. I make a warm place for the dogs. I want to be ready for bad weather. "It is easier to throw the load off the cart than to put it on," as my Czech neighbors might say.

You want to be ready for anything. My father once told me about a man in our town who had been purged by his doctor with caustic anti-parasitic potions and promptly passed a long segmented hookworm that the doctor displayed on the sidewalk in front of the man's house. It was summer, the weather pleasant, and for an hour following, the doctor, who apparently had nothing else to do, spoke to passersby about the dangers of going barefoot in places where pigs had been permitted to run.

Dad said the worm was about twelve feet in length, pale and gray like a long strip of soaked toilet paper, and had an ivory head the size of a baby's fist with a small sucking mouth surrounded by hooks the color and size of toenail parings. The sick man, recovering on a daybed on the sun porch, spoke through a screened window to people who wanted to wish him well and patiently answered their questions about how it had felt to have such a creature living inside him. You never know what can happen.

We were also cautioned about journeying far from home. As an example of the dangers, the town had a badly crippled woman named Lucy Tripp, who as a girl had traveled to New York City. As she walked along a sidewalk, sightseeing, she was struck by the outstretched hand of a suicide who had leapt from high above. Her spine had been shattered, and for the rest of her life, she was to walk bent forward at the waist, tapping the sidewalk with two black canes. Whenever the subject of travel to a big city was raised, someone would say, "Just remember what happened to Miss Tripp."

Two miles east along our road a family of beavers has dammed a creek and flooded a couple of acres of corn. The man who owns the land has tried to reclaim this part of it by pulling the dam apart, but the beavers are better at repair than he is at destruction. So that part of the cornfield stands in water, unharvested, though the rest of the field has been picked.

The farmer has built a couple of small duck blinds next to the beavers' pond, thinking to get a little something for his labor, and he's camouflaged them with a covering of corn shucks. Today he's turned his cows and calves in to the field to eat what's left of the cornstalks, and as I drove past, I saw two calves, one black and one brown, eating one of the duck blinds. The beavers and the cattle have the upper hand.

A cold morning. An old woman with a sweet shy smile—my Grandmother Moser—is turning potatoes in hot fat, the thin slices bubbling and snapping and browning. The Second World War has just ended. She is using a small, bone-handled, three-tined fork, and she has been holding it in the same hand and using it in the same way for so many years that one of the tines has been nearly worn away. Just as the fork is captive to the old woman's way of frying potatoes, just as the fork is made to sweep her skillet in the same slow circles day after day, the old woman has been caught in the habits of my memory. Whenever I think of her, she must rise from her daybed by the parlor window and return to that hot kitchen and stand on her swollen feet at the wood range and begin frying potatoes. This is not the afterlife that the Lutheran church taught her to expect.

When I am gone, she will be freed from this duty. She has been standing there in my memory for more than fifty years. Like her fork, my recollection of her is beginning to wear down on one side. I can no longer see her as well as I once could, that is, from the fixed spot at the side of the warm wood range where I always stand and look up at the side of her face, the right side, with the pale brown birthmark in the hollow of her temple, under a loose wisp of gray hair.

❧ ❧

My wife's great aunt, Helen Stetter, will soon celebrate her 107th birthday. She lives in the Nebraska Sandhills, six hours north and west of the Bohemian Alps.

She is old enough to contain within her small head, with its steel gray curls and glittering eyeglasses, the memory of Sioux dancers coming down off the Rosebud to dance and chant on the main street of her town, the dust on their bare legs streaked with sweat, their clothes in rags. In the year of her birth, old Chief Red Cloud, who had once had his run of the Powder River country in Wyoming, got arrested there for hunting without a permit.

When we attended her 100th birthday party, I made these notes:

She is wearing a blue dress with a floral print and sits on the edge of her bed. She has scraped the frosting off a piece of her birthday cake and has set the cake aside until later. She says, my, she was frightened by those Indians. She says they were doing a "war dance," and she tests the effect of this by fixing her listener with her one good eye. It is a clear and intelligent eye that has studied the world on its own since, as a girl, she blinded the other with a needle while learning to sew. Because she has only one good eye, she has seen the entire twentieth century in just two dimensions, and her mind has come to regard most things in just two ways, black and white or right and wrong. When she talks, she holds one of her ancient freckled hands in the other and kneads the knuckles with her thumb. She is wearing a pair of leather deck shoes tied with rawhide thongs.

Someone may have told her that what she was watching from behind her mother's skirts on that afternoon was a war dance, but in the late 1890s, when she was a child, the great Indian wars were over, and the mass graves at Wounded Knee, seventy miles to the west, were already beginning to sink under the prairie grass. She was born after the hostilities had ended, but there was still enough blood and smoke in the air to have kept the fear of Indians alive in her for all these years.

Her forebears settled in the area near where Minnechuduza Creek runs into the Niobrara River. There was no town there then. Her father and two uncles made their living by butchering beef and selling it to the army stationed at Fort Niobrara. The three of them, young German-Americans, had come west from Virginia and had lived for a while at Sidney, where they sold meat to the soldiers at Fort Robinson. That had been during the 1870s, and they had probably been there in 1877, when Crazy Horse was bayoneted on the grounds, but she doesn't remember the family speaking of that. Would they have spoken of that? One of her uncles was a renowned storyteller. Surely he would have mentioned it if he had been there to see it. He might even have bragged about being there on that infamous day, for this was before a white man would have felt shame at the behavior of his kind.

There are women like her in many families, ancient maiden aunts who stayed home to take care of ailing parents, who have outlived their brothers and sisters on the pure energy of bitter resentment. For nearly a hundred years she has thought about the sacrifices she made so that her brothers and sister could go on and have normal lives and raise families. At such an advanced age, she may revise her family's history in whatever way she wishes, for she has outlived anyone who might contradict her. In the past few years, she has begun to work her way back through the family, singling out specific relatives to punish for ancient slights and indiscretions.

She is not only the oldest person in her family but also the oldest in the community. She is the sole living authority on not only her own family but also the family histories of her neighbors. Not from her but from published local histories, we know that in addition to his beef business, her father was the proprietor of a tavern called the Deer Lodge—a log structure built near the fort, where a soldier could buy a drink and a woman. In his photographs, her father wears a rakehell handlebar mustache, a wide smile, a broad-brimmed western-style hat, and a full-length buffalo coat. To her, he is always "Dear Poppa, dear Poppa," delivered with a little sigh and a dainty dab at the corner of her good eye with her flowered handkerchief.

Despite her occasional sallies against the long-dead, there is nothing so spiteful about her that it can spoil her for us. She is the family miracle, a true survivor, still strong and intelligent and borne forward into a wonderful and strange new age.

❦

Lots of people on the Great Plains pack up and go south from November through February, but my wife and I enjoy winter in Nebraska.

Spring is downright impatient with people in their fifties and sixties: we're under steady nagging pressure to turn over and plant a vegetable garden, to gas up and check out the lawnmowers, to wait endlessly while the other party selects bedding plants at the greenhouse, and to begin the five-month-long, everyday chore of picking wood ticks off the dogs.

Summer is one weary, endless, hot, dry mowing of grass, with interludes of garden weeding and chigger bites, and after every thunderstorm there are fallen branches to cut up with the chain saw and drag from one place to another. It is also the time when nature's weedy disorder reclaims the little bit of territory we thought we had cleared for ourselves.

Autumn is beautiful, my favorite season, with its clear skies and long shadows arrowing across the red hills, but it is also the time when the lawnmowers have to be drained and stored, when the pressure tank in the well house must be drained and checked, when the block heaters need to be installed on the cars, and when the dead plants in the garden must be pulled up and burned. It is also a time of sighing and regret, of the admission that during the spring and summer we didn't get done what we had hoped to.

Then winter sets in, and the obligations of our sixty-two acres are buried under the blessed somnolence of snow and ice. It is the time of lingering over suppers of meatloaf and squash and of wrapping ourselves in shawls in our chairs and reading books and nodding off at eight-thirty or nine. Then to bed under heaps of blankets and comforters, my wife in wool stockings, sweatshirt, and sweatpants, and I in the long flannel nightshirts my mother made.

❧ ❧

Our food co-op has an aromatherapy display you pass on your way to the checkout counter, a couple of dozen attractively labeled vials: *Essence of Pine, Essence of Wild Rose, Essence of*

Ginger, and so on. My Grandmother Kooser would have held up the checkout line while she stood on her broken-over shoes admiring these little bottles. She was a huge woman who enjoyed things miniature and perfect, and she kept rows of empty perfume bottles along her windowsills where they caught the light of the postwar 1940s. She lived in a rented house with rented but regularly dusted windowsills and was too poor to buy perfume for herself, but her friends gave her their empty bottles. I have what's left of her collection, and the three vials with the tightest stoppers still hold the faint sixty-year-old fragrances of Evening in Paris, White Shoulders, and one other scent so frail and delicate that it has irretrievably lost its name.

A person might be tempted to make fun of people who try to make themselves feel better by sniffing fragrances, but aromatherapy appeals to me. A familiar odor can fuel the fastest kind of time travel, speeding us back across the years.

But it's the unique combination of a number of fragrances into one indefinable evocative scent that punches its fist straight to the heart. I have been thinking this morning how many laboratory trials I would have to conduct, mixing test tubes of fragrances, to come up with that exquisite blend of odors that would take me back to a deeply pleasurable moment fifty years ago. There I was, standing in Sally Martin's kitchen, with my mittened hands stuffed in the pockets of my winter coat, when Sally took me by the shoulders and kissed me full on the lips, my first real kiss, a hot, soft, deep, wet kiss.

I can recall the smell of that moment but only guess at the ingredients: essence of boiling potatoes, essence of wet rubber galoshes, essence of sweat rising out of my collar, and the fresh celery smell of Sally's long brown hair. I would like to pull out the stopper of that lost bottle and be swiftly transported back to that warm kitchen on Kellogg Avenue in Ames, Iowa, in the first winter of the 1950s, snow puddling around our rubber boots set toe to toe on the linoleum, Sally and I at the beginning of long lives of kissing other people.

The electrician didn't like snakes, not at all. I thought I'd cleared them out before he arrived. I'd taken off the Styrofoam sheets that cover the pit, so the snakes would get uncomfortably cold and slither away. But when he pulled off the lid of the junction box, two snakes tumbled out, a two-foot blue racer and a three-foot bullsnake. He hollered, "I hate snakes!" and flew up the ladder. While he stood watching and panting, I went down into the pit, picked up the snakes, which were dull from the cold, and carried them over to the barn.

After he'd figured out what was wrong with the circuits and I'd paid him and he was gone, I went to the barn to see if I could catch the bullsnake and blue racer and bring them back, but they'd already gone off to hide. I hope they can find a warm home for the rest of the winter. They certainly aren't going to try to make it fifty feet across the frozen ground just to get back into the well pit. They'd wind up like Commander Scott, who before dying of exposure left a plaintive note in his Antarctic journal, "For God's sake take care of our people." I'm doing my best.

We'd had two or three hard frosts, and there wasn't a sign of insect life anywhere outside, even though it had warmed up considerably as it often does after the annual Thanksgiving storm. I cut up a dead tree with my chain saw one morning and peered in under the loose wet bark, but there was nothing there but the abandoned meandering highways of whatever kind of bug made them. In the house, a few flies, slow and drunken looking, slapped the lampshades when we read in bed, and sometimes, early in the morning when I was wallowing up to my ears in the bathtub, a mosquito mysteriously appeared and whined in circles above me, baffled by the rising steam.

Besides the various kinds of spiders, welcome in our house, I discovered another insect that had decided to spend its winter inside. I would find it sitting motionless on the arm of the couch in the living room, watching me read. It had a tiny head and a broad flat back barred in shades of brown like a hawk or owl feather, and it looked like a painted African shield carried on the heads of four bearers.

Our insect book told me this fellow's name was the leaf-footed bug, a relative of the squash bug. According to the book, it was a predator, but I couldn't imagine what this one was finding for lunch in our house, which is usually clean and neat. He was more like a tiny camel, hopelessly trudging forever across vast deserts of plaster, no food or water anywhere in sight, condemned to never-ending exile. Over the next few weeks I got in the habit of watching for him. I was attracted to his melancholy dreariness. All day he wandered up and down walls, across ceilings, like a cardiac patient walking a shopping mall. If sometimes I felt as if I were wasting my life, well, I always had the leaf-footed bug to show me things could be worse.

Occasionally, when suddenly agitated by some mysterious force, he would fly for a short distance, awkwardly whirring down the air of a room, to smack head-on into a wall on the other side. When the house was quiet, there would be a little click. The leaf-footed bug would fall to the floor, slowly gather itself as if brushing off its coat, and slowly move on. I was reminded of Harold Stassen, campaigning for president again and again. It was encoded behavior, I suspect, deeply imprinted in his genes, a complete disregard for failure.

This went on for weeks. I learned to expect him. Often, as I sat reading in the evening, I would discover the leaf-footed bug somewhere nearby, perhaps on the arm of the chair or on the nearby table, those tiny eyes watching me.

After several weeks, he was gone. I looked here and there but couldn't find him. He was not in the jungles of the flowerpots, not tracking the dust on the Venetian blinds. He was not among the dead and entangled daddy longlegs caught up in webs under the furniture.

Then, one day as I swept the floor, I found him lying on his back against a baseboard, his legs neatly folded over his breast. It looked like a stage death, like something from a melodrama. He looked like Count Dracula, pretending to sleep. Wake up, I said, you can't just give up like this. But he was gone, having floated away on the shallow little boat of his body. I swept him into the dustpan and was done with it.

But in the evenings now, when I sit under a lamp reading, the house darkened, I find myself searching the nearby furniture to see if he is out there in the shadows, watching me to see what I might do with my life.

☙ ❧

I got out the Christmas decorations today, set up and decorated our little artificial tree, and unboxed and arranged the figures in the Kooser family crèche. Perhaps sixty or seventy years old and about the size and heft of a briefcase, it is made of thin hard-board splattered with plaster. When it was new, it was touched lightly with brown and rust-colored paints to make it look old. It is indeed a humble and even tacky setting for the birth of our Savior, who lies with His pudgy ankles crossed and His hands spread wide as if to embrace the morning of His birth. All the figures are of cast plaster, enameled in primary and secondary colors. The Savior's mother, a pretty young woman in blue with an open face, is down on one knee, hands folded in prayer. The adoptive father is down on both knees, his face pale and slack. He has the dark brown hair and beard of a man much younger than the Joseph of the Gospels, but perhaps the Gospels were wrong about this. Near these two stands an angel with broad thick wings and yellow hair. She blesses the moment by raising the broken-off stub of one arm.

Only two of the three kings have arrived, and both of them wear identical red robes and crowns that look a little like foil-wrapped kisses. Each carries in his hands a tall gilded box with a peculiar pyramidal lid, the kind of box that looks like a magic trick, that might have other smaller boxes inside and, inside those, even smaller boxes, designed to get a chuckle out of a baby. Two shepherds have arrived, wearing identical brown robes with wide-brimmed blue hats, which they have taken off to show respect (this courtesy has not occurred to the two kings, but they are foreigners). One of the shepherds has a very alert-looking lamb draped over his shoulders, so alert-looking that the shepherd can soon expect a warm trickle down his back. The other shepherd holds up one hand with his fingers folded around a hole about the size of the shaft of his missing crook. The crook has been deftly snatched from above by some divine prankster, and the shepherd has not yet noticed it is gone.

There are two donkeys, one standing wounded with a broken ear and another down on the hard brown floor, wearing a very sour expression as if terribly put upon. Another lamb stands alone with its head dropped, hoping the other shepherd will pick it up so that it too can have the pleasure of pissing down a human back.

The most unusual member of this group is a celluloid Jersey cow, orange in color and weighing so little you could blow it over with a good hard puff. How this cow got included among the plaster figures is a mystery. Perhaps my father, who was always in charge of the crèche, which once had belonged to his parents, decided that every stable needed a cow. Whatever the reason, it has a commanding presence. No matter where you place it, all the other figures immediately seem to arrange themselves in relation to it. Even the baby Jesus on his plaster cake of straw is upstaged by this cheerful-looking black-eyed cow, so light, so filled with a kind of airy joy right down to its bulging udder that it might at any moment ascend to heaven. Perhaps that's what the sour-looking donkey has been waiting for, some kind of a miracle.

❧ ❧

Few long-time city dwellers who move to the country for peace and quiet understand in advance how big an allowance of winter can get spent starting machinery, thawing plumbing pipes, or climbing down in a frigid well pit to puzzle over a sudden absence of water pressure at the moment your wife was ready to rinse the shampoo out of her hair. If a fellow has become accustomed to driving his suv into the local Firestone Car Care Center and tossing his car keys (with their lucky rabbit's foot) onto the glass counter, then striding out the door, topcoat flying, he probably has no idea what life is like in a drafty five-below-zero barn with cold feet and a runny nose, thirty miles from the nearest mechanic, praying that a fifty-year-old tractor will start.

We had six inches of snow on Sunday, preceding what the weather experts call an arctic air mass, but what I'd call a clear blue sky. That sky arrived this morning with a pale full moon in the west, lip-chapping winds, subzero cold, and a windchill of minus forty. Impassable drifts of snow blocked our driveway.

My 1947 Farmall Cub tractor was built prior to the invention of the windchill factor, and if it could scoff at such an elaboration, it would certainly scoff. Like other machines, it holds to the time-honored standard of mercury column temperatures. It was five below in the barn when I went there at six this morning to see if I could get the Cub to start. If I'd known in which of its orifices I might insert a fever thermometer, the tractor's temperature would have been precisely five below. In fact, I was the only thing within a mile that knew what the windchill factor was and was all the colder for knowing it. The radio had been tireless in reminding me of it every ten minutes while I ate breakfast, and now I was being reminded of it by my puffs of breath, which hung in a sour coffee-flavored cloud before me. The red siding on the barn, the snowdrift at its door, the dusty glass of its little windows, every tool handle, every wisp of straw, all these were five below. Alice was as oblivious to the windchill as was the tractor as she happily snorted around in dark corners expecting to sniff out a rat, a long-dead sparrow, or some other delicacy.

The Cub has a five-foot snow blade on its front and a twenty-five-horsepower four-cylinder engine that can on a good day nudge a small heap of snow from one place to another. I hooked up the battery charger with its dial set to 6 VOLT START, checked the antifreeze level and the tire chains, squirted some ether into the carburetor intake (suddenly recalling a painful childhood tonsillectomy), said a short blessing, snapped on the charger, saw its arrow go over into the red zone, turned on the ignition, and cranked the starter. The Cub started right up, its little stack trumpeting an eye-burning flatulence of exhaust.

I let it warm up for ten minutes, then folded an old blanket for the cold metal seat, sensitive as I am at my age to the caution that many farmers have picked up bad cases of prostate trouble from cold tractor seats, a rural variation on the germy toilet seats my mother had warned me about. I adjusted my cap, earflaps down, climbed aboard, and merrily lurched out into the drifts. I seemed the happy genius of the winter day, the center of our farm's attention. Every sparrow in the bushes, every field mouse in its burrow, every rat in the woodpile listened as I rattled to and fro.

Within an hour I'd gotten stuck and unstuck twice, lost my cap to a tree branch, torn up the end of our brick sidewalk with the tractor's chains, scraped a lot of gravel off the drive into the grass, given Alice reason to run in wild circles, barking, and burned a gallon of gas and a quart of oil. I had also created a high-speed bobsled chute in place of the driveway, which ascends to the county road and which my wife's Subaru had negotiated without any effort whatsoever while I was still tinkering in the barn. I also stalled the engine once, and since the battery wouldn't hold a charge and the generator didn't seem to work, I had to run a hundred-foot extension cord out from an outlet in the house, haul the charger from the barn, repeat my invocation, and start it again so I could steer it back into the cold silence of the barn.

I was able to accomplish all that in just three hours, and the guys at Firestone didn't get a cent of my money.

❦

In addition to our standard Christmas decorations, tree and wreath and candles and so on, I've arranged some dollhouse furniture and tiny dolls on the floor in front of the fireplace. These were given to me several years ago by a friend. They had been hers as a girl, and they probably date from somewhere in the fifties. No plastic pieces, such as you'd find today, but solid wood. Refrigerator, stove, and sink, solid, heavy, and serious looking in thick white enamel. A bathtub and bathroom sink the same (toilet missing). These pieces modeled on the standards of the day, kitchen sinks with drainboard surfaces to either side, all of one piece and made of enameled steel, always cold under the fingers. Then there are painted wooden beds with mattresses, end tables, and a mirrored dresser and a chest of drawers with drawers that actually pull out. And the dolls. A family, with father and mother and two daughters, tattered and missing most of their hair. One of the daughters is in bed with the flu this morning, just as my wife is. The other daughter is sitting on the uncomfortable solid green couch between her parents, who are dressed for Christmas morning, the mother in a dress, the father in a suit. I set up a

Christmas tree for them from my own belongings, one of those cone-shaped bottlebrush trees from the forties.

This once was someone's dream of family life, a dream so badly tattered today. Worn out, bent, broken. On the faces of the dolls is an expression of astonishment at what the world has come to while they waited in the darkness of their cardboard box.

❦

After I'd decorated our Christmas tree and arranged the doll furniture and set up the Kooser family crèche, I discovered the family reindeer were missing. When I was growing up, my parents had a set of eight white celluloid reindeer and another eight smaller, heavier ones made out of some kind of pre-plastic composition material painted in natural colors. These latter reindeer were antiques, I'm certain, from the turn of the century. They had once been on display in my grandparents' house. I was very much taken with them as a little boy because they looked so very real. They even had little bumps on their hard brown antlers that seemed authentic, though I don't know if real reindeer have such bumps.

Years later, after my sister and I were grown and gone, at about the time the entire country was in its antiquing phase, when people from coast to coast (including my mother) were trying to improve new pieces of furniture by making them look old and beat up, my father, then in retirement and always looking for something to do, got the idea to spray the reindeer gold. And he did. And then he put little necklaces of pea-sized red beads on rubber bands around their necks. I was disgusted.

The white celluloid reindeer that had once seemed so buoyant looked heavy as hood ornaments, and the little composition reindeer, once so very real, looked like something you'd unscrew from the top of a bowling trophy.

Then, to add insult to injury, Dad glued quarter-sized cardboard circles on their feet, like snowshoes, because the reindeer had toppled over in the draft created whenever somebody opened the living room door.

Wanting to restore as much from my childhood Christmases as I could, I asked my sister by e-mail what might have become of the reindeer, and she replied that she was certain I had them. She said that when Mother moved into her assisted living apartment and we had given away most of her belongings, I had taken the reindeer home with me.

This afternoon I undertook a lengthy search, and on a shelf at the back of a closet, I found them in a yellow hatbox from my father's store, each wrapped in a brown tissue sleeve or yoke or collar from one of Mother's Simplicity sewing patterns. There aren't as many reindeer as there once were. Only one of the composition ones has survived, and the celluloid ones are down to five big and two small. I've just finished lining them up on top of the china cabinet, and they look as cheap and tawdry as the console radio that my mother antiqued pea green. But they do look like something from home.

❦ ❦

It was eleven below zero when I got up at five this morning, and when I snapped on the light in the bathroom, I found a box elder bug stumbling along the edge of the tub. He looked discouraged, as if he'd spent the past couple of days looking for something to eat.

About a half inch long, slate gray with red trim, the box elder bug is known to rural Nebraskans, who are mostly Republicans, as the Democrat beetle, a nickname that originated at the time of the Roosevelt administration, when Democrats were everywhere and into everything. And since we Democrats are presently grieving over the recent loss of the White House, perhaps my box elder bug has lost his patronage position in the Bureau of

Wet Bark and Tree Sap and is looking for work. Or perhaps he's just beaten down by the insufferable smugness of Republicans.

The University of Nebraska's Cooperative Extension writers put out useful reports on a variety of subjects from replacing light bulbs to changing the oil in your sewing machine. You can pick them up at the county courthouse, and I happen to have their four-page bulletin on box elder bugs. The paragraph entitled "Life History" begins: "In the spring, after emerging from overwintering sites . . ." Overwintering sites. I've always fancied a name for our acreage, but the suburban subdivisions have used up the really good ones, like Bonnee View and Pumpkin Glade. So at least for this one morning, with forbidding fields of subzero snow stretching in every direction, I intend to call our home "The Overwintering Place," a name that trundles over the tongue like a bug.

The bulletin says, "When seeking an overwintering site, box elder bugs often enter buildings through small openings around windows, doors, conduits, and pipes and through small cracks in or above the foundation." I'm not surprised by any of that, and we do have small openings all over the place, even one through which these small observations creep into my days. The bulletin goes on, "They do not damage food or other items in the home, nor do they bite humans or pets." Thank God, for, naked as a jaybird, I had stepped without caution right over this box elder bug and into the tub without a moment's thought that he might try to bite my belongings as they swung above him like the loader bucket on a dragline.

Since this is now "The Overwintering Place," I am prepared to extend hospitality to any and all box elder bugs, whose ancient race sounds so much like a clutch of uncles. In the autumn, the bulletin says, "activity continues well beyond frost as insects sun themselves on vertical walls on warm fall afternoons." How could anyone object to that? Fie on the Cooperative Extension Service, whose lack of charity comes through in the following sentences: "The best method of control once insects have entered the home is to use a vacuum cleaner. If only an occasional bug is observed, a fly swatter makes an effective weapon." A *weapon*?

The Bohemians say, "An old man sees better behind himself than a young man sees in front of himself." I'm down in my pond-side library, next to the crackling wood stove. It's snowing lightly, and I've been thinking about Christmases past.

My grandmother, Grace Lang Kooser, was a large woman who spent most of her time in a favorite chair gossiping on the telephone. She was attacked one evening in the 1930s by a grapefruit-sized ball of lightning that leapt through an open living room window, burned its way across the floor to her feet, and vanished just short of the toes of her carpet slippers.

The ball of fire, which she said jumped up and down and hissed like a snapping turtle, had apparently followed the wire that my grandfather had hidden beneath the carpet as an antenna for his radio. One might wonder what made that fiery missile disappear at my grandmother's feet, but she was an imposing woman whose scorn was quite capable of stopping an act of God dead in its tracks.

The burnt carpet had been replaced long before I was born, and my grandfather had died when I was two, taking his radio with him, but the lightning ball lesson smoldered on in my grandmother's imagination. For the rest of her life, she looked with suspicion upon all electrical devices. She kept her icebox long after refrigerators had been introduced; she unplugged her toaster after every slice popped up; and she was especially wary of strings of Christmas lights. She had been a girl in the late 1800s, when Christmas trees had been decorated with real candles, and could remember stories in which trees had caused devastating fires. The fact that the bulbs in strings of Christmas lights were shaped like flames predicted danger. She insisted that my uncle Tubby, with whom she lived, set up their Christmas tree on an unheated glassed-in porch. If the lights should happen to ignite the needles, she reasoned, perhaps the firefighters could more easily save the rest of the house.

She also insisted that the tree be strung with oversized outdoor lights, which were presumed to be safer, having heavy wiring and thick black rubber sockets. This meant, of course, that the first thing one noticed about my grandmother's tree was the enormous bulbs with their red and green and blue coatings flaking away and the heavy tar-colored wiring under which the branches sagged. The wires looked thick enough to carry the power from Hoover Dam.

She had some lovely old glass ornaments, including graceful pheasants with sprays of feathery glass fibers for tails, pairs of snowy owls with glittering ruby eyes, and praying angels in fancy conical skirts. There were other glass ornaments in the shape of vegetables—carrots, turnips, parsnips. A few fruits and vegetables had been sewn from bits of cloth and stuffed with cotton—strawberries, plums, lemons, a few slices of orange. But you had to look very closely to identify any of these under the ominous cage of electrical cable.

My sister, Judy, and I sometimes spent Saturday afternoons with our grandmother Kooser. Because she was so heavy, she had difficulty moving about, and childcare was easiest for her if she could rest in her chair with us at her feet. From where we sat, her enormous legs swelled pale and white above the brown rolls at the tops of her nylon hose, and her knees were as large as the faces on Mt. Rushmore. She entertained us by reading stories aloud and scissoring the *Des Moines Register* into long strings of elaborate paper dolls.

When we got bored, we were permitted to explore the house.

Grandmother Kooser had an ill tempered black-and-white bull terrier named Fiji, who kept to himself on a rug in the kitchen. He was a great temptation to us, but if we got too close to him, he made a sound like a marble rolled across a hardwood floor. On a window ledge above the staircase, so as to catch the light, she kept her collection of miniature glass bottles. She and my uncle had bedrooms upstairs, but all I can remember of them today is the big sagging bed in the shadows of my grandmother's room and the pungent medicinal scent of Lifebuoy soap that came from my uncle's doorway.

Maybe once a year, my sister, my grandmother, and I would make a "coal plant." This was a Mister Wizard kind of scientific experiment she'd read about somewhere, recommended for entertaining small children. The object was to create a thing of beauty from something as homely and common as a lump of coal.

I would be asked to select the object of the experiment from the dusty bin in her cellar and place it in a bowl. We always used a particular mashed potato bowl, blue and white, with little Chinese fishing villages around its base. Onto the coal we poured a mixture of household chemicals—I suppose it was made up of vinegar, baking soda, and food coloring. The objective was to create, through the formation of crystals, a miniature mountain covered with snow and forest. The lump was left to steep in this concoction, and by the time of our next visit, it would have begun to look not so much like a mountain as a lump of coal upon which a fuzzy, colored mold had formed.

During the days before Christmas, we would be permitted to press our faces to the French doors going out onto Grandmother Kooser's porch and gaze at the exiled Christmas tree, its strings of lights dark, its plug drawn far back from the socket.

Slowly, as Christmas approached, presents began to collect under the tree, a few new ones each time we came to visit. Those winters were cold. We children sometimes begged to be permitted to go onto the porch to squeeze and shake the packages, but we were ordered to put on our winter coats and caps to do so. Our breaths hung in puffs in the pine-scented air.

On Christmas afternoon, Mother and Father and Judy and I arrived at our grandmother's to exchange gifts. Uncle Tubby had plugged in the tree, and the huge outdoor bulbs glared, fierce pinpoints of white light beaming through their chipped colored skins. As he brought armloads of gifts from the freezing porch, his spectacles would fog over and he would wipe them with a handkerchief he had snatched from his pants pocket and snapped in the air.

We sat on chairs drawn into a circle in the living room, our coats over our shoulders because of the chill that had entered with the packages. As we unwrapped them, the paper popped like a frozen stream. If the gift were some item of clothing, a scarf or stocking cap, we would squeeze the cold air from it. Metal toys were beaded with moisture. The faces of my sister's dolls were covered with a light sweat of condensation. All of the gifts had to be set aside until they were warm enough to touch.

Once the presents had been unwrapped and a dessert of pie and ice cream had been served and eaten, my grandmother would signal my uncle with a nod, and he would promptly step back onto the side porch and unplug the tree. He would draw the cord far back from the wall outlet and coil it neatly next to the tree stand.

As we talked, the setting December sun would, for a few moments, touch our faces with a pale pink light, and then the living room would ease into darkness. On the marble-topped table by the window, the homely coal plant mercifully disappeared into shadow. My grandmother shifted in her chair, folded her hands on her lap, and sighed with satisfaction. Once again, her family had been spared from the flames.

⛄ ⛄

We've had an ice storm. I knew a shy old man whose long hands swung from the cuffs of his shirts like the ice-coated branches sweeping our shadowy yard in the light from the kitchen window.

He was good with machines, but when his fingers were empty of work, he had no place to hide them. They never quite fit in his pockets. For more than eighty winters, he sat just inside the loose door to the world, watching his wife work in her kitchen. His fingers brushed a table there, feeling for something that ought to be tightened.

By the light of the kitchen window tonight, I see him out there on the threshold showing his hands to his wife, how clean he's got them, scrubbing them over and over.

⛄ ⛄

In the weeks just before Christmas, my father's store was busiest, its narrow aisles crowded with shoppers, its carefully arranged displays rumpled and disarrayed, and its floors slippery with melting snow. On Saturdays and when school let out in the afternoons, my sister and I helped out. She worked on the sales floor, and I made bows for the women in the gift-wrap booth.

The bow machine was set up in the furnace room. A single light bulb hung over the card table upon which it sat. Behind my chair, the great gray furnace sighed and ticked, and piles of bald and disassembled manikins watched my back with wide unblinking eyes. In the shadows, bugs rustled across the floor, and above me the footfalls of customers knocked up and down the wooden floor. There I wound green and red satin ribbon into shiny bows that I dropped into a big cardboard box beside me. It was a job like those in fairy tales, in which a child is imprisoned in a castle and made to spin golden thread from flax straw.

Occasionally, my dungeon-keep would be visited by Otto Uhley, the store's janitor. He was a friendly hump-backed man whose nose was runny from first frost until after Easter, and who frequently dabbed at his upper lip with the tip of his tongue. Because the bow machine was in his basement, he looked upon the bow making as his responsibility and included me in his rounds of mop closets, toilets, and shipping room.

As if to inspect my work, he would dip his great knobby hands into the bow box and swirl them about. The satin splashed and sparkled around his thick hairy wrists. Although it was my responsibility to deliver the finished bows to the gift-wrap booth, Otto liked to do it for me. Up the narrow back stairs he'd go, the big box in his arms, his round face buried chin deep in the shiny satin.

Sometimes, his visits to the furnace room would be cut short by the appearance of my father, who occasionally fled from the crush of customers above to stand for a moment or two in the quiet warmth of the basement. Whenever he came down the stairs, Otto would hurriedly scuffle off to the other end of the darkness under the store.

My father was then in his early fifties. As much as he enjoyed storekeeping, there were times when he was gray with fatigue. He often worked ten or twelve hours a day. As much as he liked visiting with customers, there were moments when he would fall silent and stare off into space. There were evenings when he would drive the family in our old Plymouth out to the edge of town, only to get away for a few moments. There, a farmer kept a pen of sheep, and my father would pull the car off the road and stop. "See, children," he'd say, "how much the sheep look like the people who come to the store. Why, look! There's Dr. Mason's wife, and Mrs. Fitch, and, oh, there's Gladys Fitzpatrick, bless her soul . . ."

It was at such times, when the press of the store had become more than my father could bear, that he would stop in the furnace room, his shoulders sunken, his arms hanging down as if to let his responsibilities drip from the tips of his fingers. Though he would have preferred to stand there in silence, taking a few breaths, he would ask me how the bow making was going and would answer questions about how things were going on the sales floor above. Then, as quickly as he had appeared, he would be gone.

Except for these two visitors, I was alone. As the box filled with bows, my head filled with dreams. Behind me, the furnace breathed like an enormous and motherly old woman, pleased to have a boy among the dark folds of her skirts. Above me, the footsteps resounded with the spirit of giving. I could imagine women in rich furs, smiling and chatting, their shoulders sprinkled with new-fallen snow, their arms piled high with gifts, and upon each gift, one of my beautiful bows. I could imagine the presents spread about under the Christmas trees in their houses, each package lit by the winking lights. I could hear the rattle of the colorful paper as each package was torn open, my reverie enhanced by the rustle of the insects behind the furnace.

As the days drew closer to Christmas, the store became busier, and my box of bows was whisked away up the stairs before I'd had a chance to fill it. Sometimes, one of the women from the gift-wrap booth would come running down for it, thus spoiling Otto's opportunity to bury his wet nose in the gay colors. Sometimes, my father would come for the box, having passed by the booth in his endless rounds and seen that the women were nearly out of bows. The footsteps above me flowed together into a steady rumble along the wooden aisles.

In the evening, after the store had closed, my sister, my father, and I would pass through the aisles, finding the countertops in shambles and the floors a wet black swirl of grime. At the front door, waiting to let us out and lock up behind us, stood Otto, his nose dripping, his mop bucket at the ready.

And then, suddenly, it was Christmas Eve!

Late in the afternoon, I was told by my father that I could stop making bows. My work was finished. I shut off the light, put on my warm jacket, and walked snowy Main Street down to its end and back, enjoying the rush of last-minute shoppers, the Christmas carols being piped out under the awnings of the stores. I stopped to look at the animated display in the jewelry store window, tiny elves endlessly making toys in Santa's workshop. The cold air sang in my lungs. I hummed along with the carols as I walked back to the store. Christmas at last!

By the time the store closed that day, my father's face was gray and his hands trembled. He walked through the aisles, absentmindedly touching the counters, straightening the loose piles of unsold clothing. Our family was the last in the store. Even Otto had gone home before then, his arms full of packages, the floor left dirty behind him.

On the "Hold" shelf behind the counter in the gift-wrap booth would be several packages, left by mistake, forgotten, big boxes and small, all mysterious in their gift wrappings. Thinking that someone might come for them, my sister and father and I would wait an extra half hour, standing at the front of the store and peering out into the darkening street, the diminishing traffic. But no one came back. Finally, we loaded the mystery gifts into the Plymouth to take them home, leaving a note taped to the door: "If you have forgotten your package in our gift-wrap department, you may pick it up at the home of our manager." This was followed by our address.

By that hour we were the only people in the streets, the headlights of the Plymouth searching the ruts in the snow. In every window, a Christmas tree glittered. My sister and I sat among the packages as our father drove home.

My mother met us at the door, and the smell of cookies baking poured out into the cold air. It seemed that every light in the house was turned on. The Christmas tree stood in the corner of the living room with packages spilling out from beneath it. We unloaded the strangers' orphaned gifts and put them in the entryway, leaving the porch light on to guide their owners, should they come.

Soon, my father's older brother, Tubby, would come to spend the evening. We would hear him coming across the snowy yard, ringing a belt of harness bells that had been in our family for many years. When he came in, the cold night air slid from his topcoat. His gifts for the family, left all day in the trunk of his car at his office, were like blocks of ice. We set them under the tree with the others and sat down together for supper.

All through the evening, as we opened our packages, strangers came to the door to claim their gifts. Uncomfortable, shy, apologetic, they thanked my father for taking the gifts home. As they stood in the doorway, snow melted from their boots onto the carpet and the cold air flowed in around them. What would they have done, they asked, how would they have explained to their children? Each of them glowed with good luck and gratitude.

Finally, all the mysterious packages were gone and all of the family's had been unwrapped. Our family gathered in the living room, which was lit only by the tree, my uncle Tubby dozing in an armchair, my father and mother together on the couch, and my sister and I stretched out on the floor below the tree, looking up through the glittering branches. It was quiet. Beyond the window, it was snowing. In a box in a corner of the room, the used Christmas wrappings rustled as they slowly unfolded. Near me, the shining bows sat in a little pile under the tree.

DINTY W. MOORE

Son of Mr. Green Jeans:
A Meditation on Missing Fathers

Between Panic and Desire

Allen, Tim

Best known as the father on ABC's *Home Improvement* (1991–99), the popular comedian was born Timothy Allen Dick on June 13, 1953. When Allen was eleven years old, his father, Gerald Dick, was killed by a drunk driver while driving home from a University of Colorado football game.

Bees

"A man, after impregnating the woman, could drop dead," critic Camille Paglia suggested to Tim Allen in a 1995 *Esquire* interview. "That is how peripheral he is to the whole thing." "I'm a drone," Allen responded. "Like those bees?" "You are a drone," Paglia agreed. "That's exactly right."

Carp

After the female Japanese carp gives birth to hundreds of tiny babies, the father carp remains nearby. When he senses approaching danger he will suck the helpless babies into his mouth, and hold them safely there until the coast is clear.

Divorce

University of Arizona psychologist Sanford Braver tells a disturbing story of a woman who felt threatened by her husband's close bond with their young son. The husband had a flexible work schedule, but the wife did not, so the boy spent the bulk of his time with the father.

The mother became so jealous of the tight father-son relationship that she eventually filed for divorce, and successfully fought for sole custody. The result was that instead of being in the care of his father while the mother worked, the boy was now left in daycare.

Emperor Penguins

Once a male emperor penguin has completed the act of mating, he remains by the female's side for the next month to determine if he is indeed about to become a father. When he sees a single greenish white egg emerge from his mate's egg pouch, he begins to sing.

Scientists have characterized his song as "ecstatic."

Father Knows Best

In 1949 Robert Young began *Father Knows Best* as a radio show. Young played Jim Anderson, an average father in an average family. The show later moved to television, where it was a substantial hit.

Young's successful life, however, concluded in a tragedy of alcohol and depression. In January 1991, at age eighty-three, he attempted suicide by running a hose from his car's exhaust pipe to the interior of the vehicle. The attempt failed because the battery was dead and the car wouldn't start.

Green Genes

In Dublin, Ireland, a team of geneticists has been conducting a study to determine the origins of the Irish people. By analyzing segments of DNA from residents across different parts of the Irish countryside, then comparing this DNA with corresponding DNA segments from people elsewhere in Europe, the investigators hope to determine the derivation of Ireland's true forefathers.

Hugh Beaumont

The actor who portrayed the benevolent father on the popular TV show *Leave It to Beaver* was a Methodist minister. Tony Dow, who played older brother Wally, reports that Beaumont didn't care much for television and actually hated kids.

"Hugh wanted out of the show after the second season," Dow told the *Toronto Sun*. "He thought he should be doing films and things."

Inheritance

My own Irish forefather was a newspaperman, owned a popular nightclub, ran for mayor, and smuggled rum in a speedboat during Prohibition. He smoked, drank, ate nothing but red meat, and died of a heart attack in 1938.

His one son—my father—was only a teenager when his father died. I never learned more than the barest details about my grandfather from my father, despite my persistent questions. Other relatives tell me that the relationship had been strained.

My father was a skinny, eager-to-please little boy, battered by allergies, and not the tough guy his father had apparently wanted. My dad lost his mother at age three and later developed a severe stuttering problem, perhaps as a result of his father's sharp disapproval. My father's adult vocabulary was outstanding, due to his need for alternate words when faltering over hard consonants like *b* or *d*.

The stuttering grew worse over the years, with one noteworthy exception: after downing a few shots of Canadian whiskey my father could muster a stunning, honey-rich Irish baritone. His impromptu vocal performances became legend in local taverns, and by the time I entered the scene my father was spending every evening visiting the working class bars. Most nights he would stumble back drunk around midnight; some nights he was so drunk he would stumble through a neighbor's back door, thinking he was home.

Our phone would ring. "You'd better come get him."

As a boy I coped with this embarrassment by staying glued to the television—shows like *Father Knows Best* and *Leave It to Beaver* were my favorites. I desperately wanted someone like Hugh Beaumont to be my father, or maybe Robert Young.

Hugh Brannum, though, would have been my absolute first choice. Brannum played Mr. Green Jeans on *Captain Kangaroo*, and I remember him as kind, funny, and extremely reliable.

Jaws

My other hobby, besides watching other families on television, was an aquarium. I loved watching as my tropical fish drifted aimlessly through life, and I loved watching guppy mothers give birth. Unfortunately guppy fathers, if not moved to a separate tank, will often come along and eat their young.

Kitten

Kitten, the youngest daughter on *Father Knows Best*, was played by Lauren Chapin.

Lauren Chapin

Chapin's father, we later learned, molested her, and her mother was a severe alcoholic. After *Father Knows Best* ended in 1960, Chapin's life came apart. At sixteen she married an auto mechanic. At eighteen she became addicted to heroin and began working as a prostitute.

Masculinity

Wolf fathers spend the daylight hours away from the pack—hunting—but return every evening. The wolf cubs, five or six to a litter, will rush out of the den when they hear their father approaching and fling themselves at him, leaping up to his face. The father will back up a few feet and disgorge food for the cubs, in small, separate piles.

Natural Selection

When my wife, Renita, confessed to me her desire to have children, the very first words out of my mouth were, "You must be crazy." Convinced that she had just proposed the worst idea imaginable, I stood from my chair, looked straight ahead, and literally marched out of the room. This was not my best moment.

Ozzie

Oswald Nelson, at thirteen, was the youngest person ever to become an Eagle Scout. Oswald went on to become Ozzie Nelson, the father in *Ozzie and Harriet*. Though the show aired years before the advent of reality television, Harriet was indeed Ozzie's real wife, Ricky and David were his real sons, and eventually Ricky and David's wives were played by their actual spouses. The current requirements for Eagle Scout make it impossible for anyone to ever beat Ozzie's record.

Penguins, Again

The female emperor penguin "catches the egg with her wings before it touches the ice," Jeffrey Moussaieff Masson writes in his book *The Emperor's Embrace*. She then places the newly laid egg on her feet, to keep it from contact with the frozen ground. At this point both penguins will sing in unison, staring down at the egg. Eventually the male penguin will use his beak to lift the egg onto the surface of his own feet, where it will remain until hatching.

Not only does the penguin father endure the inconvenience of walking around with an egg balanced on his feet for months on end, he will also forgo food for the duration.

Quiz

1. What is Camille Paglia's view on the need for fathers?
2. Did Hugh Beaumont hate kids, and what was it he would rather have been doing than counseling the Beav?
3. Who played Mr. Green Jeans on *Captain Kangaroo*?
4. Who would you rather have as your father: Hugh Beaumont, Hugh Brannum, a wolf, or an emperor penguin?

Religion

In 1979 Lauren Chapin, the troubled actress who played Kitten, had a religious conversion. She credits her belief in Jesus with saving her life. After *his* television career ended, Methodist Minister Hugh Beaumont became a Christmas tree farmer.

Sputnik

On October 4, 1957, *Leave It to Beaver* first aired. On that same day the Soviet Union launched Sputnik I, the world's first artificial satellite. Sputnik I was about the size of a basketball, took roughly ninety-eight minutes to orbit the earth, and is often credited with escalating the Cold War and launching the U.S.-Soviet space race.

Years later, long after *Leave It to Beaver* ended its network run, a rumor persisted that Jerry Mathers, the actor who played Beaver, had died at the hands of the Soviet-backed communists in Vietnam. Actress Shelley Winters went so far as to announce it on the *Tonight Show*. But the rumor was false.

Toilets

Leave It to Beaver was the first television program to show a toilet.

Using Drugs

The presence of a supportive father is essential to helping children avoid drug problems, according to the National Center of Addiction and Substance Abuse at Columbia University. Lauren Chapin may be a prime example here. Tim Allen would be one, too. Fourteen years after his father died at the hands of a drunk driver, Allen was arrested for dealing drugs and spent two years in prison.

I also fit the gloomy pattern. Though I have so far managed to avoid my father's relentless problems with alcohol, I wasted about a decade of my life hiding behind marijuana, speed, and various hallucinogens.

Vasectomies

I had a vasectomy in 1994.

Ward's Father

In an episode titled "Beaver's Freckles," we learn that Ward Cleaver had "a hittin' father," but little else is ever revealed about Ward's fictional family. Despite Wally's constant warning—"Boy, Beav, when Dad finds out he's gonna clobber ya!"—Ward does not follow his own father's example and never hits his sons on the show. This is an example of xenogenesis.

Xenogenesis

(zen'u-jen'u-sis), n. Biol. 1. heterogenesis 2. the supposed generation of offspring completely and permanently different from the parent.

Believing in xenogenesis—though at the time I couldn't define it, spell it, *or* pronounce it—I changed my mind about having children about four years after I walked out on my wife's first suggestion of the idea. Luckily this was five years before my vasectomy.

Y Chromosomes

The Y chromosome of the father determines a child's gender, and it is unique in that its genetic code remains relatively unchanged as it passes from father to son. The DNA in other chromosomes is more likely to get mixed between generations, in a process called recombination. What this means, apparently, is that boys have a higher likelihood of directly inheriting their ancestral traits.

Once my wife convinced me to risk being a father—this took many years and considerable prodding—my Y chromosomes chose the easy way out: our only child is a daughter.

Maria, so far, has inherited many of what people say are the Moore family's better traits—humor, a facility with words, a stubborn determination.

It is yet to be seen what she will do with the negative ones.

Zappa

Similar to the persistent "Beaver died in Vietnam" rumor of the late 1960s, Internet discussion lists of the late 1990s were filled with assertions that the actor who played Mr. Green Jeans, Hugh "Lumpy" Brannum, was in fact the father of musician Frank Zappa.

Brannum, though, had only one son, and that son was neither Frank Zappa nor this author.

Too bad.

Good, Alright, Fine

Falling Room

I t's a winter Tuesday night. I've skipped school to drive north and trip on acid with my best friend, Dean. The day has been more than unnerving; it has suggested something occult and sinister is happening in our lives, and the chill that laces my spine doesn't feel like a mere effect of chemicals—it feels scary. So I get home and nerves are whirring in me, to say nothing of the cold blades of the acid. What I know is my best friend has changed; what I don't know is if I have, too. I've missed dinner; I've not called. My brother is out of town. Only my dad and our dog, Sky, are home and the kitchen is black. The blue of the television swims faintly around in the living room. I'm wondering if school called, if my eyes are still monstrously dilated, if he's pissed I missed dinner. I turn the key, with difficulty, in the dark lock. I get a soda and the refrigerator nearly blinds me—the slices of beef and browning vegetables are grotesque—and mock my pretended sobriety and calm. I have cold sweat on me as I stand in the doorway of the living room. Sky rises and stretches, ambles over for a scratch. I'm grateful that she occupies me—but I don't show her my eyes, because *she* would know.

"Hey dad—sorry I'm late, I got stuck with Diane helping her with that research paper she's doing, not sure if I told you about it, it's on domestic violence and anyway there's like sources to cite and—"

"Eli, have a seat."

Shit. I've only recently been officially allowed to see Dean again; if Dad discovers I've been skipping school—to say nothing of tripping—with him, I'm screwed. I fold awkwardly down on the little sofa next to his chair. He pauses the film he's watching. The TV is the only light in the room and, in the film, something vague is happening in a bedroom, so there is not enough illumination for him to really see my face.

He sighs. "Missed you for dinner."

"Yeah, I know. I'm sorry; I should've called." I marvel over how good and simple the truth sounds. I drink my Pepsi.

"Oh, it's alright." He spins the remote around a couple times on the coffee table. "So how was your day?"

The words *good, alright, fine* line up like divers, ready to plunge into the room. But there's a blockage. And I realize that I want, very badly, to tell him the truth about "how my day was." I'm burning to talk. I allow myself a few seconds of heavy quiet to cobble together something safe but honest.

"I don't know. I guess kind of weird. I mean, I was talking to Dean earlier and he was telling me about some things that happened lately that are kind of strange." I gauge his reaction to this, trying to see if the word "Dean" has tripped the usual series of alarms. But there's no sigh, no eye-roll. He nods at the stilled screen, two gray lovers scowling in bed. "I mean, he's just noticed a lot of coincidences lately. In one way he seems kind of stuck on finding them but there's also been, like, a *lot* lately."

"Give me an example." The screen winks once, brightly, on his lenses as he punches the power button. Then it is black and I hear his glasses clink down on the table. And I tell my dad all of it, cutting myself and LSD from the tale carefully as I go.

"It's just, like, because of the kind of things that are happening he feels like there's something sinister going on—like there's somebody controlling things that happen to him, trying to fuck with him." I say this, I realize, breathlessly, trying to hustle it out. My father sighs again.

"Well, you know, listening to you brings up a number of things for me. First of all, it makes me feel a little bad for the way I've always thought of Dean. He's probably dealing with a lot more than I imagined. But this stuff also makes me sorry all over again that your mother and I didn't introduce you and KC to any kind of spirituality." He turns to me in the dark to which our eyes have somewhat adapted. He's trying to see if I'm with him. I nod. "I don't mean that you and Dean aren't onto anything. I don't doubt that coincidences are much more than that. I believe that there is a higher power manipulating things in a strange way—and even if I sometimes don't like it, I don't think it's anything sinister. But I can imagine what you've described is fucking unnerving."

That night my father allowed me to unload the tension that had been spun through me. Things weren't all resolved, of course—there was still Dean's disintegration to endure. But that night he listened and eased me like only a father can so I could get to rest. And before I did, in the light of the film restarting, I looked him in the eyes and there was nothing left to hide and we both smiled.

II

I might have not even noticed the arrival of "Smart Drugs" in my home were it not for the brass monkey.

I was, at the time, deeply embedded in the world of not-so-smart drugs, my friend Dean's second slide into lunacy, and a relationship with a girl that can only be described as violent—though there were very few actual blows thrown (and, for the record, none by me). But one Christmas I'd been scrambling for gifts, very late in the season, and I found myself in a mall searching for something worthy of my dad. It could have been my teenaged poor judgment, just an inexplicable whim, or my affinity for the Beastie Boys, but when I found the business card holder, I barely deliberated. It was a brass monkey standing, his arms lifted above his head, holding a tray cut to the right size for business cards.

I was pleased to see my dad put the gift to use, but it was more the content of the cards that intrigued me. They were homemade, computer-fashioned and they looked it. They read: "Smart Drugs + My Experience = Your Goals Defined & Realized."

It was only then that I started to take note of the vials of opaque liquid, the bulky pill bottles—the instructions in a strange alphabet—that lined the bathroom cupboards. Dad believed that medical research had progressed beyond what the narrow-minded FDA would approve—which explained the small parcels arriving on our doorstep with postage marks from Sweden, Canada, and other liberal nations. I began to read snatches of a newsletter called *Smart Drug News: The Newsletter of the Cognitive Enhancement Research Institute*, most of which made me glaze over. The community of people experimenting with smart drugs seemed a different species ("Could tryptophan or 5-hydroxyttryptophan function as SSRIs?").

But here and there I did come across words for the first time that I would hear constantly later: *attention deficit, Prozac, Ritalin.*

My father claimed at one point that he had cured his own biochemical depression with smart drugs, though I can't remember any elaboration. Knowing my dad, he must have explained this new dimension to his life—successful or not. He'd always been gleeful to drop his get-rich schemes and strange hobbies on us. But knowing myself, I'm sure I barely listened; knowing my brother, I'm not surprised that he did.

The drug that KC recalls first seeing my father inject (though he admits he can't remember if it was "skin-popped" or "intramuscular") was called HGH (human growth hormone). Allegedly, HGH is a naturally occurring chemical that aids stiff joints, skin elasticity, and muscle formation. But, the human body being the flawed work that it is, folks run dry of HGH by their late twenties. Dad claimed that experiments with HGH had geriatric patients starting workout routines and enjoying surging libidos.

This always reminds me of the film *Cocoon*, in which alien pods accidentally wind up in a senior center swimming pool and the residents find themselves possessed by teenage urges. But HGH is no alien pod—although it is rumored to be derived, in part, from human brains. Creepy or not, dad insisted that eight months of plunging that hormone into his arm was the main reason he recovered from the damned Costa Rican cliff.

The other specific drug that KC recalls was supposed to enhance memory and focus. Dad insisted that it was nothing short of a great medical breakthrough and, of course, only natural that he should be one of the first to learn of it. He told KC to use it "if he needed to study or something," but KC steered clear, as much out of disgust at sharing a nasal gun with our father, as real trepidation.

For a long time these substances sat in a kitchen cabinet beside the aspirin, coffee, sugar, and mugs. But eventually they petered out, like so many other revolutions of the mid-90s. In their place appeared a sledgehammer narcotic, one that surely undid any good work on my father's mood or cognition.

III

I'd been very self-conscious. Not only was my father's disability (from the eighty-foot fall from a cliff) obvious in the uneven lurch of his walk, but he was wearing an actual fanny pack, that moronic invention that acts as identification and invitation: as a tourist, to be robbed. So when Miguel sauntered up just clear of the razor wire on Mexico's side, and my father immediately told him in horrid Spanglish that he was looking for drugs, I told him in Spanish that my father was looking for drugs, and I was going to Chiapas to join the revolution.

But Miguel wasn't impressed by my Spanish or amused by my joke. He turned back to talk with my father and navigated us deftly through drug stores and to their back doors. My dad was delighted with the negotiations and transactions. Not only was he saving considerable cash, but he was circumventing all the red tape the U.S. doctors now put between him and painkillers—to say nothing of the anxiety at not knowing where his next doses would come from. Stateside the haul of pills he lined his pockets with would've cost him weeks of wrangling with physicians and thousands of dollars. Peeling off fives and tens for the little pink and blue caplets was more like turning water to wine than buying anything. As I watched my father's pleasure increase, I began to like Miguel. From time to time, when my father stumbled, Miguel steadied him; I imagine Miguel thought of finding Dad relief from his wrecked body, his chronic agony, as his duty.

After a couple of hours I could feel my dad's elation wearing off. His steps became more precarious and pallor showed on his cheeks. Miguel guided us toward the border. We passed two gringo kids my age, all tattoos, piercings, and shades, undergoing a rough interrogation by military cops in a dark doorway. My nerves wound up as the pedestrian bridge arched over the waiting line of cars. We said goodbye to Miguel on a grimy side street, exchanging addresses and laying forty bucks on him.

I was about to suggest we cross separately but my father was still chatting with me when we got in line. He was calculating his savings, praising Miguel, damning the tight fisted pharmacists of El Norte, and generally at ease. I held my breath as we were waved into our country without so much as flipping our IDs.

We collected the dingy rental car and hit the freeway that would take us to my LA County home—or, if one were to keep driving, eventually to within a mile of our doorstep in Seattle. I drove and my dad unloaded his cache into the glove box, reclining in the seat. And then the border checkpoint pulled itself around the corner: a phalanx of uniforms and rifles standing between flashing lights in the center of the freeway. My heart tried to break free of my chest, head back to Mexico.

"Hmmm," Dad muttered.

The agent leaned down to the window. "Y'all coming from Mexico?" He was a Texan; irrationally this alarmed me more. My dad affirmed we were.

"How long this car been rented?"

I was stuck on *How the fuck did he know this was a rental?* to say nothing of *Why would he ask that?* But my father didn't miss a beat.

"Oh, about a week—I got it at LAX to visit my son here at his college, sir." He smiled and placed a hand lightly on my shoulder.

"Not bringing any drugs or anything back from Mexico are y'all?" I managed a too-quick shake of the head. My father's voice was a precise blend of indignation, cooperation, and friendliness.

"Nope. No drugs."

As we drove into the poisoned sunset and I practiced deep breathing, my father unwrapped and ate a trio of oxycontin.

IV

The phone rings in the corner of the cookie-cutter apartment and interrupts my and Rudi's twentieth yelling match of the day. As I lift the receiver to my ear, I'm keeping my evil gaze against her evil gaze, both of us letting the other know nothing is forgiven simply because of the intervention. But when I say *Hey, dad!* she uncrosses her arms, walks away, and I know the tiff is over.

"Hey, Eli—I think I'm actually right outside but unfortunately I've been pulled over." He chuckles nervously. "I know I'm on your street; I think I just passed your place and, I guess, blew a red light in the process." Another little laugh. I tell him I'm on my way.

On my cheap bicycle, the curbs and driveways of Route 66 are rough drops and jolts to negotiate. I can see the spinning blues and reds a quarter mile ahead. I'm trying not to get run over, but also to hurry, not knowing for sure what sort of situation my dad is confronting. But as I cut across the wake of an eighteen-wheeler, I see through the thick breath of exhaust that the cop is smiling. Turns out he's trying to help get my father get oriented, suggesting which apartment complex may be mine, to say nothing of having waived the citation for the red light. My dad hugs me through the window and I have to question the professionalism of the cop; I immediately recognize the slur on the edges of his greeting, the sleepy tilt of his gaze. I curse myself for allowing him to rent a car. We both thank the deputy and I lead dad back to the pad, hoping he's not going to rear end me on the way.

At dinner in a New Orleans–themed restaurant somewhere in the sprawling grid of greater LA, the booths are high, affording great privacy but making us feel a bit dwarfed. Rudi and I sit together across from him; she's clutching my hand under the table, assuming, mistakenly, his state is more upsetting than expected. My dad has a mangled corn muffin and some kind of chowder in front of him; half a pilsner winks amber through a greasy glass. He is slumped both back and sideways, but slightly. The anemia that's cursed him intermittently has been beaten back by the sun, and an almost healthy pink hue is spread on his brow and cheeks. His glasses are sliding off, though, and in the way he's sitting there is a suggestion of a double chin. He's talking with a kind of languid excitement about his plans for the next weeks, which include a trip to Mexico and a fully "comped" stop in Vegas. It's basically a monologue; he's not talking much or fast but each time one of us begins to interject he starts again. He produces another pink pill and navigates it to his mouth. Rudi squeezes my hand—in alarm or an attempt to soothe me, I don't know.

"So . . . maybe Guadalajara is a place for that. I'd like to spend time in the mountains—but not far from the sea. Of course, my desire for *amenities*, as my son keeps reminding me, limits . . ."

He trails off here and his half-lidded eyes have left us and found something apparently on the floor. There is a mole on my father's right eyelid. When I can see that mole, I know we have crossed a certain threshold.

"You won't like that stuff, Sky. It's all veggie. I got something for you in the fridge, so later on . . ." His eyes are nearly closed now; now, Rudi no longer looks alarmed but, instead, embarrassed. She squeezes my hand again, but studies the decorations across the room. Our dog Sky is no doubt snoozing fitfully, readjusting her arthritic three legs back in Seattle, a thousand miles from here.

"*Dad.*"

His eyes snap open for a moment, then retreat to half-lidded. He licks his lips and sits upright with a grunt. A sheepish smile wavers on him.

"What?" By the way I'm looking at him he sort of gets it. "Did I, uh, slip over a little?" I nod. "Wow. Yeah, that happens sometimes when I'm this tired."

It would be a lie to say that I am embarrassed. I'm not; I know too much about the pain my father's broken body brings to begrudge him this vice. It would be a lie to say I'm not amused. I am; he's funny when he's this muddled, if also somewhat incoherent. But I'm also frightened: of how unpleasant I suspect he'd be if the pink pills ran out; for his safety as he drives around the traffic-clogged city; of whether he would have the ability to make any plans were it not for the balm of narcotics; of whether he would choose to live without them at all.

As we leave the restaurant I tell him I think his rented Taurus is an eight-cylinder and how I'd sure like to drive it. This allows him to pass me the keys without shame.

V

The pills were stored where the smart drugs used to be—with the sugar, mugs, coffee, and aspirin in the glass cupboard above the kitchen counter. On a summer night I remove one, slip it into my wallet on a whim. Later that night in a downtown apartment, the hours have become small, the energy has leaked out of the room, and I'm slouched on a sofa with Ike. I pull out the pill and he snaps it in two with his blade. We each take half. An hour later we are in a pub down the block, watching one another, blurry, across a sticky table. We can't put together sentences too well and the stumble home relies heavily on walls and friends. At this point, my father is eating eight or nine of these pills per day.

VI

The sun spikes off the blacktop, the morning dew magnifying the brilliance. Sun in the Northwest feels like an anomaly somehow; even in the midst of summer when it's been the rule for several weeks, it's hard to get used to—and sweet all over again each day you wake to it. I flip the visor down and suddenly see the wall of stopped vehicles. The tires give a tearing sound and my dad is jolted mildly forward, his broad brow dipping like a quick prayer.

"Shit. Sorry 'bout that."

He dismisses it with a grunt. He's uncharacteristically pensive, sunglassed eyes playing the Everett skyline. We're headed for a detox hospital in this small city north of Seattle. I can't remember now what it was that finally compelled my father to check in, but I doubt it was pressure from alarmed others. More likely it was reaching a personal zenith of frustration: wanting desperately to read a certain book; angered by his inability to sit through dinner and a movie without dozing; wanting seriously, earnestly, to begin to write stories again, which I knew would do more for him than any quantity of narcotic, meditation, or prayer.

"Take this exit, Eli."

We find the correct avenue after some haggle and he tries to make light of the coming week, but his reservations still shoulder through.

"I really don't know what to expect, you know? They won't tell you shit; I guess it's some kind of security thing. I just hope that it's not a bunch of goddam group therapy with zombies—though maybe I'll get some great material for stories." He's trying to be social, to bring me in by way of subject matter here. I nod my agreement, feeling nervous myself. I don't know whether to be serious, try to give him a pep talk, or to take a swing at the weight of it all with humor. "When I get back maybe we can plan a camping trip with your brother." I say I'd like that, and I would—though I'm concerned by how frustrated my father gets with his disabilities out in the woods.

After a couple of false passes, we find the hospital. The lot is full so I drop him off and go find parking. When I finally locate the tiny intake room, he's already finishing his paperwork and a portly male nurse is standing like a bailiff in wait. I hug him quick and hard, one of those embraces that says, simultaneously: *No big deal, see you soon* and *it's so heavy, a hug is so absurd.* At the door, backlit by the bright interior of detox, he turns and gives me a look of nervousness, embarrassment, guilt, and amusement, a look you might, at age ten, give your best friend as your mother hauls you away from your mischief. I leave with stifled, vague emotions and his confiscated mouthwash, chocolate, and aspirin folded in a sack under my arm.

My brother thinks that having "Dad in detox" programmed into his cell phone is about the coolest thing ever. We both find it cool, after my brother makes the drive to Everett to collect him, that my dad has riveting stories about his time in there: elderly junkies and their hand-wringing wait for phenobarbitol; the nurses cloned directly from *One Flew Over the Cuckoo's Nest*; the seventeen-year-old tweeker who refused to participate because they wouldn't let her smoke. Neither of us knows exactly what to think as dad half-heartedly claims he's learned what he needed to and consumes more narcotic.

VII

In January 2000, nearly three years since he plummeted from that Costa Rican cliff, my father returns to the hospital for the final major spinal surgery. This time it is to remove the considerable hardware clamped around his backbone that could, with time, cause fatal infection. I've spent a strange New Year's Eve at my mother's mountain home with a gaggle of friends. On the day Dad's surgery is scheduled, I drive over a hundred icy miles to plead guilty to felony possession of magic mushrooms in a desolate little county in the center of the state. Luckily, the judge opts to send me back to college instead of back to jail. Luckily, dad's surgery goes as planned.

I creep precariously through a blizzard, the two hours back to the city morphing into six.

When I arrive at the hospital, my father is recovering on the ninth floor. I can hear him before I see him.

"Right, right, I understand that is the situation. What I'm asking you is to explain *why.*" Dad is using his tough business tone; it only surfaces when he really feels he's being jerked around.

I stand in the doorframe, snowflakes in my bangs transforming into cold beads on my brow. My father's glasses are crooked; his face is beet red. But his arms and lower legs, where they stick out from the gown, are anemically white. He sees me and smiles with relief. He waves in greeting and a couple of IV tubes wave with him. The doctor is a forbidding man, bald and huge and a face redder than my dad's. He swivels toward me and realizes who I am. As he does, I see some relief in his expression as well. He takes me out in the hall as dad curses under his breath and punches the morphine button with a dull violence.

I get very angry when doctors act as if my father is irrational; it's almost invariably the case that he is simply challenging their dismissive explanations. They are accustomed to passive patients who take orders and news at face value; it's far easier to ascribe "irrational" or "problematic" to them. The doctors do not appreciate my father's pointed inquiries and insatiable need for information. I learned the hard lessons of medical hubris and negligence many times after my father's fall in 1997. But I also learned, slowly, how to keep my temper in the face of it.

"Your father is in quite a bit of pain, so he is very concerned about his medication," the doctor says, avoiding my gaze by rubbing his lenses clean. I know what this means is *your father is an addict.* He will not say this, of course, because he is one of those responsible for said addiction. "You're going to be taking care of him this week, yes?" I nod. "Well, I'm going to give *you* the prescription—you need to be responsible for his medication, make sure he doesn't take too much."

I hold the post of narcotic dispenser for approximately thirty hours before handing the pills over. Dad has plenty squirreled away anyhow—combined with what the doctor prescribed, enough for weeks—but he paces the apartment cursing and raving behind his walker because there is a problem with conflicting prescriptions and he doesn't yet know how he is going to get more. We do the math several times, count the pills again, and he spends hours haggling with a slew of medical personnel on the telephone. I remain in noncommittal solidarity with his rants against the paranoid, meddling doctors and pharmacists and the cheap-ass insurance bastards. But I realize that my silence is wearing on me and that the alarm I feel is, by way of repression, slipping toward anger. Because he is wound so tight, stressed, and in pain, when I make some smart-ass remark because I can't get any of his six remote controls to turn on the TV, he snaps.

We have it out right there, me pouring out all the nasty alterations in his personality, how "*everyone* is alarmed," him fighting back with all the defensiveness and denial he's not yet had reason to use against me. I unload the details of his addiction: the nodding off in restaurants, the slips in and out of reality, the weaving into the opposite lane driving, the stack of books that he's "reading" but hasn't yet started. He perches on the edge of the sofa, fitfully rearranging his agonized body, firing back with everything he has: I don't understand a goddamn thing about it, I'm selfish, I'm trying to love him conditionally just like everyone else, I don't respect him, if I really knew how hard it was I'd be impressed that there was still a full clip in grandpa's service revolver.

It doesn't end in a long, firm, father-son embrace, sobbing and pledging to fight through to some solution. He doesn't promise to quit and I don't promise to stand by his side. It doesn't end that way at all. I leave him there, curled on his bed, the pills and gun in reach, an impossible distance in his eyes. I leave him there alone and partially helpless; in pain, depressed and crippled and addicted. I leave him there in unspeakable shame. I leave him there to go get drunk carrying the same in me.

VIII

In 2000 my father packs his bags and flies to London, where my brother KC is in his first year of college. After three or four days amid the perpetual drear of the city, they rent a car and split for Hastings, the 1066 battlefield to which some scholar has traced our surname. In the course of conversation, my brother lets it slip that Amsterdam is a mere six hours' drive, and in a vague, twisted manner, sort of on the way back to London. My father decides they will leave the next morning for the fabled city, which he hasn't visited in more than two decades.

My brother, still young enough to feel nervous when it comes to an intersection of *drugs* and *parent*, is shy about procuring grass in the first coffee shop they visit, but my father encourages him and soon they are giggling at a counter, sipping from hot tea and hash joints, watching the carnival city unroll through a misty rain. My father, however, in the vernacular of my brother, is far more "stoked about the smart shops." The first one they enter sends my father into wide-eyed shock and glee, which he overcomes in order to grill the clerk on every product. He says he'll pay top dollar for the peyote on display high on a shelf, but they're not selling. Eventually they leave the smiling merchant and make their way through the twilight back to the boat hotel, rocking softly along one of the canals, with an assortment of magic mushrooms.

My brother makes the decision to play the role of caretaker, not being entirely sure how my overly analytical father might respond to being hurled into a mystical and chaotic experience in a strange city on a "botel." My father settles on the bed and throws back the first trio of slimy, fresh fungi. But after a mere half-hour has passed, he becomes impatient, claims he isn't feeling a thing and wants to take more. My brother's cautions manage to hold dad off for ten minutes before he reaches for the next (different) dosage and gobbles those. He's accustomed to only a momentary wait before he reels into the comfort of his painkillers. Again, a small chapter of time passes, during which my brother smokes Dutch grass and loses track of exactly how much time, and my father wants more. Despite KC's protestations, Dad eats a third and final dose, of yet another type. All told, he has eaten between two and a half and three and a half doses of strong psylocibin (six months later, I eat a half dose, which my father thoughtfully smuggled back across the Atlantic for me, and damn near lose my mind in the Cascade mountains). My brother shakes off his own high and watches our father carefully as the night thins over the red light district.

It is hilarious when the toxins really began to twirl in his bloodstream, KC tells me. He invites Dad to the porthole to check out the night sky. Dad reportedly withdraws with a gasp, then recovers and claims he's "never seen a *real* star before." They spend some time at that tiny window, their two heads crammed side by side, my father aghast at the wonder of it all, my brother laughing himself to fatigue.

When they settle back onto the twin beds, my dad's gaze finds the bedside table which holds the customary alarm clock, jewelry, drugs, rolling papers, passports, and cartoonish currency of Holland. He proclaims it an incredible work of art and can't take his eyes off it. Trying to get Dad more active in his trip, KC moves the articles around on the table, rearranging them, but dad shrieks in horror that KC is ruining the masterpiece. They laugh about the severity of Dad's response for a bit, but some hours later, Dad still glances painfully back at the table.

"Jesus, KC, you really did fuck it up," he complains, shaking his head.

As the night winds down, my brother turns his attention to the television and begins a search for an English channel. When he curses his lack of luck, my dad seems baffled.

"Hey, what's the matter—that's a good movie!"

When KC explains slowly that there is nothing on in their language, my dad turns incredulous. He insists that *every* program is in English.

"Okay, pops, what did that dude *just* say?" KC tests him.

"Oh, shit, I missed that. That actor just mumbles," Dad shoots back, still convinced.

Dad finally wanders into the tiny bathroom where he remains in the shower for over forty-five minutes. When he finally emerges, KC is dozing off. The last thing he remembers is Dad sitting on the bed in silence a moment. Then he turns to my brother and announces, deadpan, "I think I just had an identity crisis."

He is snoring earnestly at his ordinary volume within minutes.

DINAH LENNEY

Acting

Bigger than Life:
A Murder, a Memoir

get my call time from *Cracker*. Wednesday midmorning I'm due to drive up the Golden State Freeway to the flats of Valencia to play a scene with the star; he's the genius detective, and I'm a psychiatrist to a transsexual killer with baby lust who has stolen an infant from a hospital nursery. The Monday before, I go for my fitting with my pager clipped to my jeans. The sizes I asked for are too big and they have to pull more clothes from the wardrobe truck. I stare into the mirror at that peculiar face—almost gaunt—and I have fantasized gaunt for as long as I can remember. But gaunt or not, I hardly recognize her, that woman in the mirror whose father is missing.

Tuesday night Paul calls to say the real-life detectives are getting close, they know where he is, helicopters are hovering over the New York side of the Hudson, searching in circles, a loud light show along the Hudson River.

"It's not good, Dine," he says. "It's not good."

I call my stepmother and leave a message on her machine.

Everything is the same gray color at five o'clock Wednesday morning, when I open my eyes just before the phone rings on my side of the bed. I pick it up and stumble over to the window, where the buzz in the line goes away, blocking my left ear with my index finger to hear better. Fred is beside me, his hand on my arm.

"Dinah, they found him," says Paul.

"Is he dead?"

"Yes—yes."

He tells me he will call later in the day to tell me about the memorial service and to get my flight information.

"Paul, can I ask you a favor?"

"You'll say a few words at the service," he answers, but that's not what I want. I ask him to get me something, anything—a watch, cufflinks—before it's all gone, something that belonged to my father that I can have for my children.

No reply, something muttered, muffled, a shuffling in the background, a woman's voice rises in a question. "Paul? Hello?" I press harder against my left ear with the heel of my palm.

"Dinah," says Gayle, who has taken the phone, "he's crying, honey, what did you say to him?"

It's just after seven that morning when I call my manager at home.

"They found my father," I say. "I can't work today."

"You can't work?"

I woke her, I can tell, she's confused, distracted by her own small daughter who is whining in the background. In a voice that's higher and flatter than my own, I explain that my father is dead, found in the woods in a ravine by the Hudson River. As I speak it's as though I'm on the other side of the room, watching, listening, wondering who can be saying these words.

After I hear from Paul and once we've gotten the kids off to school, I clean up my desk, make phone calls, reservations, pack an overnight bag. That afternoon, Fred and I retrieve Jake from the JCC and we drive all together to pick up Eliza from her school, in the flats of West LA. We park, as always, in the lot behind Winston Tires, next to an overflowing dumpster. The sun, a washed out ball in a no-color sky, is September hot in this part of town, all squat and the same, no relief from the scorching, and the hills in all directions have disappeared behind the smog.

We buckle the kids in behind us, then turn around in our seats to talk to them: family conference in the car. Eliza, initially delighted to see us both, grows suddenly suspicious, knows something is up, leans forward in her seat and knits her brows.

"Pop died," I say.

Jake struggles to understand. "So we will never see him again?"

There was an accident involving the car, we explain, and Eliza asks, "Was he wearing a seat belt?"

"Pop never wore his seat belt," says Jake, and then, "Too bad we won't get to see him one more time." He begins to cry, silently.

Eliza, studying her lap, says, "I need privacy to think about this."

"I wish," Jake chokes out, "I wish I was with Pop right now."

Before we start home, we tell them that I must go back East for a few days, to say good-bye.

"I want to say good-bye," says Jake. "I want to come with you to say good-bye to Pop."

My uncle has pressed me to leave the kids home, as if I needed convincing. Back in New Jersey the smallest of the cousins know the details of what happened to their grandfathers' brother, but I'm not ready to tell my own children, and I'm grateful not to have to.

That night, just hours after my father's body has been found, we have tickets to see the Dodgers, and we cannot disappoint these kids. Do I look different, I wonder, sitting in the stands, a week after my father has been kidnapped and murdered, the day his body has been discovered on the banks of the Hudson River. Do I smell funny, I wonder, sitting next to my daughter who eats half of her cotton candy, a handful of popcorn, a bite of a hot dog, and hands the remains each in turn to me.

An acquaintance, a mother from the preschool, catches sight of us and wanders down from her seat to whisper in my ear. "Have they found your father?" she wants to know.

"Yes, this morning," I whisper back. "He's dead. I'm leaving tomorrow."

We both stare out over home plate and she knows not to say any more.

"Will you miss me?" I ask Jake, when I kiss him good-bye the following day.

"Mom," he says, "how can you miss someone when you know they're coming back?"

At the airport, I buy the *New York Times*. There he is on the front page of the metro section. "Youths Accused of Killing New Jersey Millionaire," reads the headline, and there's a photo—not the prison mug shot from 1974, a smiling one this time—later I will get a condolence note that remarks on the twinkle in his eye.

Bludgeoned, says the paper, pistol-whipped, hit with a rock in the back of the head, stabbed multiple times, and his throat, says the article, *may* have been cut.

A large black lady in a navy polyester suit sits beside me at gate 40-something, puts her hand on my shoulder. "You all right, miss? Honey? You all right?"

I nod in her direction, focusing on the lint on her shiny sleeve, willing her to leave, willing her to stay, willing myself to disappear, willing it to be yesterday or the day before yesterday, or the week before last.

"You know that man?" she asks, pointing with one dimpled finger, and now the self-conscious dilemma begins, for I am the actress, the eldest, the only child from the first marriage, the one who talked too much, the one who needed too much attention. But if I deny who he is, isn't that wrong? Mustn't I shout this to the terminal? Mustn't I call attention to this evil? Mustn't I stand up and tell everybody, *This is my father!*

She calls to the stewardess who's involved in preflight procedures near the security doors, "Look here, miss, this is awful, this is her *daddy*! Give me this a minute," she says, taking the paper from me. "Look at this here." She's jabbing the photo with her index finger. "This is her *father* in this picture here."

Somehow I rise. "Please," I say, "please, I'm sorry," and I take the newspaper and walk in the direction of the pay phones to call Fred, to tell him, when I can breathe again, the *New York Times* says maybe they cut his throat.

"Oh no," says my husband. "Can you sit down, do you need water, oh, Dine, what can I do?"

Fred has always regretted that he didn't come with me. With his own parents dead, he saw this loss as an inevitable—if extraordinary—rite of passage, one through which he'd always intended to hold my arm, support me, stand at my side.

When Rose died of natural causes, neither of us thought twice about Fred's staying in LA with Eliza and Jake. No point in dragging everybody east for three days, and who else to march the kids through soccer and T-ball and the weekend birthday party parade? I was relieved to learn Leah and Ron would actually be in town for business reasons. Fortuitous, that, especially with Fred suddenly knocked flat by a terrible cold. But when I suggested they coordinate with him and the kids, my mother's fury was unmistakable. As was her contempt for my grandmother, her ex-mother-in-law.

"Dinah," she spat over the wires, "don't expect me to grieve for that woman! She betrayed me!"

Nobody was asking her to grieve, I protested, only to spell Fred for a bit, to take the kids for ice cream, to play a couple of rounds of gin rummy with one or the other and give the poor man a break. My mother was damned, she announced, if she'd facilitate my mourning.

"Don't presume, Dinah," she admonished, opting not to see her own grandchildren that weekend rather than to pick up the slack.

This time, in the wake of my father's murder, Fred felt truly conflicted about letting me fly east alone. Who could blame him under the circumstances? But who else to stay with our children, who only knew their grandfather was dead, and not the truth about how he died? Who better to hold them, and love them, and protect them from the dark?

NATALIA RACHEL SINGER

And There Fell a Great Star

Scraping By in the Big Eighties

And it fell upon the third part of the rivers, and upon the
fountains of waters;
And the name of the star is called Wormwood: and the third
part of the waters became wormwood; and many men died
of the waters
Because they were made bitter.

➤ THE REVELATION OF JOHN 8:11

What is history? Is it a theory? I no longer live in the place
where I and those who look like me first made an appearance.
I live in another place. It has another narrative.

➤ JAMAICA KINCAID, "In History"

I was leading the cool-down in AM Aerobics when someone
announced that the space shuttle Challenger had blown up
in the sky. Not only were seven talented people struck down
in their prime, but school children had to watch their beloved
teacher, the one civilian crew member, explode on live TV. It was
too awful.

That night, I forced myself to watch Reagan's State of the Union
and immediately wished I hadn't. After he asked us to pause to
mourn and honor "the valor of our seven Challenger heroes,"
Reagan implored us to "go forward America and reach for the
stars." There it was—an infomercial for Star Wars. Reagan was
using the death of the Challenger Seven to legitimize the nearly
trillion dollars we were spending on a program inspired by a bad
sci-fi flick he'd starred in.

By now it seemed that every public event—the release of the Iranian hostages on Inauguration Day in '81, the wag-the-dog invasion of Grenada in '83, this mission to the stars—was timed to provide content for the Great Communicator's next speech. And just as planned, after this one his ratings soared, despite rumors that NASA felt pressured to launch in dangerously cold weather—frozen O-rings be damned—so that Reagan could deliver yet another triumphal American tale in this State of the Union address.

I had just decided on my own triumphal tale for 1986. Claudia had called from Seattle with an appealing invitation: she and her boyfriend were traveling to Europe that summer and wanted me to sublet their apartment. I knew what I would do: I'd bill myself as a freelance "physical fitness specialist from Boston" and teach around town, transformed, at last, into the serene, fit, confident creature I'd first gone west to become.

Although presenting myself as *from* Boston was a bit misleading, I actually did possess the rest of that credential: my reward, on paper, for enduring a weeklong course with some boisterous jocks at Springfield College. I could calculate target heart rates; lead a snappy routine of aerobic dance moves, calisthenics, yoga stretches, and guided relaxation; pinch an inch with skin calipers to measure your fat; even resuscitate you from cardiac arrest (*Annie, Annie, are you all right?*) although I'd never tried this on an actual human and hoped I never would have to. I pictured the posters Claudia would put up in advance of my arrival with the extravagant promise, GET IN THE BEST SHAPE OF YOUR LIFE, blazoned across the top.

I also applied to the writers' conference in Port Townsend, this time as a fellow. Raymond Carver would be on the faculty again and I was determined to get in his section. I needed a letter of recommendation and I knew just who to ask: Tamas Azcel, my advisor. "Aim high," he said often, encouraging me to reach for the stars.

The call came at the end of April—I was one of two fellows selected, and I'd been awarded a scholarship to the conference. I was high on this achievement until that evening when, perhaps as a corrective for too much joy, my mother phoned with terrible news. She had just learned that my father was dead and that my grandmother, as suspected, had Alzheimer's disease. I hadn't intended to go to Cleveland that year, but I took the first train I could get.

As much as I'd dreaded the visit, when the cab dropped me off in front of my grandmother's red brick house, I felt oddly comforted by the familiar: the cooing mourning doves in the front-yard oak tree, the money-tree bushes lining the driveway, the backyard flowering magnolia tree, even the yellowing Formica kitchen floor.

"Tell your mother the house is going to blow up if she doesn't stop smoking," my grandmother called to me by way of greeting. I was relieved that she knew who I was. She sat on her overstuffed blue chair in her pink duster, sifting through old utility bills from the seventies and drinking, then discarding, endless cups of tea. The year 1986 flickered in and out of her radar and I tried to keep up. Sometimes I was me at thirteen on my way to school, sometimes I was my sister hyperventilating beneath a table during a family quarrel, and sometimes I was my mother returning home from her triumphant debut piano recital just before America entered World War II.

My mother waited until my grandmother was napping to hand me the file with her correspondence from Social Security about my father. "You won't believe this," she said.

It turned out that my father had been dead for a long time— since December of 1980, my first winter in Seattle, when I was living on unemployment in the Ballard duplex with Joe. And now I knew: after romanticizing him all these years, still half-believing he would return to save me from my mother, or that I'd find him in Mexico, or that he'd come looking for me (after he saw my name on the *New York Times* bestseller list), he was to remain my imaginary father, my creation. I thought of all the unsent letters I'd written him during his life and after. I thought of how much space he had occupied in my psyche. I had spent an unhealthy chunk of my life having an intense conversation with a dead guy.

My mother's detective work had uncovered that he had not been in Mexico, or Europe, but in the capital of Boozehound America, New Orleans. In 1979, when I was writing my senior honors thesis on Tennessee Williams, my father was like a char-acter in one of Williams's plays, drinking himself to death in a rented room for transients on Napoleon Street. I should have known.

I held his death certificate in my hand and tried to glean the story behind the words: *marked fatty liver, cardiomyopathy, chronic pancreatitis.* I found out later that he'd been standing on his balcony, opening a beer at 10:30 in the morning when he dropped dead of a heart attack at the age of sixty, having never become the big success he'd abandoned his family to become.

I told my mother I needed a nap and went upstairs to the den, a small room with a sleeper sofa and a green hatbox from the 1930s on an antique Chinese table in which my grandmother kept old photos. I wanted to contemplate the news in private. Outside I heard birds singing, the coo of those mourning doves. I opened my journal and wrote the date, May 2, 1986, and tried to write. Nothing came.

What I'd carried with me all these years, the most persistent of my stories about my father, was that he had left us to do something more important than be our father. I had few memories of him but the one I treasured most was of climbing the attic stairs to visit him in his study when he was writing. I had always believed that even if he changed his name to elude my mother, I'd open a book someday and recognize his voice. His were the potato rhythms of the American heartland, flavored with the paprika of his Hungarian gypsy ancestors. I liked to think they were my rhythms too.

And yet, in the end, all that my father had in his possession were his portable typewriter, five brown suits, a passport, and a six-pack of beer. He'd been with us when he published his one novel, at the age of forty; he was supposedly at work on what would be his masterpiece when he left. What had happened with this manuscript was anyone's guess. All I knew was that he had resisted the gravity of home, family, love, and community for a solitary flight to the stars only to crash-land below sea level in swampy Louisiana, unloved and unmourned, where he would linger in perpetuity not on the American lit syllabi across the lands, but in an unmarked pauper's grave.

A year into my MFA program, barely scraping by on a first-year fellowship of $2500 and my YMCA wages, I still believed that a true artist must relinquish all materialistic urges in the service of that higher calling. And despite my persistent desire to find love and family and security, a part of me still believed that such longings were a sign of weakness I needed to transcend, just as a part of me had always been proud of my father for refusing to be a conventional postwar father—indeed, I loved the idea, if not the reality, that my father had descended from a nomadic, restless, transgressive people. The gypsy identity softened the blow of his abandonment and, in turn, made *me* sound more interesting than I was. I had even played that Hungarian gypsy card when I first met Tamas Azcel. He himself was a Hungarian who fled the Communist takeover of 1956, and I sometimes wondered if it was our shared "homeland" more than the quality of my work that made me one of his pets.

But I would later learn that the Hungary gypsy story was just a story. After meeting another of my father's abandoned children in the 1990s I would discover that he was of Swiss-German Mennonite origin, the descendant of five generations of Indiana chicken farmers. He had told my mother he "worked his way through college in Indiana plucking chickens," but he hadn't told her they were *his parents'* chickens! And though he started college at Purdue, he completed his education in California on the GI Bill. The biggest revelation to me was that my father was a veteran of World War II—something my mother never mentioned. Maybe she knew, but maybe he somehow kept this a secret so that he could deprive her of his GI benefits, or maybe when they met in Los Angeles—she a twenty-two-year-old olive-skinned beauty just out of the mental hospital, he the dapper man in the white suit (like Faulkner's) who at twenty-nine was already a veteran of two marriages, a war, and a master's degree program—he decided to rewrite his biography to impress her, slipping in just enough facts (chickens, Indiana) to give the fiction the stuff of real life. In the end, the most enduring fiction of my father's career was the one he fashioned of his life.

And this fiction had been passed on to me. I had identified with his path, despite my feminist critique of it. Why did my life choices still seem so dialectical, with family and its sacrifices at one pole and creativity and its sacrifices at the other? I wrote in my journal: "Is this my fate too? To be buried by the state with no evidence of ever having family or friends?"

I sifted through the photos in the green hatbox in search of some record that I'd ever crossed paths with this man: my father holding me in his arms in our apartment when I was a baby, my mother and father standing in front of one of his paintings. I felt a pressure in my chest, but nothing more. I studied a picture of my grandmother in a plaid skirt wheeling me in my stroller through a park. I could not cry for her either, my Grandma Anna whose past was eroding like the silt on a riverbed: *Annie, Annie, are you all right?*

I set the photos aside and switched on the news. There was a story about a candlelight vigil: Clevelanders of Russian descent were grieving their loved ones who had been hurt or killed in the recent Chernobyl disaster. I stared at the broad faces and cheekbones of these mourners holding candles, singing and weeping. They had the short torsos, broad shoulders, and wide faces of the women in my family: peasant bodies built for work. I had often thought I'd go to Russia one day to trace my grandmother's roots, perhaps with her by my side, but I saw from the map that she was from the area where the worst radiation had settled.

And that's when I began to cry. For these strangers, whose family members resembled mine. For my grandmother, whose parents were born in Minsk and whose memories of them, their stories as Jews in the Old Country, their stories of the land, had turned to mishmash. For my father, who had left his home to pursue ambitions that never bore fruit and whose ancestral memories would never be passed on to his children. And for our ravaged earth, storied now with the scars of cold war overproduction and the toxic aftermath of the nuclear age.

I imagined the geography of Belarus and the Ukraine: ice carved valleys of snow and pine-cool forests fragrant with mushrooms laid to waste by the cooling towers of nuclear power plants, the eroded soils of collectivized farms, the crowded city buses, the ugly factories. According to Adi Roche, author of *Children of Chernobyl*, almost 2,200,000 Belarussian people were subjected to permanent radioactive contamination by the explosion. Of the country's forests and farmlands, 25 percent became a nuclear wasteland and only 1 percent remained unharmed. And yet the Politburo wrote forty secret protocols to conceal the dimension of the disaster from the public. One, for example, authorized that the so-called acceptable level of radiation be raised by a factor of fifty. In this way the Russian leadership was mirroring a move made by Ronald Reagan, who set out early on to reclassify documents about nuclear testing and nuclear plant safety that had been opened in the Carter years, thus re-concealing information on public risks to human health and enabling the Nuclear Regulatory Commission to abandon some of its most important safety regulations without the knowledge of the people who lived near the plants. In addition, as Carl Pope wrote in *Sierra* in 1984, Reagan authorized the Environmental Protection Agency's toxics chief, John Todhunter, to increase the pre-Reagan rate of the "risk of cancer from exposure to toxic substances" of "one additional case of cancer for every million people exposed" by a "hundred fold." In Gorbachev's case, had he let the public know the truth of the devastation and relocated the millions who should have been evacuated, and not the four hundred thousand that he did, it would have cost him his career.

Countless thousands of children became afflicted with, or were born with, leukemia, lymphoma, thyroid cancers, deformed limbs, and the whole range of cancers and ailments that weakened immune systems bring. Because many of them were radioactive to the touch, they were abandoned, or exiled into makeshift orphanages in Belarus, without medical facilities, toilets, or hot water.

Imagine having to abandon your home in a forced evacuation. You are sick, vomiting, dizzy, and have to decide what to carry with you when in truth, everything you own, even you, yourself, are contaminated. You, your home, your family are now the carriers of death and suffering. All that gave you comfort brings unthinkable misery.

I wanted to discuss the news with my grandmother, but Chernobyl would have baffled and upset her and perhaps added to her conviction that the house was going to blow up. She also seemed to think her husband was still among us. When I asked her if she could name the year and the current president my mother laughed and said, "I think she'd rather not think about *that*."

My mother was in surprisingly good spirits. She was taking her medication and had resigned herself to a responsibility that would have been daunting even for someone without a history of mental illness. With the present and the future indecipherable texts, the three of us spent the weekend enjoying a half-invented version of the past. Grandma showed me her treasures—Cleveland teachers' glowing reports of her and her daughter and her daughter's daughters—the testimony that at one time we were all destined for the stars.

The folly of that summer's get-solvent-quick scheme did not hit me until I arrived in Seattle a few weeks later and met my first class of aerobics students—all three of them. With the money I'd spent on ads and studio time, I would need three times that many students just to break even. If I didn't recruit a lot more fitness enthusiasts, I'd have to find an actual job.

After three days of plastering the city with posters, I took a day off with a friend from the MOM-era: a tax attorney named Jerry. A veteran of financial trouble (he was one of the many lawyers MOM fired and locked out without notice) he had survived a spate of recent disasters that made my concerns seem trivial. Two years ago his wife had given birth to twins who were born several weeks premature with serious physical problems. The babies showed up before Jerry and his wife could get on a new health insurance plan and the bills—for which they were 100 percent responsible—came to over two hundred thousand dollars. They had yet to find a subsequent provider that was willing to cover the costs for the babies' preexisting heart and kidney problems. Under the strains of these pressures, the couple had separated, and Jerry had filed for bankruptcy.

"Heck, it's only money," he said. "Let's have fun."

Claudia had loaned me her bicycle for the summer, Jerry had packed a picnic, and after we crammed the bikes into his Saab station wagon, we were off. We took the ferry to Vashon Island, where I'd once daydreamed of becoming a back-to-the-land homesteader with Joe. Soon I was soaring downhill past a cedar-tree-lined beach, inhaling the salt air and with it a glimmer of the glorious summer days ahead.

And then I hit a bump in the road. The front wheel of the bike *fell off*. I careened over the handlebars and was airborne for a minute, flying past a field of blue lupine, feeling the wind on my neck. I wasn't wearing a helmet because I thought I'd be too hot. I landed on my head.

An hour later an emergency room nurse was plucking gravel out of my face and my hands. A doctor was asking me who the president was and I said, "I think I'd rather forget." The nurse cut a gauze tent under which the doctor seamed my face and scalp back together. A numbing solution, cold as metal, dripped into my ringing ears. The doctor explained that I was getting a lot of stitches on my face and I would look "a bit beat up" for some time. "Wait as long as you can before you look in the mirror," he said.

Beyond the threats to my vanity, the real problem was my brain: if it swelled much overnight, it would need to be pried surgically loose from my skull. I would have to stay in the hospital so they could watch me. Plus, when I'd landed on the asphalt, I had also managed to scrape off the first few layers of skin on my palms. If I touched anything, I could get a staph infection. Gauze bandages held my fingers together, and until they healed, I would not be able to use my hands to cook, eat, or bathe.

Having just heard Jerry's story about going bankrupt over medical bills, I refused this care. I had no idea if my UMass student health insurance kicked in through the summer, and if it would cover an out-of-state emergency room visit, let alone a stay in the hospital. And even if they paid 80 percent, I had no way to pay the rest.

"I can only let you go home if you can guarantee you'll have people with you every minute," the doctor said.

"We've got it covered," Jerry said.

I could not imagine asking for this much help from anyone, not even my sister. Who could I burden? With Claudia gone and Joe off with a new girlfriend to Alaska, I only had Jerry and Neal. Neal had already played nursemaid when Ethan and I visited after Mexico; what had I ever done for him? I'd only been in Seattle for three days and instead of getting its citizens into the best shape of their lives, I was in their care, an invalid.

After Jerry got me home, Neal brought over soup and sandwiches and fed them to me. To pass the time, we invented a game called Fact or Fiction. We would ask each other questions, then either make up lavish lies that sounded like the truth, or tell true stories that were so strange and packed with coincidence as to seem fictitious. "What was the most embarrassing thing that ever happened to you?" he asked.

"Well, one day I was in my apartment in Northampton taking a shower," I began, inspired by a whiff of my body odor. "I was scrubbing away, and somehow I lost my balance and fell through the wall into my neighbor's bathroom where he was sitting on the toilet playing 'The Girl from Ipanema' on his accordion." I started laughing; I've never been a very good liar.

"I would believe it if the guy was playing 'Hey Jude,'" Neal said. "But come on, 'The Girl from Ipanema'?"

We sang the song, which I had always secretly liked.

The falling-through-cardboard-thin-bathroom-walls story was one of those urban legends I'd picked up in Boston. And I actually did have a neighbor in Northampton who played "The Girl from Ipanema" on his accordion. But perhaps the most potent fact in this dopey fiction was that very soon I would have to get naked in front of a man who was not my boyfriend. I was already embarrassed.

A few days later, it was Jerry who led me to the bathroom, covered the mirror with a beach towel so I couldn't see myself, and drew me a bath. As he unwrapped the gauze from my arms, legs, and skull I felt like a mummy being brought back from the dead. I lowered myself carefully into the tub, trying not to gasp as my wounds came in contact with water.

As I bent over, Jerry carefully lathered my hair, avoiding clumps of dried blood, and then rinsed pitcher after pitcher of warm water over my head. I thought of Jerry's toddlers getting washed by their father, and of the public baths for women in Orthodox Jewish ritual, and of the baptism I might have had if I'd remained a Christian. I closed my eyes.

"I'm not going to try to get the tangles out because you might start bleeding again," Jerry said, patting my hair gingerly later with a towel. "That's okay," I said, looking down so he wouldn't see my tears of gratitude. "I've always wanted to be a Rastafarian."

In my bedridden days I tried not to picture the puffball above my right eye where a dozen wire stitches zigzagged up into a nest of scabrous dreds. But one day when I was ambulatory again I couldn't stop myself: I *had* to look. I made my way to the dresser mirror and stood there for several seconds beholding the bride of Frankenstein: her red lips protruding like grapefruit sections, the black narrow slit of an eye peering blankly out of the bandage on the right, creating the effect of someone permanently, grotesquely, winking.

Several days later, the scabs fell off my face and turned to purple blotches that looked, from a distance, like radiation burns, or Kaposi's Sarcoma lesions.

Since I had literally shed my skin, it made sense to keep going. I walked into the salon at the Bon Marché and asked the stylist to hack off the hair clumps and give me a perm. Why I did this, I still don't know. What is it about our culture that bullies us and beats us down until finally, after months or years of seeing something as ugly and vulgar, it begins to look pretty? My friend Robin Hemley used that same word, *bullying*, to describe the way our current revival of Bigger-Is-Better makes him feel like he should be driving a Range Rover. What is it that makes the outsized, the synthetically shiny, and the hideous start to look the way things *should* look, and why do we capitulate?

The chemical treatment burned my wounds and the stink made me queasy, but I was resolved. I bought a pick to fluff up my stiff curls and marveled at how small my face looked under all that hair, how well the wiry tendrils covered the scars on my forehead.

Thus transformed into Every Woman, circa 1986, I followed my hair out the door to the nearest temp agency. In the strangest déjà-vu of all, I found myself a few days later in a typing pool with Barbara, my supervisor in MOM's office until she was fired and I got her job. I was worried she might resent me, but she did not even recognize me. I, who had tried to reinvent myself at every turn, had finally succeeded. I hadn't written myself into a cheerful, revisionist version of my past, I'd written myself out of the story completely.

Even Port Townsend was a bust. The conference staff had lost my paperwork; they had no place for me in the Carver workshop and no housing even though, on the phone, I'd been promised a single. It was as though I'd never applied in the first place. At the last minute, I was placed with a chain-smoking roommate. My first night there, I came down with a violent stomach flu and spent the better part of the week vomiting. I missed the conference almost entirely.

On the day I finally emerged into the world, the conference director told me she was looking forward to my reading, which was scheduled for four that afternoon. A reading? All I had with me was the second draft of a story I'd hoped to get advice on in the workshop: a not-ready-for-primetime player if there ever was one.

And so this was how it was to be: instead of a triumphal return to the West as an emerging literary star with great quads and perfect skin, I would survive a summer of head wounds, projectile vomiting, and the public humiliation of a lousy reading. I was living proof that what goes up—rockets, the human ego—must come down.

Meanwhile, back at the ranch, Ronald Reagan was not in the best shape of his life either. One day, when questioned by reporters about the U.S.-Soviet talks on nuclear weapons, he paused, momentarily unable to speak. Nancy whispered his cue: "Tell them we're doing everything we can," and Reagan delivered the line. But he would never again sound as convincing and winning as he had the night he comforted America over the loss of the Challenger Seven. That summer his symptoms of Alzheimer's, though not quite as advanced as my grandmother's, were forcing his wife to write cheat-sheets to help him remember the names of world leaders and members of the Cabinet.

Those U.S.-Soviet talks resumed in October, when Reagan and Gorbachev met in Iceland for a summit. Gorbachev pushed hard to negotiate the most massive weapons reductions in history and Reagan wondered if the apocalyptic Chernobyl disaster had been the catalyst for the Russian leader's new pacifism. In *Dutch: A Memoir of Ronald Reagan*, Edmund Morris remembers Reagan telling him that "Chernobyl means 'Armageddon' in the Ukrainian Bible." Actually, Chernobyl is Ukrainian for Wormwood, a name that Revelation applies to the "great star" that descended from heaven, "burning as it were a lamp" and falling into a third of the earth's rivers, whereupon "many men died of the waters, because they were made bitter." I know Morris's opus is half fiction, half fact, but I believe that a star falling from heaven would capture Reagan's imagination, as it did mine.

Whether or not Chernobyl, the greatest ecological disaster in human history, was Gorbachev's motive to disarm, he came close to getting Reagan to sign a unilateral nuclear disarmament treaty. Imagine what the world would look like now if nuclear weapons had been obsolete since that summit. There were moments of great progress in their talks but Reagan would not let go of his dream to be able to launch or sabotage first-strike weapons from space, to turn our share of the hemisphere into one big gated community with a shield that could zap intruders like an electric fly swatter. The year that had begun with an explosion above the horizon would end with the threat of many more to come as the superpowers played a high-stakes game of fact or fiction.

In *Murder in the Air*, the 1940 movie starring Ronald Reagan, our hero has to protect a wonder weapon from some wicked enemies who would want to steal it from America. This technological marvel is called an "inertia projector"; it disarms enemy planes by dismantling their electrical systems. "It not only makes the United States invincible in war," one line from the film begins, "but in so doing promises to become the greatest force for world peace ever discovered." In Orwellian terms, war is peace. As conceived by Reagan, Star Wars was a "nice" weapons system: it killed missiles, not people. Garry Wills points out that space, the final frontier, would also be the landscape where Reagan's blind optimism put a literal lid on all our problems and fears. Space would be the biggest movie screen ever.

Don't laugh. As I conclude this chapter, Son-of-a-Bush is planning to blast Son of Star Wars, the multibillion-dollar millennial sequel, into a theater near you.

AARON RAZ LINK AND HILDA RAZ

Not Coming Out

What Becomes You

H i, Paul," I said. "Boy, what a beautiful day. Look at those trees. When did everything get so *nice*?"

Paul gave me his best Disapproving Look. "Your mother called," he said.

"What did she have to say?"

"She wanted to know where you were."

"Okay," I said, somewhat confused. "What's the problem?"

"I told her you were out with Dawn." Paul pursed his lips and looked thoughtfully at the ceiling. "Oh, yes, *Dawn*. She seems to be seeing a *lot* of her friend *Dawn* recently. So, Paul, what's *Dawn* like? Is she *nice*?"

"Oh. Psychic Mom Powers."

"She wanted all the gossip."

"Paul, what the hell did you say?"

"Nothing! That's the *problem*. I felt *terrible*. She *trusts me* for all the details; out here I'm her only source. You have no idea what it's like." Paul put his hands on his hips and said sternly, "You have got to tell her about Dawn."

"What about Dawn?"

"Everything."

"That's none of my business. If Dawn wants to tell my mom the story of her life . . ."

"That's not what I meant. All about you, then."

"What about me?"

"You're evading the issue."

"I am not. Just because, um, uh . . ."

"You're madly, passionately in love."

185

"Uh, yeah, that. Anyway, it doesn't mean anything about either of us. I'm exactly the same person I always was."

"You didn't used to hum."

"Look, Paul, none of this 'I'm a new person!' bullshit. No 'I was incomplete without you!' I was plenty complete already, thank you very much."

"What's wrong with admitting you're soul mates?"

"Paul!"

"Oh, all right, but the next time she calls, don't ask me not to tell her all about it."

Faced with the picture of Paul spinning hordes of pink cotton-candy cherubs all over my carefully polished fuck-you image, to my *mom*, of all people, I sat down and tried to face the problem.

If I told my mother I was in love with Dawn, she would think I was a lesbian. Well, she already thought I was a lesbian. Everybody always thought I was a lesbian. Women seemed to want to give me things, be my friend, help me out, and worship me in a deeply satisfactory recognition of my many superior qualities. Of course, women said I was superior because I had finally achieved freedom from contaminating Maleness. Ugh. I never had sex with women, never had a girlfriend, I didn't even *like* hanging out with women. I even told people I was gay. Nothing I did seemed to have any effect on people's idea that I was a lesbian. I never could figure out why. My mom loved lesbians, which people thought was great for me.

And if I told my mom I was in love, she'd think *Dawn* was a lesbian. If there was anything worse than your mother thinking you were a lesbian, for Chrissakes, it was your mother thinking your lover was one. I mean, what did that say about me? No, we definitely weren't going there.

Of course, as Paul had gently pointed out, the obvious alternative of just not telling my mother anything could easily be stretched out for a few more days. Weeks. Years. The rest of our lives. Having chosen this alternative in his own life, Paul could spot it coming a mile away. No, we definitely weren't going there, either. Losing touch with my mother was about the only thing I could think of that was worse than her thinking Dawn was a lesbian.

Eventually, a brilliant plan struck. Since neither Dawn nor I were lesbians, the *actual issue* was that Mom would think she was the *mother* of a lesbian. Yes, this whole identity business was clearly her problem, not mine. Aha! In a stroke of generosity, I decided to offer my mother the option of maintaining separate but equal universes. I raced down to West Hollywood, purchased a glossy anthology of essays by the mothers of lesbians, and sent it off to her along with a note to make sure, one more time, that she didn't think I was a lesbian. There. I knew she loved books. I didn't open the book, much less read it; I didn't care to know what was inside. She could come out as the mother of a lesbian if she damn well wanted to; that was her life and her business, not mine.

On the hottest July morning in her town, Sarah's mom sprinted over the hot sidewalk to the metal mailbox and pried open the door, pulled out the mailer stuffed behind the Visa bill, and raced back to the house shaking her burnt fingers. The mailer was from Sarah, good news. She pried off the three staples instead of pulling the red tab and discovered inside the glossy book written by a group of mothers. Good. She was a mother. For a long time Sarah and her mom had exchanged interesting books, mostly about science. She put away her manuscripts and read the book. After a while she understood that the only two things these mothers had in common were lesbian daughters and not being writers. The essays were sappy, silly, conventional, and badly written. If Sarah had meant to come out as lesbian to her mom, this book was a bad way to do it. She remembered stories from her own youth in which the parents of her friends told them about sex by leaving a pink or blue pamphlet on the dresser. She'd spent a lot of time telling Sarah about sex. In person. Without metaphor and with diagrams and correct terminology. The fact that Sarah hadn't been interested hadn't affected her mother's diligence at all. Obviously Sarah as an adult didn't think that her mom knew anything at all about lesbians. And worse, Sarah thought her mother would have the same kind of response that these mothers had. Sarah's mom was really pissed off.

So Sarah's mom sat down and began to write a thank you letter in response. She chose a scroll of beautiful laid paper from the going-out-of-business sale of the local printer. Her best ink pen. A big envelope without a clasp, with a glued flap. This is what she wrote:

22 July 1991

Dear Sarah,

Your coming out letter and the gift of the book are important to me in several ways. But I'm angry at the responses of some women in the book (especially the Jewish mom, who is NOT ME or my community of Jewish women. Did you know, for example, that Susan Jacobsen, one of my best friends, who died and was buried as an Orthodox Jew, was gay?) and angry at your assumption that the issues central to lesbian identity are not and have not been (WITHOUT your ever asking ME) central to my own life.

I love YOU and what and who you are. I've cherished and protected you (not always well) as you are and will be and raised and supported your nature since you were conceived. Who and what you are I've been witness to for twenty-six years, one of the major pleasures of my life, and the one that draws my attention most truly, as you—or anyone—can see in my WORK. The complex blend of Sarah always delights and teaches me. You ALWAYS have and ALWAYS will have my total interest and support. You.

I'm sad you won't have (or raise) a child. Your child might have advantages other children don't. But I'm not VERY sad. I hope and expect you'll have contact with some kids along the way. Or not.

I'm sad not to have known your identity as male-identified in a lesbian culture that insists on another configuration these days. I don't believe you won't find companions who are women and can be your friends but I see the problem more clearly now. (I've always known you were male-identified, of course, but not that you were trying to find . . . what? Acceptance among feminists who embrace what you deplore.)

Please remember the circle of stories you bring again and again to my attention: take heart and believe that just as you were born and grew to be Sarah at twenty-six, some other women are having a similar experience now. In LA, perhaps you'll find them. All women of ambition are male-identified in some major ways just as your friend Paul in his most flamboyant-sock mode can be called female-identified.

I hope you'll find women of talent, intelligence, and good humor to love and/or hang out with.

Hilda never sent this letter. Years later we found it in a pile of papers, still sitting on her desk. When she handed it to me, she said she'd meant to write more at the time, but whatever was left unsaid she couldn't find a way to say.

Excerpt

Phantom Limb

Excuse me . . . excuse me,' I call out, trying to get the attention of the woman I spotted in the rearview mirror on the way to meet Ellie.

I run to catch up with her. 'I hope you don't mind my asking but . . .'

She swings around, pivoting on a crutch. I'm surprised; from the back, I'd imagined her older, not a handsome woman in her forties who, with an inquiring tilt of her blond head, seems open to my question.

'. . . did you have a problem afterward with phantom pain? My mother lost her leg and . . .'

With a thick accent, she says that she has only just come to this country six months ago. Her operation was done in Russia, where, she claims, they do it so well that people don't suffer. She has heard that in America, surgeons cut the nerves badly. 'I hear it can be excruciating,' she says with the commiserative air of the fortunate. As she pivots away, she wishes my mother good luck.

I surprised myself with my brashness, running after a stranger to ask such a personal question, but my mother's situation has become extreme. New tests have revealed a serious blockage in the so-called good leg. Dr. MacKenzie, her surgeon, advises another bypass. She's dead set against it.

He says, 'The vast majority need five, six, seven days in the hospital; it's not that much of a deal. Look, this isn't God's work; it's human engineering.'

He did add that some surgeries are more difficult than others, and indeed, the incision will be groin to ankle. He says my mother can expect to have 'local pain for two or three weeks on the way to healing.'

This is the doctor who said that virtually none of his patients ever experienced phantom limb. He's either living in a dream world or a believer that a stiff upper lip produces better results. Nuts! I want a true assessment, even if it errs too far in the direction of predicting pain.

When my mother continues to refuse, he says, 'All we can do is hope she'll be lucky this time. If she lives very quietly and does nothing to disturb the leg, she might be okay.'

Shall I tell her how limited her choices really are?

'Have you noticed how many little details you have to deal with all the time?' asks Ellie when we meet for coffee. She's her usual self, handbag and shoes matching, but the strain shows around her eyes and she has gained a few pounds.

'It's no fun. Do you know what I do when I leave my parents' apartment? You must never say another word about this, but I get into my car, roll up all the windows, and I scream.'

All over America, adults are screaming. I hear them in small towns in Maine, in front of doormen buildings on Park Avenue, and along the Wilshire Corridor of Los Angeles, screaming in sealed cars in border towns in Texas, in the driveways of two-family homes in Wisconsin, in Boston and La Crescenta. I hear America screaming, its grown children trying not to be heard.

MARY FELSTINER

Alternatives, 1979

*Out of Joint: A Private and
Public Story of Arthritis*

Three years later whenever John asks, after a long day, "Swim with me?" I shake my head. I have to admit my sweet remission has vanished, lingering no more than a year. Sarah has turned ten, and my old premarriage desire—"children (optimally four)"—seems cruelly out of bounds. But I still have a longing for optimally two, so once in awhile John and I weigh the alternatives. I say, "I'm not sure it's possible." He sits down while I take a breath to add, "Antimalarials and gold would overdose a fetus . . . even if we're ready, you know, for a baby again."

For hours we turn the question over, but it's beyond us. Without pills for nine months would I collapse, or would alternative treatments steady me till another child? Then would my joints be able to deal with taking care of one? Finally I remember a trick of my parents, who never lazed around in their personal lives if they could expose segregated housing or steelworker wages. They passed to me their fact-finding drive and their dissent, which could help now: I'm foundering in my condition and need a different take on it.

That's how I come to Susan Sontag's *Illness as Metaphor*, a dissenting 1978 book claiming that the early seventies distorted cancer into a metaphor (John Dean: "we have a cancer within—close to the presidency") and that this misuse reflected anxiety about an uncontrolled economy. Suddenly I'm able to see arthritis as a metaphor for more recent years: it's the sluggish aftermath of growth, the frazzling of energy since the '73 oil crisis. It stands for recession, as in "the economy moves at arthritic speed." No wonder it's abhorred: incurable, unspeakable, recessionary.

Until reading Sontag, or Ivan Illich's 1976 *Medical Nemesis*, I do not realize that recession doubles the patients on Medicare and Medicaid, that medicine can add to the suffering it's supposed to fix, or that nonurgent operations end the lives of twelve thousand people yearly—more civilians dying on nearby gurneys than U.S. soldiers in Vietnam. I do not realize the "failure of heroic medicine to cure" till reading Regina Morantz. But I do know it's perilous to start doubting medicine's claim of helping bodies and improving lives. It would throw me into the hands of alternative healers. And what if I doubt these too?

This question leads to the next one, as I make my commute after teaching: what do I want now?

I want to blame my stinking joints on . . . John. OK, this is promising, but don't ride the brake.

I also want to be worthy of—watch that station wagon on the left—worthy of mothering again. But suppose a tiny baby is a sinker on my body.

I better get off the freeway at Sand Hill Road before the after-school program closes. "How was school?" I ask as Sarah jumps in the car.

"Fine."

"After-school?"

"Fine."

"How was the lunch John made you?"

"Fine."

"Oh honey, I hope it's all true, all fine."

At home I empty her lunchbox, with one crescent bitten from the whole-wheat-and-tofu sandwich, then realize I've been wanting to answer "Fine" too for quite some time. In the air of the seventies there's faith that people will do fine with alternative medicine, fine with Chinese remedies now that diplomatic lines are open, fine with the organic sandwiches that Sarah leaves in the lunchbox. Even RA patients do fine on their own, if a third of them go into remission whether treated by doctors or not. But I'm not in that third. By now I've tried and failed to get relief from acupressure, macrobiotic and high-protein diets, massage, self-hypnosis—every decent alternative the seventies has on offer—and I'm wary of the sting in other self-treatments. Arthritis consumers are shelling out $950 million on unproven remedies: copper bracelets circle fifty million wrists at $35 per arm; for every dollar going to arthritis research, $25 heads toward "mistreatment," as I read one day in *Consumer Reports*. The members of my slow-moving subgroup—and here's an irony for you—are the nation's speediest spenders on "do-it-yourself" cures.

The next day I'm in Stanford Library, handling the do-it-yourself book of 1979, *Anatomy of an Illness*, in which Norman Cousins masters a severe rheumatic attack by rejecting a "cycle of fear, depression, and panic," by "bucking the odds." His self-treatment: laughter, because it seems to "reduce inflammation in my joints." I like the cut of his cure. Why don't *I* just buck the odds? Then I remember that his ailment came from exposure to jet fuel, while mine lives deep in immune cells where ignorant armies clash by night.

It's Cousins's view of pain that finally throws me off. He blames "promiscuous use" of painkillers for creating "psychological cripples and chronic ailers." Promiscuous and cripples? I have to block those metaphors with hands that can't hold the hardback between them, with smoldering shoulders that hurt when I laugh. "Pain-killing turns people into unfeeling spectators of their own decaying selves," writes Ivan Illich. Uh, I'm afraid it's pain that does that. I shove the books back on the shelf, then stop and admit they've taught me lessons anyway—that I need to read about health to make decisions for my life, that I can't swallow heroic medicine whole and can't fall for alternatives either, and that I'm ready to try *something* new.

I try imagining my hard-working grandma with arthritis, which no one in my family ever had. She'd have called on public health in the 1920s, and they'd have said, "REST," and she'd have said, "On the *bed*?" Later, if her daughter Anne, my mother, had suffered arthritis, which she didn't, her doctor in the 1930s would have suggested, once again, rest. Even today, I realize, most arthritic joints are told to go easy, and that's about that.

But now there's a turnabout in treatment starting a mile from where I'm strenuously resting. Dr. James Fries, director of Stanford's Arthritis Clinic, claims that every single joint will profit from exercise. His popular 1979 book, *Arthritis: A Comprehensive Guide*, says exercise helps joints by squeezing waste products out of cartilage (which is three-fourths water and compresses like a sponge), then sucking back joint fluid, nutrients, and oxygen. Dr. Fries cautions that rheumatoid arthritis ("the most destructive kind of arthritis known") causes "erosions of the bone itself, rupture of tendons, and slippage of the joints" and makes most sports (except swimming or walking) a danger. Still, if exercise can "fight anxiety and depression," it tucks nicely into the view that upbeat moods heal illnesses. There's also news of mutual-aid groups like the National Black Women's Health Project, or Stanford-run support groups helping thousands of arthritis patients exercise so that they live in less pain and actually drop some disability. This sounds so good I might take up self-help or exercise. Then pregnancy.

At the end of a decade that assures me, wrongly, any health dilemma can be dealt with, my doctor once again reviews the dilemma he calls "the desirability of her getting pregnant vs. the desirability of taking gold."

Of those two choices I chose gold—actually pain chose it for me. But now I'm open to any reason to reverse. Dr. B. says, "If you want a baby—"

"I think so."

"What's your husband say?"

"That it's exhausting with RA, two jobs, shared childcare . . ."

"If you want a baby, stop the gold."

"I want a baby being *well.*"

"You'll feel better during pregnancy. Women with RA usually do."

This is such good news I decide not to know what happens afterward. Soon I start tugging on John. Suppose I go without gold? Suppose we rouse our energies for another child? John says it's finally up to me.

Once I'm gold free and pregnant, my body slips into charmed remission again. I'm springing around the neighborhood, thinking health thoughts that aren't about joints. Thinking how my obstetrician says I'm a natural for pregnancy, and that's true: I'm overjoyed with it. I'm also a natural for women's choice, which he doesn't see when declaring he "won't do Roe v. Wades."

Still, I like his sharing his new technology with me, offering a pair of earphones to track a fetal heart. "Hear that?"

"No."

"Listen again. Hear it?"

"YES."

How astonishing. Each visit for months I strap on the earphones, and the heart's *there* again, the thrilling autonomous thump.

I feel so good I need to look good too and go off to a spa so I'll end up after birth as slim as before pregnancy. I soak in a hot tub (no warnings that pregnant women shouldn't) and three days later, at a Passover Seder, feel a very slight trickle on my leg.

"Doesn't sound too serious," the obstetrician says on the phone. "Come tomorrow around ten."

Right at ten I'm on the examining table, strapping on the earphones for the heartbeat. Nothing there. I do *not* need to not hear that.

The doctor orders, "Bear down, Mary! Push," and I deliver: a late-fifth-month miscarriage, technically a stillbirth, what the doctor calls a "baby boy!"

John glances at my jammed-shut eyes and on the next beat says, "Don't you mean fetus?"—words that matter a good deal, even at that moment, words at war. I never again want a doctor who does miscarriages but refuses abortions, who would call this stricken thing a "baby boy!" And I never again want to get intimate with *anything* perishing inside my skin.

Pregnant one week and not the next, I hear my colleagues, to a man, assure me I'll be pregnant again, but all I see is a perfect sphere of loss. Then a colleague who's hardly noticed me looks straight in my eyes and says the one true thing: "This is heartbreaking."

Heartbreaking to follow pregnancy, again, with pain. This is the loss that finally assembles ten years of losses, tangling them into one undeniable knot. On the sofa between John and Sarah I reach for that knot, visible to no one else. In one decade I've lost my guarantee of good health, lost fluidity, lost ease in the physical acts of parenting, lost a fair practice of equal tasks, lost nouns like *energy* and *swiftness*, lost my lifelong singing voice and even a speaking voice free of crackles and pops, lost my elbow grease for vacuuming and yard work and tearing full speed down a swimming lane, lost any assurance I could run from threats, lost my trust in feminists to name my woes, lost my reliance on medicine and also on alternatives, lost my remission, lost my pregnancy. Amid all the losses what can never be found again is my old sense that each loss must be a fluke.

Each one is knotted in. For this is RA, this is chronic, this has design.

I try to focus on my terrific child and partner and job. Look how I've come through the decade—with tenure, with essays on revolution and on feminism, with phone messages from friends, with care for their problems, with adventures watching our fourth-grader. Look at her swimming the crawl with a flutter kick to die for. Or racing down the soccer field with energy enough to yell as she passes the bench, "What's for snack?" And look at her sitting beside John and unrolling her day, as I ask them to tell me about it, then tell me more. Here's John handing me a peeled carrot, saying "You're beautiful," as he looks at my tight-ribbed sweater and newly narrow waist. Here's Sarah trying out tunes on her new flute. And here's a wingbeat passing over, the Angel of Anatomy, my votive figure, my imagined tribune, announcing: I give you all of the above, but I also take away.

Some months later, by good fortune, I'm expecting again—thrilled, wary, skeptical, thinking no one congratulating me understands my disease.

Well, do *I*? Most days arthritis just takes me over, puts me down to nap. I've never yet stood back to question how it's *working*. I've detested it too much to give it features and causes, a meaning in the world. But now that a new baby's coming, I've got to get wise to it. I call this out, banging the kitchen table, surprising Sarah and John.

And soon enough I get wise to the worst part about it.

JONATHAN JOHNSON

Excerpt from
"The Second Trimester"

Hannah and the Mountain:
Notes toward a Wilderness Fatherhood

T he next few hours we did better. We were relieved that the end had begun.

Dr. Bowden came in after visiting a delivering mom down the hall, gave Amy a quick check-over, told us the labor was progressing, then plopped down in one of the chairs beside the bed. We asked her how she was holding up.

"Me? I'm fine. It's you guys I'm concerned about."

"Yeah," Amy said. "But still, you look beat."

"Okay, I confess. Long day."

We asked her about herself and she sat back, deep in the chair, and exhaled. Grief-filled though our room was, Dr. Bowden seemed at ease with us.

She told us stories of her years in northern Pakistan and Mozambique. She said she'd come to Idaho and accepted her job in the practice because of a stray dog that the senior doctor had taken home and for which he was trying to find a new owner. When Bowden was in town interviewing, she'd met the dog and that was it. "I told him I'd take the job if I could have the dog."

Amy and I welcomed the distraction. Bowden's company reminded us that our own lives were, until recently, also adventure-filled and wonderful.

She talked about her new marriage, how it was an adjustment after so many years alone.

"I've always been fiercely independent," she said. "When I was a kid I was a tomboy, and I've never found someone I wanted to commit to. At thirty-nine, I figured I never would."

In her wire-rim glasses, short-cropped hair, green surgical scrubs, and hiking boots, she looked the very picture of independence. Since June she's been married to a widower, the Lutheran minister in Sandpoint, who has three teenage boys.

We talked about marriage and love. Every few minutes Amy rubbed her abdomen and lower back and said she felt a contraction. Bowden asked her to rank its intensity on a scale from one to ten. They were holding around three or four. When each one passed we kept talking.

Amy confided that I sometimes crowd her. "That's been one of the hardest parts of marriage for me," she said.

Bowden nodded and smiled at me. "I can see it," she said. "And it's the same for me. I'm a doctor for cryin' out loud! And Steve drives me to work, which is fine. But then he gets out and hands me my stupid briefcase. I told him it makes me feel like I'm in kindergarten." Amy and I chuckled knowingly. Though we haven't even been married three years, we felt like a couple of old hands.

"But we're good together," Bowden said as much to herself as to us. "He's this conservative, traditionally religious preacher, and I'm more of an Earth Mother–worshiping liberal, and we respect each other deeply."

She was quiet a moment, then said, "The biggest difference in my life is the male perspective. In my practice, it's all these women, all female energy. Like the shelter I suppose," she said to Amy. "But at home, it's my husband, these teenage boys, and their teenage buddies."

Amy told Bowden about the Johnson family ranch and all my father's brothers who grew up there and still visit often. "Masculine power permeates that place," she said.

Earlier that evening Bowden had left the hospital for an hour to watch the oldest of her new sons fight in a boxing match over at the high school. More guy stuff.

"He's a writer for the paper, not a tough guy at all, but intelligent and witty," she shook her head and laughed. "He does these things so he can write articles about them."

"How'd he do?" I asked with a grimace, feeling a bit of kinship with the young would-be pugilist writer.

"He's going to have a bruise across both eyes and the bridge of his nose for a week," she sighed. "But I think it was more traumatic for me than him."

Here we were in this dimly lit room in the middle of the night. Our baby was soon to be born dead, and this woman, our doctor, when she could no longer do anything medically, was helping to soothe our wrecked spirits with her presence.

And Bowden did another thing that helped Amy and me cope. We told her how guilty we felt for allowing ourselves to get stuck on the cabin road, and for the subsequent long walk Amy had to take to get out of the woods. Amy especially wondered aloud if she hadn't actually caused this. Bowden told us that, given how weak we now know it to be, in all likelihood Amy's cervix would never have held this baby to viability. She said it's natural to want to feel somehow responsible, that something could have been done differently and we are not powerless in the face of catastrophe.

"I feel guilty myself," she said quietly. She paused a moment before going on, then said, "I've been thinking how maybe I should have put you in the hospital sooner, kept constant watch over you. I'm such a positive person, maybe I wasn't cautious enough. What I'm saying is, it's natural to want to have an explanation. If I did something wrong, I'm not so fucking powerless." She sighed a long, empty sigh.

I realized immediately how vulnerable such an admission makes her. If only for a moment, Bowden placed our need for solace and reassurance above the safety of her own career. Amy and I will still feel guilty, I'm sure, probably for the rest of our lives, but as a result of Bowden's willingness to admit she's human and trust us with her self-doubts, we'll have the comfort of knowing we aren't alone, that our guilt is natural and not a sure sign that we have wronged our child beyond forgiveness.

❧ ❧

How do I tell what I have seen? At 2:55 a.m., Friday, March 8, Hannah Marjorie Howko-Johnson was born.

She was born dead, a deep rose color, with bruises on her back and chest. She hung limp like Michelangelo's Pieta, the veins in her foot like veins in perfect marble.

We held her to our chests. She was long and slender, with thin toes and feet, and none of the baby fat of a full-term baby. Her eyes were still closed, and her face held the expression of a sleep deeper than I can imagine.

I performed a brief baptism, dripping water from a syringe on the baby's forehead. "I baptize you in the name of the Father, the Son, and the Holy Spirit, Hannah Marjorie Howko-Johnson."

Yesterday, when they learned that our baby would be born soon and very tiny, the nurses here had the hospital laundry alter a little receiving cape to fit her. They also gave us a fleece blanket with a teddy bear print. I am so grateful we will have these things to take home and keep.

We wrapped the cape around our baby and the nurse took her away for a birth photo and measurements. Dr. Bowden hugged us good-night, told us what a beautiful little girl our daughter was, and left.

The nurse returned in a few minutes with the baby and left the three of us alone. Amy held Hannah in her blanket, folding down the corner to kiss her good-bye.

❧ ❧

Where was she? Where was my Hannah? It was so sunny. Someday, she would have wanted to play outside. Where was Hannah?

I didn't want to leave the hospital. It was as if our daughter were somewhere just a couple blocks away and if I watched for her out that second-story window long enough, I might see her pass between the trees. In these scenarios she was about five years old.

I knew that, after being with Amy through the delivery, my mind, the mind of a new father, naturally, *biologically* yearned to take care of my child. I knew that Hannah was gone, and any thought otherwise was not rational or grounded in truth.

I also knew that I ached for her ghost, that I worried she was alone and lost. I thought of the other babies leaving the hospital and the children they will grow into. They could have been Hannah's playmates, all of them turning somersaults and laughing under the trees. But they wouldn't want to play with her. They'd have no use for her ghost.

Before we left that room the cries of newborns came to us from down the hall. Amy lay still in bed, curled on her side and slipping in and out of sleep. I stared out into the fresh snow that had fallen and wiped out the previous day's bit of spring. The snow clung to the cottonwoods, and for the first time in my life I thought about how it would be to kill myself. It wasn't that I wanted to be with Hannah, that I thought I could somehow go to her or hold her, but that I would at least be *like* her. I wanted to be dead to be the same as Hannah.

I wouldn't do it though. Of course I wouldn't do it. I loved Amy now more than I ever had. I would stay with her and hold her and wait for days I knew would come when I would want to be alive.

But still I keep picturing that foot emerging from my wife, that minute, purple, translucent, perfect foot that made it suddenly, shockingly clear to me that this was real.

When Amy was discharged I wheeled her down to the hospital entrance and left her there while I went to get the truck. When I returned and saw her small and sunk down in the wheelchair in front of those doors that slid open for the people coming and going around her, she looked completely alone and exhausted. She had her elbow on the chair arm and her chin propped up on her palm. As if her head were too heavy to hold up otherwise. She looked blankly off toward the houses beyond the parking lot.

I got out and opened the door for her. She got in and patted Yukon on the head. "Hello boy," she said. "Let's get out of here."

A couple hours after we came home, the sun broke out again— the latest chapter in the unfolding struggle between winter and spring. Amy slept more and I walked up to Carlson's Field with Yukon. He'd gone into town with us the day of Amy's ultrasound, before we knew she'd wind up in the hospital and we'd be there for four days. Except for a walk every few hours, he'd been in the pickup in the hospital parking lot the entire time, and now walking up the cabin road, he was giddy, bounding through the melting snow and rolling in it, kicking his absurdly big paws in the air.

I hiked up to the spot where we think Hannah was probably conceived. The ground was still a couple feet down under snow, but a few tufts of the tallest shafts of hay grass showed through and bobbed in the wind that rode along the snow's surface.

I took off all my clothes and paced a circle in the snow. I was amazed at how far off the icy pain on the bottom of my feet was, at how insulated I felt from the wind that moved near my skin. I put my clothes back on and pulled up my heavy pack boots and sat down and stared at the snow between my knees.

I looked up toward the trees at the edge of the field in every direction and the valley and mountains beyond. When the sun had dropped into the dark row of white fir behind me, I saw that, on the now slate-blue surface of the snow, my disappeared shadow was indistinguishable from the shadow not cast by my daughter.

I left before the sky darkened deeper, before night could find us up there.

❧ ❧

Today, Amy packed up Hannah's clothes—the OshKosh railroad overalls, the red fleece jumper with white polar bears. Quickly, and without faltering, she put the clothes in a box with the oversize books and teething ring and big plastic keys. She packed up all of this and the yellow rubber ducky and found a marker and wrote on the box BABY THINGS.

The things of this world are still the things of this world. The only difference is Hannah will never see or hold them. Walking the aisles of Safeway, looking for medicine and high-iron foods— broccoli and asparagus—for Amy's recovery, I saw wine bottles, bagels, shopping cart wheels, and faces, and all of it, every single thing, was another thing Hannah would never know.

The world when Amy was pregnant seemed a world waiting for its full truth, a world only half created, waiting to be filled by our child's perceptions. Other children will be born, maybe even Hannah's siblings to come, but the world will never be what it could have been through Hannah's eyes.

❧ ❧

I put on my empty backpack, and Amy and I set out for the cabin. In four days we'll be going back to northern Michigan, to Marquette, her hometown, and we needed to retrieve a few books and clothes for the trip. We walked down the road from my uncle's place and past my grandparents' old ranch house, where smoke from the evening fire was drifting up from the chimney into a slate sky. At the machine shed we turned and started up the steep climb to the cabin.

The hill road was thigh deep with snow so we stopped every few minutes for Amy to catch her breath. She is getting better physically. Her shuffle is gone and she's started walking with her back straighter, her shoulders not rolled so far forward. And, despite my objections, she had insisted on coming. As we stood there, huffing clouds of breath and looking back over the valley that was falling away beneath and behind us, I found myself ready for us to get out of Idaho for a while. I feel as though Amy will survive her grief if we can just get her home to Marquette, to the streets of her childhood—those woods, movie theaters, and restaurants filled with the comforting familiarity of her past.

There will be Lake Superior. That biggest freshwater lake in the world. Amy's known its sound since her own infancy, and if the flat cover of ice has broken up or drifted off toward Canada when we arrive, she'll be able to hear the cold waves in the wind as we lie in bed across town. I have imagined those waves might speak to her with our daughter's voice.

And in Marquette will be Amy's own family. My family here—Steve, Marguerite, my cousins and grandparents—have been quiet around us, speaking in hushed tones about neutral things, giving us room. But what Amy needs now is not more calmness, more repose. What she needs now is not my family and not Idaho. She needs that primal embrace only her own mother can give her. Her mother, with whom she can, I'm hoping, open completely and weep without stopping herself.

I am worried about her, and getting her home is the one thing I know to do. She's so often steady, so seemingly balanced, like she was when she told me she wanted to go with me up to the cabin. "It'll be good to get outside," she'd said this morning.

But this afternoon, getting dressed after a shower at Steve's house, she called out to me. I came in to the bedroom and found her sitting on the edge of the bed, looking down at her swollen breasts. To reduce the swelling she's been holding ice packs on them several times a day for the three days she's been home from the hospital. She's even spread cabbage on them in accordance with one of the nurses' suggestions, trying to get her breasts to realize they are not needed despite this recent birth, that they should sink against Amy's ribs again and wait.

But there, after her warm shower, a single drop of milk had formed on the end of one nipple. Tears streaked her cheeks and she looked up at me. "I thought it was over," she sobbed. "Now this."

"My belly is so hollow," she said, her voice quiet then as I held her. "I wish they could put her back inside me and I could make her better."

It was frightening to see her so shattered, but I was more frightened by her steady eyes when she looked up at me after catching her breath on the hill below the cabin and said, "Okay. Let's go on. I'm fine."

Maybe in Marquette she will be able to let her sorrow run loose. Maybe.

I must remember to stay close. I reminded myself of this as we trudged through the snow. I must remember to keep watch.

The cabin was cold and empty. The daffodils in the plastic mug on the windowsill were still in full bloom two weeks after I'd given them to Amy. The recent freezing and thawing temperatures apparently had been ideal for keeping them alive.

"Let's leave them here," I suggested.

"Yes. The place ought to have a touch of color, of life," Amy said.

I thought how, if some small spirit should pass through this otherwise abandoned home while we are gone, those bowed yellow heads might be some version of company.

We stood at the shelf and each of us pulled down a few books and then shuffled through our stack of CDs. These we stuffed down into my backpack; then we climbed the narrow stairs to the loft and went through the steamer trunk for clothes—underwear, socks, T-shirts, jeans, flannel shirts. We stacked them folded on the bed as we have for so many trips before, then packed them in the backpack too.

When I clicked closed the cabin door behind us, the sky was

darker. The day was about over, and it occurred to me that it was Wednesday and Hannah has been cremated for two days.

I have always believed my life was my own. Not simply in the sense that I could quit a job or declare my love for someone, but I've always believed that my very experience emanated from some magical marriage between the world and my own will. If I really, really focused on Amy making it home through the blizzard, I knew I'd see her headlights soon, coming up the road. And, sure enough, there she'd be, every time. If I pictured our life, Amy's and Hannah's and mine together in the sunshine and cut-hay smell of a late summer afternoon, I'd be in that vision come September, natural and inevitable, certain as my hand holding this pen. I believed I was writing a life for us to live. Now, nine months before my thirtieth birthday, my beautiful illusion had dissolved and the world had been revealed distant and indifferent.

Near the cabin, in a tall stack of building scraps the snow had melted enough to reveal, I found a foot-long piece of larch pole that we had cut off one of the wall logs.

I had been hoping to find a short length of log like this to hollow out for Hannah's urn—a piece of our house, her house, in which to carry her back to Marquette. I stuffed it down into the pack, pulled the drawstring closed around the top again, and lifted the strap back to my shoulder.

Amy didn't ask me what the piece of wood was for. She was somewhere far off inside herself, and neither of us spoke on the way back down.

❧ ❧

For the first time in my life I had arrangements in that sense of the word that means those things you have to do when someone dies. I rented a car down in Spokane yesterday for the drive back to Marquette. I finished Hannah's urn last night, wood shavings accumulating around my feet as I hollowed out a bowl shape in the end of the short piece of log from our cabin. When I was done, it was a crude job, something that looked like a first-year, high school wood-shop project. I carved and carved but the wood was wet from sitting in the snow all winter. Instead of cutting smooth and dry, the log seeped gold water when I pressed the knife into it. And I was tired from the long drive from Spokane, my hands clumsy and thick. Despite sanding until my fingers were raw, the bottom and sides of the bowl were still rough, almost fuzzy with wood fibers.

"It's exactly how I want it," Amy said when I showed her my work.

"I wish I was a skilled woodcarver," I said.

"Don't say that." She rubbed her fingers around the lip of the urn. "It should be natural, how it was as a tree."

Amy had her own arrangements to make at work. In the morning she went in to prepare the shelter staff for her absence. They have four clients, the most they've had in two months of operation. Four battered women. All this late-season fluctuation between fresh snow and melt is pushing people to the brink. There is violence behind people's eyes in the grocery store and post office in Sandpoint, and even out here at the Westmond General Store. It's good that the sun is out today. And it is good that we are leaving northern Idaho for a couple of weeks.

After dropping Amy at the shelter, I went by the funeral home to pick up Hannah's ashes. The young man there handed me a little envelope, the extra small kind where you have to fold the paper up and fold it again on one side to make your letter fit.

"That's her?" I asked.

The funeral home man set the envelope on his desk beside some papers for me to sign. "That's her. I'm so sorry," he said as I lifted the ashes. "This is hard."

"Yes," I said back to him, feeling how light the ashes were in my hand, "hard."

I signed where the papers were highlighted in yellow.

The funeral home doesn't charge to cremate babies, so I was done and free to leave with the envelope.

"Thank you."

"Give my condolences to your wife," he said and stood as I stood to leave. He offered me his hand. "Let us know if we can do anything else."

"Thank you," I said again, accepting the handshake and really noticing him for the first time since I'd walked in, his brow furled in an earnest expression under his thick dark hair. He was younger than I am.

I sat the envelope in the urn in the back seat of the rental Pontiac and drove out of town, up toward the Canada line, passing the occasional log truck along the otherwise deserted highway. The sky was razor bright, and the deep snowpacks of the Selkirk Mountains rose around the car, fresh snow weighing down pine boughs and barn roofs.

I had Willie Nelson on the tape deck. His voice came bright and clean through those speakers, and I turned it up until I couldn't hear any of my own thoughts over his words.

I was fine, driving eighty on a dry, sunbaked road, the ashes silent in the urn in the back seat. I was fine. Until the first few lines of "Angel Flyin' too Close to the Ground" brought an overwhelming wave of sadness. All the selflessness of fatherhood that my life had been moving toward had evaporated, and I was back in my skin, in this self-indulgent drive into the sun-bleached, snowy mountains alone.

Hannah was the other, the one who was to have pulled me out of myself. With her gone I will have to work to stay connected to this world. I know Amy will need me like never before, and I am making a deliberate effort to hold on.

But speeding along Highway 95, I could feel the Canada line up ahead, the give of that new accelerator pedal under my foot as I pushed down coming out of the curves and straightened that tight steering wheel. The low, near sides of mountains blurred. Summit crests above the canyon moved toward and past me like crests of waves. Willie sang loud his song of a fallen angel, and I wept, and Hannah was Hannah in her envelope in the hollowed-out log in the back seat as that seafoam-green Pontiac sailed us toward what might as well have been the edge of the earth.

❧ ❧

At Amy's follow-up appointment at the Sandpoint Women's Health Clinic, Dr. Bowden gave us the okay to travel back to Marquette. Sheepishly we told her we'd already rented a car for the trip. "We're a little on the willful side," Amy admitted.

Bowden listened to us tell of the crushing grief we'd been through the last week, and she reassured us when we asked about future babies that, "Yes, there's every reason to hope Amy's next pregnancy will be successful. The key will be getting a stitch around that cervix early in the second trimester."

Next pregnancy. The words sounded to my ear like blasphemy. I knew though that they wouldn't always, and I was glad there would be something that could be done to keep this from happening again.

Before we left we asked if she'd want to step out of character and have dinner with us when we got back.

She brightened. "I'd really love to," she said. "And, I'd love for you to meet Steve. He's heard a lot about you guys, anonymously of course. I really leaned on him last week when this was happening."

Friends. It looked as though we might end up making bright, worldly, compassionate friends out of this. Pain can draw people together, can strip away pretense and leave the kind core of empathy, as we sit together in the truths of our fragile, precious lives.

May it be so with Amy and me, I thought to myself. May we find and hold each other through this suffering.

❧ ❧

If your wife dies, you are a widower. If your parents die, you are an orphan. I know of no word for what you become when death leaves you childless. There should be a word.

We crossed the Montana line, heading east out of Idaho toward Michigan. Amy slept while I drove, then just north of Missoula I looked over at her and she was awake, her eyes were wide and filled with tears, and she'd been watching me. I held her hand and cried silently with her as the car moved down through its long turns into that gray valley. At the edge of the city, we passed a small herd of elk grazing on the steep earth-cut above the highway. They will have begun their migration back up into the high country by the time we pass through there again in April.

❧ ❧

We're back in that other hometown, Marquette, Michigan. A couple days after we got here, Amy and I drove up to Big Bay, a little lumber town a half-hour north of Marquette. The Big Bay Road winds along Lake Superior and through the low Huron Mountains. On one side tens of thousands of acres of hemlock and white pine and birch give shelter to moose and black bears and a healthy number of timber wolves; on the other side the lake widens like a flat desert of ice falling over the horizon toward the Arctic.

Because it is frozen over, we won't be able to spread Hannah's ashes in the water this winter, which is just as well. We aren't ready to let them go.

I don't know where to turn now that landscape is not enough

to sustain me. If any place could call me back to the goodness of life, the Big Bay Road could. Instead, Amy and I fought.

Amy told me that she is deeply angry, enraged at herself and me—angry at herself because she kept working, which she believes could well be the reason Hannah is dead, angry at me because I was very much in favor of her working so I could keep writing and building the cabin.

I reminded her that Dr. Bowden had said she could keep working, and I insisted this terrible thing hadn't been anyone's fault. "I admit I wanted to keep writing, but God, if I'd known, if I thought that you would lose the baby because you were working . . . I didn't want to believe it."

"I don't care. My baby is dead and I never get another chance. I was supposed to be her mother, her *mother*, and I didn't take care of her because I was working."

"I looked for work. At the Forest Service and with that log home builder. We only had a few weeks," I said quietly, but I knew I had been greedy, jealously guarding my writing time and the life we had in the cabin as I assured her everything would be all right.

Amy just watched the woods slip by. I'd never seen her so inconsolable. I was frightened to feel so far from the one person who shared this grief with me, frightened that I would wind up alone after all this. Beyond that, I was frightened that I might believe what she was saying, that it was our fault, this thing that had happened to us.

"And I'm mad at you because I didn't feel like you were there emotionally when I came home from the hospital," she added finally.

I wanted to jump out of the car and run into the woods or into the lake and disappear.

"Jesus Christ, I was out of my mind then. I could hardly speak."

"I know it. But you weren't there to listen to me. You were so upset."

"I never left your side," I insisted, though I knew that she wasn't talking about a physical absence.

The world seemed foreign. I didn't recognize the trees along the road. My own hands on the wheel. Where were we going? Amy had already told me she was having a difficult time thinking about returning to the cabin with no running water and lumber stacked everywhere and no fridge or kitchen stove. "I just want to have a normal, settled life," she'd said. Now she was telling me that at her most desperate time I'd failed to provide the economic and emotional support she needed.

She looked very much alone, staring out the window, her hands together in her lap.

We turned around in Big Bay, in the parking lot of the General Store with the plastic moose on the roof, Christmas lights still strung in his antlers. We didn't stop into the Big Bay Hotel restaurant for a bowl of whitefish chowder as I thought we might. We didn't go into the Lumberjack Bar for a quick drink. We headed back onto the highway toward Marquette in silence.

"I'm sorry," I said after several minutes. "I wanted so bad to pull myself together for you last week. I want to finish the cabin for you, to make it comfortable. I wish to hell I'd found a job and hadn't clung to my precious writing time like a spoiled kid."

"You were wonderful," she sobbed and grabbed hold of my arm up near my shoulder. "You never left me in the hospital, and all the women at the shelter are jealous of how kind you are and of our relationship. Oh, I'm just so fucking mad! I never sang to her or rocked her or was alone with her." Amy was clutching my arm harder now, crying into my shoulder. I pulled off the road and we held each other in the idling car and wept.

"What am I supposed to do with all the baby clothes?" she cried. "The toys and the books? What will I do with my maternity clothes? I don't want to have more children. I want my baby. I wanted to ask Dr. Bowden to take my incompetent cervix and cut it up into a thousand pieces. That way I'll never let another baby down."

The air was quiet in the wake of her rage.

"We don't get another chance," she said finally and sighed a deep, deep sigh. "I just want her back."

I am determined that our marriage will hold together. It must. But what are we holding on for? What is left of our lives?

Each other. That is the answer, of course. But how we keep each other in sight as we wander so far into the blackness of our individual griefs, I don't know.

We sat there for a moment longer.

"God, how will I function at work?" Amy said, rubbing her eyes.

"You really want to go back?" I asked, pulling the car onto the road again.

"The shelter is a way out of how I feel. It's the only thing I can imagine that will keep me from sinking forever into this," she answered.

"For me it's the same with the cabin," I said. "I need to finish that place, to feel the wood in my fists, to make it happen."

"We'll go back," she said. "We've got to live someplace. But I am fed up with exposed insulation and midnight outhouse trips."

"I'll work faster, stay focused," I assured her.

"I'm not saying that. I'm just so damn tired of struggling."

"I know. Me too," I said. "It's good we're here for a while." The highway hummed under us. "Marquette and our families can't save us, but at least they can help us endure. For a few weeks, anyway."

"I guess, yeah. I'm glad we came," Amy said.

A dozen miles outside Marquette, we turned from the Big Bay

Road onto a plowed two-track where people have been feeding corn and hay and rotten lettuce to whitetail deer.

We got out and stood with our arms around each other beside that aqua-colored rental car covered with the dried mud and road salts of the northern United States. I rubbed her back. The fleece of her coat was soft under my hands.

"People ask me how I'm doing," Amy said. "Do they want to know the truth?"

"Some of them," I said.

The deer, maybe a hundred in among the woods, only glanced up and went back to their food, less afraid of us than of the burning hunger in their guts.

"They're thin," Amy said.

"Yes. If the snow gets too much deeper they'll be in trouble."

"I hope they make it to spring."

"They're almost there."

❦

In our grief and exhaustion we've grown passive, giving ourselves over to our families and to Marquette. And it would be easy to just stay. Old friends have started to call to get together. Amy's folks take us cross-country skiing and out to dinner. When we can't sleep, my folks stay up late and keep us company while we watch the local TV news.

Some nights, when Amy does sleep, I walk.

I walk the neighborhoods of my high school and college years, past bars I know too well, past the King Koin Laundromat on Third Street, the smell of moist, warm, lint steam drifting down from the roof exhaust. The streets of town have narrowed with snow that tumbles back down the high banks after plows pass, their six-foot-tall blades not high enough to toss all the fresh powder clear. Walking Marquette is like navigating a maze of trenches, the branches of oak trees and gables of houses above, on the new, elevated surface of the world.

When I return to whichever of our parents' houses we're staying at that night, I stand outside for a while, across the street. It's comfortable to stand there in the cold, perfectly still air and know that Amy is inside, warm and asleep. The windows are all dark, including the one behind which she is sleeping. It looks like all the other dark windows in town, and it seems such a small space when I think that behind it is so much of what I call my life.

❧ ❧

I sat in the Marquette Village Pub on Third Street at one in the morning with my friend Mac, both of us drunk. I hadn't had a drink since Amy's pregnancy was first diagnosed as risky, but I wanted to drink with Mac. He told me everything about his son's death six weeks before. He showed me Shaun's new driver's license and told me how it'd been covered in blood. He told me about sitting in his office at the University Counseling Center, listening to troubled students, trying to focus on their pain and their self-doubts while his own grief stormed inside him.

Mac goes to the cemetery every day. He is buying up grave plots around Shaun for himself and his other kids. He had Shaun's fleece jacket professionally cleaned of blood and flesh for Shaun's younger brother to wear.

"I didn't want to wash out all the body stuff, didn't want to clean off the license, to wipe off the blood. It's real, I need that. I love that," he said, staring into his beer.

He held his head up with his hand at his temple. His fingers were ashen and wrinkled, like bark. Older than mine. And the straight black hair that leaked like water between his fingers was streaked with gray.

Mac honks his horn when he passes the spot of the accident. Someone has inscribed a cross with the words "God Bless You Boys" in big black letters and driven the cross into the top of the ten-foot snowbank beside the road. The entire town is mourning.

When I told him that I feel distant from what he must feel, unraveling his heart from the daily threads of Shaun's presence, Mac lifted his eyes to mine. Deep in their wrinkled, freckled folds of skin those eyes were kind and knowing and unspeakably sad when he answered, "But Shaun got to live. Shaun got sixteen years. One of his friends, a beautiful girl a year older than him, was teaching him to kiss. Hannah won't have that."

I didn't want my loss to be in league with the black hole of Mac's, and it *is* different. But Mac was right. Hannah has been robbed of all of it, of the touch of her face by some high school kid's hand as he leans in to kiss her. And for me, just as for Mac, any future I thought I had a hold of, any sense of owning this life beyond the present moment, was gone.

Earlier that day, eating breakfast at my parents' dining room table, watching children at recess at the school across the street, I was overwhelmed by hopelessness. I thought of how, only a couple weeks before, my father must have sat at that same table watching those same kids climb and tumble down that giant snowbank and thought, with the deepest satisfaction, how his own grandchild would be among them.

Walking home from the closed bar in the falling snow, through the deserted town under the blinking stoplights, I loved Mac with a compassion and understanding I'd never felt toward any friend before. I've had close friends all my life, people whose stories I weave gratefully into my own. Now though, stopping to watch those stoplights pulse yellow and red, back and forth, lighting up the snow in the air with yellow and red light, I knew I'd crossed over into some new level of human connection.

Mac spoke of a fence between the living and the dead that he now gazes across daily. I think there is also a fence between those, the grieving, who can see into that furthest region and those who cannot. I have Hannah to thank for much of who I become from now on, for leading me here. If not for Hannah, I would never have had the honor of hearing Mac describe how, when he got to the hospital, the nurses had laid out Shaun's body on a bed in a normal hospital room, how he held his son and stroked his hair and drank in, for the last time, his musky, adolescent smell. If not for Hannah, Mac could not have told me how, despite having been killed by a combined collision speed of a hundred miles an hour, Shaun had looked worse with bad cases of childhood flu and tooth-breaking falls off his bicycle. If not for my own daughter and her death, Mac would not have been able to tell me how the only thing wrong with his son that night in the hospital was that he kept growing colder. Because of Hannah, I knew exactly what he meant.

FLOYD SKLOOT

A Measure of Acceptance

In the Shadow of Memory

The psychiatrist's office was in a run-down industrial section at the northern edge of Oregon's capital, Salem. It shared space with a chiropractic health center, separated from it by a temporary divider that wobbled in the current created by opening the door. When I arrived, a man sitting with his gaze trained on the spot I suddenly filled began kneading his left knee, his suit pants hopelessly wrinkled in that one spot. Another man, standing beside the door and dressed in overalls, studied the empty wall and muttered as he slowly rose on his toes and sank back on his heels. Like me, neither seemed happy to be visiting Dr. Peter Avilov.

Dr. Avilov specialized in the psychodiagnostic examination of disability claimants for the Social Security Administration. He made a career of weeding out hypochondriacs, malingerers, fakers, people who were ill without organic causes. There may be many such scam artists working the disability angle, but there are also many legitimate claimants. Avilov worked as a kind of hired gun, paid by an agency whose financial interests were best served when he determined that claimants were not disabled. This arrangement was like having your house appraised by the father-in-law of your prospective buyer, like being stopped by a traffic cop several tickets shy of his monthly quota, like facing a part-time judge who works for the construction company you're suing. Avilov's incentives were not encouraging to me.

I understood why I was there. When the Social Security Administration had decided to reevaluate my medical condition, eight years after originally approving my claim of disability, it exercised the right to send me to a doctor of its own choosing.

This seemed fair enough. But after receiving records, test results, and reports of brain scans, and statements from my own internal medicine and infectious diseases physicians, all attesting to my ongoing disability, and after requiring twenty-five pages of handwritten questionnaires from me and my wife, scheduled an appointment for me with Avilov. Not with an independent internal medicine or infectious diseases specialist, not with a neurologist, but with a shrink.

Now, twelve years after first getting sick, I can say that I've become adept at being brain damaged. It's not that my symptoms have gone away: I still try to dice a stalk of celery with a carrot instead of a knife, reverse *p* and *b* when I write, or draw a primitive hourglass when I mean to draw a star. I place newly purchased packages of frozen corn in the dishwasher instead of the freezer; after putting crumpled newspaper and dry pine into our woodstove, I strike a match and attempt to light the metal door. Preparing to cross the "main street" in Carlton, Oregon, I looked both ways, saw a pickup truck a quarter-mile south, took one step off the curb, and landed flat on my face, cane pointing due east.

So I'm still much as I was in December 1988. Along the way, though, I learned to manage my encounters with the world in new ways. Expecting the unexpected now, I can, like an improvisational actor, incorporate it into my performance. For instance, my tendency to use words that are close to—but not exactly—the words I'm trying to say has led to some surprising discoveries in the composition of sentences. A freshness emerges when the mind is unshackled from its habitual ways. In the past, I never would have described the effect of that viral attack on my brain as being "geezered" overnight if I hadn't first confused the words seizure and geezer. It is as though my word-finding capacity has developed a buckshot associative function to compensate for its failures of precision, so I end up with *shellac* instead of *plaque* when trying to describe the gunk on my teeth. Who knows, maybe James Joyce was brain damaged when he wrote *Finnegans Wake* and built a whole novel on puns and neologisms that were actually symptoms of disease.

It's possible to see such domination of the unexpected in a positive light. So getting lost in the familiar woods around our house and finding my way home again adds a twist of excitement to days that might seem circumscribed or routine because of my disability. When the natural food grocery where we shop rearranged its entire stock, I was one of the few customers who didn't mind, since I could never remember where things were anyway. I am more deliberate than I was; being attentive, purposeful in movement, lends my life an intensity of awareness that was not always present before. My senses are heightened, their fine-tuning mechanism busted: spicy food, stargazer lilies in bloom, birdsong, heat, my wife's vivid palette when she paints have all become more intense and stimulating. Because it threatens my balance, a sudden breeze stops me, so its strength and motion can register. Attentiveness may not guarantee success—as my pratfall in Carlton indicates—but it does allow me to appreciate detail and nuance.

One way of spinning this is to say that my daily experience is often spontaneous and exciting. Not fragmented and intimidating, but unpredictable, continuously new. I may lose track of things, or of myself in space, my line of thought, but instead of getting frustrated I try to see this as the perfect time to stop and figure out what I want or where I am. I accept my role in the harlequinade. It's not so much a matter of making lemonade out of life's lemons, but rather of learning to savor the shock, taste, texture, and aftereffects of a mouthful of unadulterated citrus.

Acceptance is a deceptive word. It suggests compliance, a consenting to my condition and to who I have become. This form of acceptance is often seen as weakness, submission. We say "I accept my punishment." Or "I accept your decision." But such assent, while passive in essence, does provide the stable, rocklike foundation for coping with a condition that will not go away. It is a powerful passivity, the Zen of Illness, that allows for endurance.

There is, however, more than endurance at stake. A year in bed, another year spent primarily in my recliner—these were times when endurance was the main issue. But over time, I began to recognize the possibilities for transformation. I saw another kind of acceptance as being viable, the kind espoused by Robert Frost when he said, "Take what is given, and make it over your own way." That is, after all, the root meaning of the verb "to accept," which comes from the Latin *accipere*, or "take to oneself." It implies an embrace. Not a giving up but a welcoming. People encourage the sick to resist, to fight back; we say that our resistance is down when we contract a virus. But it wasn't possible to resist the effects of brain damage. Fighting to speak rapidly and clearly, as I always had in the past, only leads to more garbling of meaning; willing myself to walk without a cane or climb a ladder only leads to more falls; demanding that I not forget something only makes me angrier when all I can remember is the effort not to forget. I began to realize that the most aggressive act I could perform on my own behalf was to stop struggling and discover what I could really do.

This, I believe, is what the Austrian psychotherapist Viktor E. Frankl refers to in his classic book, *The Doctor and the Soul*, as "spiritual elasticity." He says, speaking of his severely damaged patients, "Man must cultivate the flexibility to swing over to another value group if that group and that alone offers the possibility of actualizing values." Man must, Frankl believes, "temper his efforts to the chances that are offered."

Such shifts of value, made possible by active acceptance of

life as it is, can only be achieved alone. Doctors, therapists, rehabilitation professionals, family members, friends, lovers cannot reconcile a person to the changes wrought by illness or injury, though they can ease the way. Acceptance is a private act, achieved gradually and with little outward evidence. It also seems never to be complete; I still get furious with myself for forgetting what I'm trying to tell my daughter during a phone call, humiliated when I blithely walk away with another shopper's cart of groceries.

But for all its private essence, acceptance cannot be expressed purely in private terms. My experience did not happen to me alone; family, colleagues and friends, acquaintances were all involved. I had a new relationship with my employer and its insurance company, with federal and state government, with people who read my work. There is a social dimension to the experience of illness and to its acceptance, a kind of reciprocity between Self and World that goes beyond the enactment of laws governing handicapped access to buildings, or rules prohibiting discrimination in the workplace. It is in this social dimension that, for all my private adjustment, I remain a grave cripple and, apparently, a figure of contempt.

At least the parties involved agreed that what was wrong with me was all in my head. However, mine was disability arising from organic damage to the brain caused by a viral attack, not from psychiatric illness. The distinction matters; my disability status would not continue if my condition were psychiatric. It was in the best interests of the Social Security Administration for Dr. Avilov to say my symptoms were caused by the mind, were psychosomatic rather than organic in nature. And what was in Social Security's interests was also in Avilov's.

Anyone who observes me in action over time can see that I no longer have "brains." A brain, yes, with many functions intact; but

I'm not as smart or as quick or as steady as I was, or as a man my age and with my education should be. Though I may not look sick and I don't shake or froth or talk to myself, after a few minutes it becomes clear that something fundamental is wrong. My losses of cognitive capability have been fully measured and recorded. They were used by the Social Security Administration and the insurance company to establish my total disability, by various physicians to establish treatment and therapy programs, by a pharmaceutical company to establish my eligibility for participation in the clinical field trial of a drug that didn't work. I have a handicapped parking placard on the dashboard of my car; I can get a free return-trip token from the New York City subway system by flashing my Medicaid card. In this sense, I have a public profile as someone who is disabled. I have met the requirements.

Further, as someone with quantifiable diminishment in IQ levels, impaired abstract reasoning and learning facility, scattered recall capacities, and aptitudes that decrease as fatigue or distraction increases, I am of scientific use. When it serves their purposes, various institutions welcome me. Indeed they pursue me. I have been actively recruited for three experimental protocols run by Oregon Health Sciences University. One of these, a series of treatments using DMSO, made me smell so rancid that I turned heads just by walking into a room. But when I do not serve their purpose, these same institutions dismiss me. Or challenge me. No matter how well I may have adjusted to living with brain damage, the world I often deal with has not. When money or status is involved, I am positioned as a pariah.

So would Avilov find that my disability was continuing, or would he judge me as suffering from mental illness? Those who say that the distinction is bogus, or that the patient's fear of being labeled mentally ill is merely a cultural bias and ought not matter, are missing the point. Money is at stake; in our culture, this means it matters very much. To all sides.

Avilov began by asking me to recount the history of my illness. He seemed as easily distracted as I was; while I stared at his checked flannel shirt, sweetly ragged mustache, and the pen he occasionally put in his mouth like a pipe, Avilov looked from my face to his closed door to his empty notepad and back to my face, nodding. When I had finished, he asked a series of diagnostic questions: did I know what day it was (hey, I'm here on the right day, aren't I?), could I name the presidents of the United States since Kennedy, could I count backward from one hundred by sevens? During this series, he interrupted me to provide a list of four unconnected words (such as *train, argue, barn, vivid*) that I was instructed to remember for later recall. Then he asked me to explain what was meant by the expression "People who live in glass houses should not throw stones." I nodded, thought for a moment, knew that this sort of proverb relied on metaphor, which as a poet should be my great strength, and began to explain. Except that I couldn't. I must have talked for five minutes, in tortuous circles, spewing gobbledygook about stones breaking glass and people having things to hide, shaking my head, backtracking as I tried to elaborate. But it was beyond me, as all abstract thinking is beyond me, and I soon drifted into stunned silence. Crashing into your limitations this way hurts; I remembered as a long-distance runner hitting the fabled "wall" at about mile twenty-two of the Chicago Marathon, my body depleted of all energy resources, feeding on its own muscle and fat for every additional step, and I recognized this as being a similar sensation.

For the first time, I saw something clear in Avilov's eyes. He saw me. He recognized this as real, the blathering of a brain-damaged man who still thinks he can think.

It was at this moment that he asked, "Why are you here?"

I nearly burst into tears, knowing that he meant I seemed to be suffering from organic rather than mental illness. Music to my ears. "I have the same question."

The rest of our interview left little impression. But when the time came for me to leave, I stood to shake his hand and realized that Avilov had forgotten to ask me if I remembered the four words I had by then forgotten. I did remember having to remember them, though. Would it be best to walk out of the room, or should I remind him that he forgot to have me repeat the words I could no longer remember? Or had I forgotten that he did ask me, lost as I was in the fog of other failures? Should I say, "I can't remember if you asked me to repeat those words, but there's no need because I can't remember them"?

None of that mattered because Avilov, bless his heart, had found that my disability status remained as it was. Such recommendations arrive as mixed blessings; I would much rather not be as I am, but since I am, I must depend upon on receiving the legitimate support I paid for when healthy and am entitled to now.

There was little time to feel relieved because I soon faced an altogether different challenge, this time from the company that handled my disability insurance payments. I was ordered to undergo "a Two Day Functional Capacity Evaluation" administered by a rehabilitation firm the company hired in Portland. A later phone call informed me to prepare for six and a half hours of physical challenges the first day and three hours more the following day. I would be made to lift weights, carry heavy boxes, push and pull loaded crates, climb stairs, perform various feats of balance and dexterity, complete puzzles, answer a barrage of questions. But I would have an hour for lunch.

Wear loose clothes. Arrive early.

With the letter had come a warning: "You must provide your best effort so that the reported measurements of your functional ability are valid." Again, the message seemed clear: no shenanigans, you! We're wise to your kind.

I think the contempt that underlies these confrontations is

apparent. The patient, or—in the lingo of insurance operations— the claimant, is approached not only as an adversary but as a deceiver. *You can climb more stairs than that! You can really stand on one leg, like a heron; stop falling over, freeloader! We know that game.* Paranoia rules; here an institution seems caught in its grip. With money at stake, the disabled are automatically supposed to be up to some kind of chicanery, and our displays of symptoms are viewed as untrustworthy. Never mind that I contributed to Social Security for my entire working life, with the mutual understanding that if I were disabled the fund would be there for me. Never mind that both my employer and I paid for disability insurance with the mutual understanding that if I were disabled, payments would be there for me. Our doctors are suspect, our caregivers are implicated, and *we've got our eyes on you!*

The rehab center looked like a combination gym and children's playground. The staff was friendly, casual; several were administering physical therapy, so the huge room into which I was led smelled of sweat. An elderly man at a desk worked with a small stack of blocks. Above the blather of muzak, I heard grunts and moans of pained effort: a woman lying on mats, being helped to bend damaged knees; a stiff-backed man laboring through his stretches; two women side by side on benches, deep in conversation as they curled small weights.

The man assigned to conduct my Functional Capacity Evaluation looked enough like me to be a cousin. Short, bearded, thick hair curling away from a lacy bald spot, Reggie shook my hand and tried to set me at ease. He was good at what he did, lowering the level of confrontation, expressing compassion, showing concern about the effect on my health of such strenuous testing. I should let him know if I needed to stop.

Right then, before the action began, I had a moment of grave doubt. I could remain suspicious, paranoia begetting paranoia, or

I could trust Reggie to be honest, to assess my capacities without prejudice. The presence of patients being helped all around me seemed a good sign. This firm didn't appear dependent on referrals for evaluation from insurance companies. It had a lucrative operation, independent of all that. And if I could not trust a man who reminded me of a healthier version of myself, it seemed like bad Karma. I loved games and physical challenges. But I knew who and what I was now; it would be fine if I simply let him know as well. Though much of my disability results from cognitive deficits, there are physical manifestations too, so letting Reggie know me in the context of a gymlike setting felt comfortable. Besides, he was sharp enough to recognize suspicion in my eyes anyway, and that would give him reason to doubt my efforts. We were both after the same thing: a valid representation of my abilities. Now was the time to put all I had learned about acceptance on the line. It would require a measure of acceptance on both sides.

What I was not prepared for was how badly I would perform in every test. I knew my limitations but had never measured them. Over a dozen years, the consequences of exceeding my physical capabilities had been made clear enough that I learned to live within the limits. Here, I was brought repeatedly to those limits and beyond; after an hour with Reggie, I was ready to sleep for the entire next month. The experience was crushing. How could I comfortably manage only 25 pounds in the floor-to-waist lift repetitions? I used to press 150 pounds as part of my regular weekly training for competitive racing. How could I not stand on my left foot for more than two seconds? You shoulda seen me on a ball field! I could hold my arms up for no more than seventy-five seconds, could push a cart loaded with no more than 40 pounds of weights, could climb only sixty-six stairs. I could not fit shapes to their proper holes in a form-board in the time allotted, though I distinctly remember playing a game with my stepson that worked on the same principles and always beating the timer. Just before lunch, Reggie asked me to squat and lift a box filled with paper. He stood behind me and was there as I fell back into his arms.

I may not have been clinically depressed, as Dr. Avilov attested earlier, but this evaluation was almost enough to knock me into the deepest despair. Reggie said little to reveal his opinions. At the time, I thought that meant he was simply being professional, masking judgment, and though I sensed empathy I realized that could be a matter of projection on my part.

Later, I believed that his silence came from knowing what else he had to make me do. After lunch and an interview about the Activities of Daily Living form I had filled out, Reggie led me to a field of blue mats spread across the room's center. For a moment, I wondered if he planned to challenge me to a wrestling match. That thought had lovely symbolic overtones: wrestling with someone who suggested my former self; wrestling with an agent of THEM, a man certain to defeat me; or having my Genesis experience, like Jacob at Peniel, wrestling with Him. Which, at least for Jacob, resulted in a blessing and a nice payout.

But no. Reggie told me to crawl.

In order to obtain "a valid representation" of my abilities, it was necessary for the insurance company to see how far, and for how long, and with what result I could crawl.

It was a test I had not imagined. It was a test that could, in all honesty, have only one purpose. My ability to crawl could not logically be used as a valid measure of my employability. And in light of all the other tasks I had been unable to perform, crawling was not necessary as a measure of my functional limits. It would test nothing, at least nothing specific to my case, not even the lower limits of my capacity. Carrying the malign odor of indifference, tyranny's tainted breath, the demand that I crawl was almost comical in its obviousness: the paternal powers turning someone like me, a disabled man living in dependence upon their finances, into an infant.

I considered refusing to comply. Though the implied threat (*you must provide your best effort . . .*) contained in the letter crossed my mind, and I wondered how Beverly and I would manage without my disability payments, it wasn't practicality that made me proceed. At least I don't think so. It was, instead, acceptance. I had spent the morning in a public confrontation with the fullness of my loss, as though on stage with Reggie, representing the insurance company, as my audience. Now I would confront the sheer heartlessness of the System, the powers that demanded that I crawl before they agreed temporarily to accept my disability. I would, perhaps for the first time, join the company of those far more damaged than I am, who have endured far more indignity in their quest for acceptance. Whatever it is that Reggie and the insurance company believed they were measuring as I got down on my hands and knees and began a slow circuit of the mats in the center of that huge room, I believed I was measuring how far we still had to go for acceptance.

Reggie stood in the center of the mats, rotating in place as I crawled along one side, turned at the corner, crossed to the opposite side, and began to return toward the point where I had started. Before I reached it, Reggie told me to stop. He had seen enough. I was slow and unsteady at the turns, but I could crawl fine.

I never received a follow-up letter from the insurance company. I was never formally informed of its findings or given documentation of my performance, though my disability payments have continued.

At the end of the second day of testing, Reggie told me how I'd done. In many of the tests, my results were in the lower 5 to 10 percent for men my age. My performance diminished alarmingly on the second day, and he hadn't ever tested anyone who did as poorly on the dexterity components. He believed that I had given my best efforts and would report accordingly. But he would not give me any formal results. I was to contact my physician, who would receive Reggie's report in due time.

When the battery of tests had first been scheduled, I'd made an appointment to see my doctor a few days after their completion. I knew the physical challenges would worsen my symptoms, and wanted him to see what had resulted. I knew I would need his help. By the time I got there, he had spoken to Reggie and knew about my performance. But my doctor never got an official report either.

This was familiar ground. Did I wish to request a report? I was continuing to receive my legitimate payments; did I really want to contact my insurance company and demand to see the findings of my Functional Capacity Evaluation? Risk waking the sleeping dragon? What would be the point? I anticipated no satisfaction in reading that I was in fact disabled, or in seeing how my experience translated into numbers or bureaucratic prose.

It seems that I was of interest only when there was an occasion to rule me ineligible for benefits. Found again to be disabled, I wasn't even due the courtesy of a reply. The checks came; what more did I need to show that my claims are accepted?

There was, I suppose, no real need for a report. Through the experience, I had discovered something more vital than the measures of my physical capacity. The measure of public acceptance that I hoped to find, that I imagined would balance my private acceptance, was not going to come from a public agency or public corporation. It didn't work that way, after all. The public was largely indifferent, as most people, healthy or not, understand. The only measure of acceptance would come from how I conducted myself in public, moment by moment. With laws in place to permit handicapped access to public spaces, prevent discrimination, and encourage involvement in public life, there is general acceptance that the handicapped live among us and must be accommodated. But that doesn't mean they're not resented, feared, or mistrusted by the healthy. The Disability Racket!

I had encountered the true, hard heart of the matter. My life in the social dimension of illness is governed by forces that are severe and implacable. Though activism has helped protect the handicapped over the last four decades, there is little room for reciprocity between the handicapped person and his or her world. It is naïve to expect otherwise.

I would like to think that the insurance company didn't send an official letter of findings because it was abashed at what it'd put me through. I would like to think that Dr. Avilov, who no longer practices in Salem, hasn't moved away because he found too many claimants disabled and lost his contract with the Social Security Administration. That my experience educated Reggie and his firm, and that his report educated the insurance company, so everyone now understands the experience of disability, or of living with brain damage.

But I know better. My desire for reciprocity between self and world must find its form in writing about my experience. Slowly. This essay has taken me eleven months to complete, in sittings of fifteen minutes or so. Built of fragments shaped after the pieces were examined, its errors of spelling and of word choice and logic ferreted out with the help of my wife or daughter or computer's spell-checker. It may look to a reader like the product of someone a lot less damaged than I claim to be. But it's not. It's the product of someone who has learned how to live with his limitations, and work with them. And when it's published, if someone employed by my insurance company reads it, I will probably get a letter in the mail demanding that I report for another battery of tests. After all, this is not how a brain-damaged man is supposed to behave.

MIMI SCHWARTZ

The New Kitchen

Thoughts from a Queen-Sized Bed

A fter five months of cooking in a dark makeshift pantry with a ten-inch sink and a hot plate, we now have a brand-new kitchen with everything working and in place: spices in the spice drawer, knives in the knife rack. Even the garbage can pulls out below the butcher block so veggie scraps fall right in.

Five years ago such order was not my thing—even with a mother who complained for eighteen years about my messy room and a husband who has wanted the neatness of his mother's house ever since. My attitude was: This is who I am, a domestic free spirit. Take me or leave me. And dinners turned out, one way or another, no matter what the setting.

But lately domestic order pleases me. The regrouting I did in the bathroom makes me smile every time I walk by, so do the screens, no longer ripped, on the porch. I think of my mother who, at my age, sold our house in Queens when I left for college and moved into a brand new apartment, even if her daughter lost her room.

Why? I thought then. She's lived so long with what she's had, why change it? It was *my* life that was beginning; hers should stay the way I was used to it being. Now, as buckling linoleum makes me feel like 102, I understand her impulse (and my mother-in-law's, who did the same thing). I need new, too—even if it means a second mortgage, which we did take out to pay for the new kitchen. "It's worth it," I keep telling Stu, who has finally stopped grumbling that the old, one-windowed, 1940s kitchen was nice enough. He, too, likes light streaming in from three sides and how we can control the sink, stove, and refrigerator with five

steps—and how I no longer leave a nightly trail of chopped onions across the kitchen floor.

My old self resists, thinking of Madeline Roth's mother when I
was in high school, always re-covering chairs, beds, and couches
and repapering the walls. We'd have to step over books of fabric
samples, propped against chairs and walls, to get to Madeline's
bedroom, where we'd listen to Pete Seeger songs of the working
man and sneer at such bourgeois materialism.

What will be next? I am thinking about my grandfather who,
from age sixty on, put on his blue suit and tie to eat wheat germ
on his grapefruit every morning. I open the refrigerator with see-
through drawers and spit-shine the chrome trim on the cheese
drawer.

A friend calls to tell me that she and her husband bought an
1850 farmhouse on five acres, twice as big as their old split-level
and in need of lots of work. "But your kids are grown," I say, feeling wonderfully modest all of a sudden.

"We want a guest wing for grandchildren."

"But you don't have grandchildren."

"We will."

"Oh."

". . . besides, we need a change."

So, evidently, did the three couples we had dinner with last
week. One has remodeled, the other two are talking to contrac-
tors. It's either that or moving or getting a divorce, we decided
over dessert. A kitchen is cheaper than a lawyer, and so what if
no one cooks much anymore?

I do plan to cook—even with the kids out of the house and a
new Tex-Mex takeout opening up the street. Stu and I will even
cook together; we've found out that neither of us needs to be the
General when making carrot curry or black bean soup. There's a
rhythm to chopping vegetables that seems to work for us when
we have enough counter space. We sit down to eat our creation

and all our many years together seem fine. Instant gratification, I guess, like good sex.

It must be that when our bodies disappoint us, we who stay together invest in home improvement. We can't change electrocardiograms, blurred vision, and dulling passion, but we can buy fresh paint, new gutters, and new kitchens of light and order. We will start again, we tell ourselves. Illusion, of course, but with a physicality that's comforting. My shoulder may still hurt from swimming too hard to stay in shape, there's a scar on my chest, stretch marks on my stomach, but at least my silverware drawer opens effortlessly.

LEE MARTIN

One I Love, Two I Love

Turning Bones

The facts are these:

On February 28, 1848, in Lukin Township, Clarissa Ridgley married Jonathan Inyart. Eleven months later, on January 13, 1849, she gave birth to their only child, Mary Ann. Jonathan died soon after from summer complaint, a common and dangerous digestive illness of the time that usually struck children. Clarissa and Mary Ann went to live with Clarissa's parents until August 1, 1856, when she married William Bell. Mr. Bell, a widower, had a child of his own, a daughter, as fortune would have it, named Mary Ann. Clarissa left her own Mary Ann to stay with her grandparents and moved a few miles east to Mr. Bell's farm. Never again did she live under the same roof as her daughter.

Because my mother and father were older, I often imagined that they weren't my real parents, that someone had abandoned me, like Moses left in the bulrushes, and this aging couple had found me and taken me in. For that reason alone, the story of Mary Ann Inyart compels me. I keep imagining that she must have felt betrayed, deserted, rejected for another little girl who shared her name.

Deb tells me that I should be careful not to assume too much. "Maybe Mary Ann was happy to stay with her grandparents," she argues. "Or maybe Clarissa didn't take her because she and Mr. Bell couldn't support her. Maybe it was just a matter of economics. Maybe Clarissa went to visit Mary Ann all the time, and everyone was happy."

These are all, of course, plausible scenarios. Last night, on a news program, I saw the story of a couple who had seventeen children. When the city condemned their house, the parents, unable to afford other housing, divided the children among various family members. Economic necessity sometimes forces families apart; this was particularly true at the time of Clarissa Ridgley, when parents often sent their children off to work as farm hands or housemaids.

So Deb is right; maybe Clarissa made the decision that she did and everyone was happy with it. Deb was an only child for ten years, but her parents were very young, having had her when they were both in their early twenties. She never grew up, as I did, with the haunting dread that her parents would die and leave her an orphan. When she considers Clarissa's story, she thinks first of this young widow, forced now by her husband's death to live again in her mother's house, to give up whatever independence her marriage had brought her. Deb and I married when she was seventeen, and she'll be the first to admit that, when she met me, she saw a chance to get away from home, where she felt imprisoned by her mother's nagging and her forbidding manner. She brings her dread of entrapment to bear on Clarissa's story, just as I bring my own fear of abandonment.

"And Clarissa must have been lonely," she says. "Six years without a husband."

Deb admits that she sometimes has dreams that I've died and left her alone for the rest of her life. She sees her widowed mother and how bleak her life is. She doesn't want to think of Clarissa in a similar situation, so she imagines that she found happiness with William Bell. I hope that's the case, too, but still I can't stop thinking about Mary Ann and how she must have felt in her heart of hearts to live apart from her mother.

When I imagine her now, it's a summer day in 1862, and she's just come out of the woods with her aunt Sally, whose given name is Sarah, their pails full of blackberries. The men are working hay in the meadow behind the house. The sun is high, and it glints off the tines of the pitchforks as the men toss the cut timothy grass into stacks. The forks whisk through the timothy, making a noise that reminds Mary Ann of the whispers she heard from her bed the night her mother announced that she was going to marry William Bell. "I've been a widow nearly six years," she said. "It's lonely without a husband. I can tell you that."

Mary Ann and Sally are some one hundred yards away from the men, half-hidden behind the honeysuckle that grows along the tree line. "Crouch down." Mary Ann grabs Sally by the sleeve of her shirtwaist and pulls her to her knees. "They don't even know we're here. We're like spies."

"They're just bringing in the hay." Sally's bucket has tipped over, and she's trying to gather the berries that have spilled. Her fingers are stained purple from the juice. "What's so interesting about that?"

Mary Ann loves everything about men. She loves the way her uncle Benton keeps his wide-brimmed hat straight on his head even as he pitches the hay, and the way her uncle Alfred, Sally's husband, wipes his face on his shirt sleeve. And she feels herself go woozy—that's the way she imagines her mother saying it, *woozy*—when she sees Henry Martin, Sally's brother. He's stripped himself to the waist, and Mary Ann can't stop looking at his bare chest, his arms corded with muscle.

"There's Henry." She whispers this to Sally. "Look at him. Oh, would you just look? He makes me woozy."

"Mary Ann, you're a scandal," says Sally.

"Tell me all about how it happens." The sun is shining on Henry's broad chest. "You know, between women and men."

"I'll tell you no such thing. You're not but thirteen."

"Thirteen's a woman. Some girls have got babies by then."

"Well, you don't need to be thinking of following suit."

"Mama said it was lonely without a man. She waited six years after Papa died. 'Six lonely years.'" Mary Ann puts the back of her hand to her forehead and tosses her head back the way she imagines her mother did the night she said she would marry William Bell. "'Would you have me suffer an eternity?'"

"Don't make fun of your mother."

"She never loved me," Mary Ann says. Then she comes out from behind the honeysuckle and goes running through the cut hay.

Maybe Deb is imagining the moment when William Bell first hints to Clarissa that they might make a pair. Maybe it happens at the Ridgley farm, where he's come to help with the threshing. At noon the men wash the wheat chaff from their hands and arms. Some of them douse their heads in the horse tank and come to the table, their hair slicked back as sleek as seals. Clarissa thinks of babies—their bright eyes, the way their skin pinkens when it's washed, its sweet smell. She's only had a chance to be a mother once. Jonathan died, and here she is nearly thirty, feeling that her best years are slipping by her. In a wink she'll be as old as her mother, Mary. She'll be an old widow woman, wizened and humpbacked, relying on the kindness of her neighbors.

She likes the way the men become polite and soft-spoken in the company of women. They say, "Please, Miss," when she asks them whether they'd like a powder biscuit, and "Thank you, Miss," when she pours them another glass of tea.

After they've eaten, William lingers outside while the other men go back to the field. He's there in the yard when Clarissa comes out to throw the table scraps to the hogs.

"It was all fine eats," he says. "Did you make them biscuits?"

"No," Clarissa says. "Mother did."

"I bet you make some fine biscuits yourself."

"I learned how," she says, "back when I set up house. Now Mother won't hardly let me touch a rolling pin."

"I'd let you make biscuits for me, Clarissa."

William is looking down at his feet. Clarissa can see his pink scalp where the hair is thinning. She knows he's trying to play the spark with her, and he's so shy about it she finds his clumsy attempt endearing. His wife has only been gone a year—cholera—and this must feel so odd to him.

Clarissa thinks of Jonathan lying those three months in his bed, death coming to him, and she wishes for the umpteenth time that she could have done something to save him. She made poultices from tansy leaves, steeped bloodroot in milk, made syrup from rhubarb, but nothing worked. He went away from her, and now here she is looking into William's eyes. He seems so afraid, she imagines that if she said, "Boo," he'd crumple to the ground. How helpless a man is, she thinks, how sweet, when he's trying to tell a woman that he needs her.

"How do you like your biscuits?" she asks him. "With melted butter? Honey?"

"Oh, I like my biscuits just about any way."

"I can make them that way." She takes a step toward him. "Believe me, I can. If I ever get the chance."

"I'd like to give you that chance," he says, and she knows that, in their awkward way, they've just agreed to marry.

My own proposal to Deb was nearly as haphazard. We had been dating barely a month, a courtship that started in the spring of 1975 when I was finishing my sophomore year at the community college in Olney. Deb was about to graduate from high school, and I suppose we were both at pivotal moments, when we would take a step this way or that and everything would change for us. I was making plans to attend Eastern Illinois University in Charleston; Deb was imagining that she would keep working at Burger Chef until she could get a job at the shoe factory or the garment factory and make enough money to finally move out of her parents' house.

And then one Saturday night I walked into Burger Chef. It was late, and the restaurant was nearly empty, just a few people like me and my friends, hanging out because there was nothing better to do. I remember so well the feeling I had in those days—a nervous energy, a restless expectation. My friends and I would cruise Main Street, making the turnaround at the east end in the Kentucky Fried Chicken parking lot, and then head back west to the bowling alley or the skating rink, anxious for something to happen. And, of course, what we hoped for most of all was that some girls somewhere would fall for us. It was spring, the air finally warm after winter's long freeze, the scent of the thawing earth all around us, the sweet perfume of lilac. We drove down Main Street with the car windows down, the tape deck playing something throbbing—Deep Purple, Alice Cooper—or something sweet with yearning—the *American Graffiti* soundtrack, which had started the fifties revival—or something even more sentimental—Bread or Jim Croce. By evening's end our bravado would be gone, and we would make the quiet drive home.

I had been in the Burger Chef before when Deb was working, and I had noted her bright smile and the friendly way she had with the customers. Her face was alive—that smile, those green eyes, a laugh that charmed me, not to mention the smoothest skin I had ever seen and a blond ponytail that bounced against her back as she moved about behind the counter. Her vitality won me.

One day, when it came time to pay my bill, I was a penny short. "I'm sorry," I said, embarrassed.

"Don't worry," she told me. "I'll pay it." And she took a penny from her apron pocket and dropped it into the till.

That Saturday night I finally worked up the nerve to talk to her. I leaned on the counter and tried to think of something flirtatious to say, something to let her know I was interested but nothing that would make her think I was one of those dangerous guys her parents had surely cautioned her to avoid. Earlier in the evening I had heard some people at the bowling alley talking about a late-night party out in the country by Noble—one of those beer blasts in a field—and though I had no desire to go there, now it was the only ammunition I could muster. "I hear there's a big party tonight," I said, trying not to seem lecherous. "Maybe we could go."

"We don't even know each other." Deb was sweet but timid. Later she admitted that she didn't want me to think that she was, in her words, "an easy-sleazy." "I can't go to a party with you."

"We could get to know each other," I said. Where was the generous girl who had been so quick with the penny? Couldn't she see I was harmless?

"I don't know," she said, and then her attention was diverted to something in the parking lot. "Hey, someone's taking my car." It turned out to be her father, driving the car to the filling station next door and then bringing it back. When he came into the Burger Chef to tell Deb what he had done, I went to the booth where my friends were sitting, thinking that I had lost my chance.

Our lives can turn on the smallest of things. In my case it was a piece of ice as big around as the end of my little finger. If Deb hadn't thrown it at me after her father left, I may have never spoken to her again. But because she did—"I had to do something," she told me later. "I couldn't stand to think that you might walk out of there"—I went back to the counter and said, "We could go out next weekend, maybe out to Art's Truck Stop. I like to get coffee there. Maybe we could just sit around and talk."

And she said that would be fine with her.

The night of our date, we did what I had promised; we drove out to Art's Truck Stop, and over coffee we talked. Our conversation, if anyone had preserved it on tape, would probably embarrass me now. In those days I could be earnest and impassioned.

I could rail against the capitalists, denounce the conservatives, quote Whitman and Thoreau. At the drop of a hat, I could turn sentimental. I could recite passages from Kahlil Gibran's *The Prophet*, Rod McKuen poems, pop-song lyrics. I thought such sources scripture when it came to love. I could even quote from the Bible. "There is no fear in love," I easily might have said, "but perfect love casteth out fear."

Part of me wants to be ashamed of such blathering now, but another part—the one that remembers what it was to be young—feels sweetly seduced. How passionate we were then—how unaware that generations and generations before us had been passionate, too.

I told Deb that I was an only child, that my father had lost his hands in a farming accident when I was barely a year old. I told her he wore hooks now, that he and my mother were in their sixties, that my biggest fear, when I was growing up, was that they would die and leave me an orphan. I said I believed in living a spiritual life, in being kind and good. I said, "It's the first thing I noticed about you. The way you treat people."

She told me that when she was young, her mother had refused to let her grow her hair long. "I always had to have a pixie cut," she said, "because it was easier to take care of. Straight hair, round face: it wasn't a pretty sight." Her mother, a child during the Depression, valued practicality over fashion. She bought sturdy oxford shoes for Deb instead of penny loafers and patent-leather Mary Janes. She sewed together polyester slacks that would last instead of buying Deb Levi jeans that would eventually fade and wear thin. "Now I've got my own job," Deb told me, "and I can buy whatever I want."

Her problems with her mother ran much deeper than arguments over clothes. In her mother's house she felt imprisoned, never allowed to be herself. She couldn't even have privacy. Her mother refused to let her have a lock on her bedroom door, insisted that it stay open. The only place in the house where Deb could be alone was the bathroom, which did have a lock, but even then her mother would bang on the door and shout, "What are you doing in there?" She was a woman driven by fear and paranoia and a powerful desire to control her surroundings. And Deb's father was reluctant to involve himself with his family. He was willing to spend his time puttering around in the garage, sacrificing the house and what went on there to Deb's mother.

These were the sorts of things we told each other that night at the truck stop, and when I think of these two people now, the people we once were, I feel a great tenderness toward them. There they sit at a Formica-covered table in the corner of a truck stop out on Highway 50, miles from town, far away from the houses to which they'll soon return and the people there—their parents—who have no idea that their very presence has started to determine what will happen next, who do not know that their children lie awake in the dark, dreaming about leaving them.

"The times are always so beautiful when we are together," Deb said to me in a letter that I've saved from those days. "One day has gone by and I feel as though it has been weeks since I've seen you."

"When did you know I was the one?" I ask her now from time to time.

"I knew it then," she says. "That night."

I knew it, too. I knew that we were connected in a profound way that was, perhaps, beyond words or understanding. Or maybe we were just so restless, so fearful, so anxious, that we clung to each other, barely able to believe our luck.

One night, as we sat on a blanket at the farm my father still owned though we had moved into town—a farm first owned by Henry Martin—I said, "What would you say if I asked you to marry me?"

Deb didn't hesitate. "I'd say yes," she told me, and I knew my life had changed forever.

So when I think now of Mary Ann running through the hayfield toward Henry on that day in 1862, I already know what they don't; they're in the middle of a love story. I wonder whether Henry has even paid her any mind, only to know her as his sister's niece. After all, he's nineteen, and his head is full these days with the talk of war.

He knows a boy from Wabash County who mustered in the summer before, when he was seventeen. He marched with Grant into Kentucky and took Fort Henry and Fort Donelson and then moved on to Shiloh in Tennessee and took it, too. Henry has listened to the Ridgleys as they've read aloud the newspaper accounts of the battles, and he's dreamed himself in those places amidst the cannon fire and the drums and the pounding of horses' hooves. He's seen boys there in Lukin on their way to Sumner or Lancaster to join up, and he's been ashamed for them to see him, still hoeing corn and pitching hay when there's a war to be fought, gray-coats to be killed. Here he is now, working with the old man, Alfred—only thirty-three, he seems ancient to Henry, who notes his slumped shoulders and the gray already starting to speckle his beard—and the objector, Benton, twenty-one, who leads singing at the Gilead Methodist Church and believes killing to be wrong, no matter the circumstances. "What about if those rebs came up here and killed your ma?" Henry said to Benton just that morning in the hayfield, and Benton quoted scripture back at him: "Vengeance is mine; thus sayeth the Lord."

Henry wants to go to war, but his father, John, has forbidden it. "I lost one child," he's told Henry. "I'll not be losing another."

It's been less than eight months since Henry's sister Nancy died. She was only twenty-one, and the typhoid took her. Out of John and Elizabeth Martin's eight children, she's the only one they've lost, a blessing that astounds them, given the fact that so many of their neighbors have put young'uns in the ground. Just look at the Ridgleys, six lost and Alfred's wife to boot. They've buried them all atop the hill on the east edge of their farm, a spot they've cleared of timber and seeded with bluegrass. Often Henry, because the Martins hire themselves out to the Ridgleys from time to time, mows the grass at the cemetery. He swings his scythe from side to side, uses his hand sickle around the ornate gravestones: the ones topped with cornices, the ones that have angels etched on them or hands with fingers pointing up to Heaven. He knows the names by heart: Charles, Sarah Ann, Eliza, Richard, Mary Jane, Sintha, Elizabeth. His sister Sally has married into this family, but he wonders whether Alfred really loves her or whether he simply needs a woman to look after his children. It's the Ridgleys' way to get whatever they want: wives, land, fancy tombstones, another family even, if Clarissa's any gauge. She traded in her daughter for another one of the same name, and now here she comes—the brat, Mary Ann—tromping through the hay, not caring a whit that she's scattering blackberries from her pail.

"Aw, look at you," Henry says. "Throwing good berries to the birds."

Mary Ann reaches into her pail and chants as she drops berries to the ground. "One I love, two I love, three I love, I say." She holds a berry up to Henry's lips. "Four I love with all my heart." He keeps his mouth closed. "Four I love with all my heart," she says again, this time with more force, and he opens his mouth and lets her lay the berry on his tongue. "Is it sweet?" she says to him.

"It's sweet," he says.

"That's because I picked it." She smiles at him, and he notices for the first time that she's growing up, that she'll be a pretty woman like her mother, that she'll know exactly what to do to snag a man.

That evening Clarissa and William come for supper. They have the children with them: Mary Ann, whom they've started calling Annie; William Jr.; and the three Clarissa has brought into the world—Marion and Amy and John. The women dish up the food and set it on the table while the children play bullpen in the yard and the men talk horses out at the stable. Soon someone will call them in to eat.

Annie is fifteen. She's wearing a tight-waisted dress that shows off the curve of her hips, her full breasts. Clarissa has helped her curl the ends of her hair, and Mary Ann, though she would never admit it, adores the honeyed spirals bouncing along Annie's slender neck. She flits about the kitchen, chattering on and on about the box supper at the Gilead Church that coming Sunday.

"I'm making a chiffon cake," she says. "Mama's helping me." Mary Ann takes a dish of boiled cabbage from her and wrinkles her nose at the smell.

"Is there some special beau you're hoping buys it?" Grandma Ridgley asks.

"Might be," Annie says. "I'm not saying."

"Chiffon." Her grandma shakes her head. "I swan. That's fancy."

Grandma Ridgley has told Mary Ann that she'll teach her how to bake a pound cake. How boring, Mary Ann thinks: sugar and flour and water and shortening. She imagines the chiffon cakes she saw her mother make before she married Mr. Bell: the satiny smooth batter, how she folded the egg whites into it, how light and sweet.

"It's not that hard," Mary Ann says.

Annie puts her hands on her hips. "I suppose you could make one."

"No, I couldn't make one." Mary Ann knows she's trying to force her mother to feel sorry for her. "Not unless Mama helped me."

"Why, Mary Ann," Clarissa says. "I never knew you to take an interest in such things."

Mary Ann wants to tell her that she's becoming a young lady, that she has interest in all sorts of things. She wants to tell her how the sight of Henry Martin can make her woozy. But she can't without validating the very thing that took her mother away from her—the desire for a man. She can't let her mother know that she's exactly like her.

A few years ago Deb's mom started giving her keepsakes: letters she and her husband, Loren, had written each other before they were married; a wooden plate someone had made for their wedding, *Wilma and Loren* hand-painted above a dove and a sprig of daisies, the date, *April 30, 1955,* inscribed below; a silver platter from their twenty-fifth anniversary.

Deb was embarrassed to accept such items. "Oh, don't you want to keep them?" she finally said to her mother.

"No, go ahead," Wilma told her. "You'll end up with them anyway."

Loren had been gone two years. Early one morning in 1993, he had stepped from his bedroom into the hallway and fallen to the floor, dead from a heart attack. Wilma had been sleeping on the couch in the living room, as was her habit those days since Loren, afflicted with sleep apnea, was often a difficult bed companion. I imagine her waking to the sound of his falling and finding him collapsed there in the hallway. Her house must have seemed like a strange place to her then and for the two years she remained there before moving into town. Though the Regulator clock still ticked along in the bedroom, and the sunlight came through the living room's picture window each afternoon, it must have felt so odd to be alone there, without the man she had loved nearly forty years.

Perhaps she thinks back now to the summer of 1975, when

Deb and I married without her blessing, and she understands exactly why we did it. I like to believe that in her widowhood she recalls the power of love and how once we fall under its spell all we can do is follow it to its end, no matter the voices telling us to have more sense.

"How will you live?" Wilma said when Deb told her we were going to marry and then move to Charleston so I could finish college.

"I'll work," Deb told her, "and so will Lee."

My parents had already agreed to go ahead and pay my tuition.

"Work at what?" Wilma was wiping off the kitchen table, around which Deb and I sat. Loren was in the living room reading the newspaper.

"Something will come along," Deb said.

Wilma scrubbed furiously at a stubborn spot on the table. Suddenly she placed her hands flat on the table and leaned toward us. "Well, I won't sign for you. I'll tell you that."

The wedding date we had chosen, August 10, was a week before Deb's eighteenth birthday. "I'll get Daddy to do it," she said.

"Did you hear that, Loren?" Wilma shouted into the living room, where Loren was hidden behind the newspaper he had spread in front of his face. "Are you going to sign for her?"

His voice, when he answered, was quiet but sure. "I guess I will," he said. And that was that.

Perhaps he remembered, better than Wilma, their own anguished yearnings when they weren't much older than Deb and I were then and everyone was telling them not to do anything foolish.

Loren was a private in the army, stationed first at Fort Leonard Wood in Missouri and then later at Fort Sam Houston in San Antonio. He enlisted in 1954, when he was twenty and Wilma was nineteen. Their letters to each other, from his time in the army, are filled with talk of marriage. In one Wilma reports how her sister warned her not to marry him when he was home on leave: "Now don't get married when he's home," her sister said. "You better wait until he's out, and then both of you will be happier."

Wilma writes to Loren: "Darling, of course I doubt if my folks and your folks wants us to, but I know what our mothers said on the Monday we was up there. My mother and your mother both said we can only tell them and the rest is up to them."

In a letter from Fort Sam Houston postmarked August 10, exactly twenty years before Deb and I would marry, Loren writes to Wilma about the length of his time there: fourteen weeks. "After I find more about it," he says, "I will tell you just how long it will be before we can get married. It will be as soon as possible, and I think you know I mean it. I will get an emergency leave and come home and get you and bring you back with me."

A few months later, in December, he writes about his parents' objections to his plans to marry Wilma, objections he quickly overcomes with his fervent desires:

Honey, I called home tonight and talked to mother, and she asked if we was planning on getting married when I come home for Christmas, and I told her that we had no plans, then she said she would rather for us not to. Honey, every one says that we should wait, and we both know it would be better if we did, but I don't know if we can wait, I don't think we can. I love and want you with all my heart. Sweetheart, I wish that we could be married right now, but we are going to wait at least one more week and a half. I love you sweetheart, and I don't care who knows it. I long for you every night darling, I won't be happy until you are in my arms again.

He didn't marry Wilma that Christmas, waiting a few months more. He married her in April and promptly got his orders for Frankfurt, Germany, where he spent the rest of his enlistment working as a technician in a dental clinic. Wilma kept living with her parents in Illinois, a married woman now, but with no man to show for it.

After Jonathan died, Clarissa did the only thing she could; she came home to her mother and father. She brought her baby, Mary Ann, and right away it felt as if she were handing the child over to them. How they doted on their little Mary. And Clarissa, sinking into the blackness of her grief, was glad not to have to worry about caring for the baby. Six years went by, and as Mary Ann grew older, she came to look more and more like Jonathan—the same slender nose, the curl in her dark hair, the heavy-lidded eyes that always made her look sleepy, and oh so beautiful, and oh so full of mystery. She resembled Jonathan so much it was sometimes painful for Clarissa to look at her.

"You're a little Indian girl," Grandpa Ridgley often told her. "We stole you away from the Shawnees."

What foolishness. But what else was there to say, since at first no one wanted to tell Mary Ann about her father and how he had died? "I'm an Indian," she often told people, and they agreed that she was a wild one all right, a real hellion, so different from Clarissa, who spent her days shuffling about the house, hardly making a sound. She sewed, washed clothes, made lye soap, did whatever chore her mother gave her, glad at first to have someone tell her how to get through the days. "Yes, ma'am," she said to her mother as if she were once again a girl.

When all the work was done, she sometimes sat in her room and idly plucked the strings on the fiddle that Jonathan used to play. She pulled her rocking chair close to the window and held the fiddle on her lap. The rosewood body gleamed in the sunlight. She watched Mary Ann scampering about in the farmyard—trying to ride baby pigs, to catch guineas—and Clarissa was surprised to suddenly find herself crying. She cried because the black-haired girl, laughing and squealing, seemed so strange to her. And she cried because she knew how difficult it would be to ever feel such joy herself as long as she lived in her parents' house, where it was so painfully clear that she was a widow.

So when William Bell finally gets around to officially proposing—"Tying the knot good and proper," he says—she doesn't hesitate. She can already imagine the changes she'll make at his house—the new curtains she'll sew, the hollyhocks she'll plant by the door, the quilt she'll make to cover them in their bed. She dreams of the new clothes she'll sew for the boy and girl, William Jr. and Mary Ann. She imagines waking them each morning and helping them dress, brushing Mary Ann's hair. If she marries William, she can see herself stepping back into the life that she and Jonathan would have had if he hadn't died.

"I've been so lonely," she tells her mother. "I'm not sure I even knew it until that day William was here to help with the threshing."

"What about Mary Ann?" her mother says. "*Your* Mary Ann."

"She's happy here," Clarissa says, and she knows she won't even ask Mary Ann whether she wants to go with her. She can't afford to, because if the answer is yes, Clarissa will never be able to escape Jonathan's death. Mary Ann—*her* Mary Ann—will always remind her of the way her life stopped those six years. And how will she be able to lie down with another man if Mary Ann, who looks so much like Jonathan, moves through the same house? "Happy," Clarissa says again, trying to convince herself it's true.

And maybe it is. Maybe Mary Ann, for a while, thinks nothing at all of the fact that her mother no longer lives with her. There's her uncle Benton, who lets her sit on his lap by the fire in the evening while he reads his Bible. The Bible has a drawing in it of Mary anointing the feet of Christ. She kneels on a rug, her fingers dipping into a clay bowl, Christ's naked foot resting on her thigh.

Her long hair trails down her arms, falls over her bosom. "That's your name," Benton says, and he points to the word *Mary*.

Mary Ann likes the way she feels when Benton smiles at her—protected, safe, warm there by the fire. Later, her uncle Alfred tucks her into bed. He lets her open his watch, teaches her to tell the time. He keeps the watch in the pocket of his vest at the end of a gold chain. Mary Ann dreams of all things golden as she falls asleep: the watch chain, the wheat ripening in the fields, the honeycomb her grandfather finds sometimes in the high hollow of a tree.

"Sweet dreams," her uncle tells her, and she falls asleep to the gentle drone of voices, her grandparents and her uncles speaking softly because their darling Mary Ann—their little princess—has gone to bed.

Her favorite story is the one of the sleeping beauty who pricked her finger on a spindle and slept for a hundred years until a prince kissed her and she awoke. At first Mary Ann imagines that her father will come back, that one day she'll wake and find him sitting on her bed. She imagines him playing the fiddle, the one her mother used to let her pluck. Then, as she grows older, her father, whom she has only imagined, having no image of him, only the gleaming rosewood of the fiddle, the horsehair string of the bow, recedes. She's thirteen, and her father is gone, and her mother, and she dreams of boys—boys like Henry Martin, who she hopes will buy her cake, even if it is a wretched pound cake, at the Gilead box social come Sunday.

Deb and I married on a Sunday afternoon. I went to church with my parents that morning and came home with them and sat at their table as I had for nearly twenty years. It seems such a short time, now that I've lived twenty-six years beyond it, now that I've spent a longer time on my own than I did under my parents' care.

My mother was sixty-five that day in 1975; my father was sixty-two. They had fallen in love twenty-four years earlier. My mother was an old-maid schoolteacher, living at home with her parents; my father was a bachelor farmer, caring for his aged mother. How happy I am that they found each other. I can't bear the thought that they might have lived out their lives never having shared a passage through the years. That passage was pocked with pitfalls, but my parents' years together contained much joy as well. When I think of them now, I remember them as partners—helpmeets, in the language of Genesis.

I think of them most poignantly in spring, when Deb and I plant our vegetable garden, set out begonias and coleus and daisies, watch our rosebushes burst into flower. Evenings, as my parents often did, we work in our garden, tend our flower beds. We check on the bud swell of our red oak, note the peonies growing up from their winter's sleep, the blackberry canes green with new growth. What I feel is what my parents must have felt with each turn of the season—thankful to walk the earth with each other, their union easing them through the unforgiving march of time.

When I think of my parents, I think of swans, who mate for life, each partner devoted to the other. I think of my mother and father working side by side all those years, tending gardens, farming their eighty acres, synchronizing their rhythms with those of the planet. I think of them each time I watch rosebuds open, tomatoes bloom, blackberries set fruit—all things moving according to the seasons. I watch the slender branches of our red-tipped photinias sway in the wind. Each branch moves of its own accord, but because the photinias are so thick, so lush, what I see is a wave, an undulation, a singular swell and ebb that repeats itself.

That Sunday in 1975 my parents were nearing the end of their time together. They had only seven years left to them. Deb and

I were at our beginning, and now I can admit what we didn't know then: we were just kids; we had no idea what it meant to be married, to be like the swans, like my mother and father, devoted for a lifetime. We didn't know, and still don't, the length of our journey and all it will ask of us. When I think back to the people we were that day—young and naive—I feel a tender pity. There's so much we don't know. But mostly I feel love—love for the fact that we've found each other, love for all our hope and courage and foolishness.

In our wedding photo, the one the newspaper will print, we're standing outside the church in front of a bed of cleyera and spruce and sumac. I'm wearing a cream-colored suit that my father gave me the money to buy, a red rose pinned to my lapel. Deb has on a dress that her mother sewed from polyester crepe, white with an empire waist and double-layered sleeves. Deb's hand rests in the crook of my elbow. One moment more, while the photographer holds us still. Then we'll move. We'll step from the frame and into the years. Deb has a 1975 penny in her shoe, a penny her father gave her for luck.

The afternoon of the Gilead box social is glorious. And why shouldn't it be? Mary Ann thinks, in love suddenly with the way the sunlight splinters through the treetops in the grove beside the church. The men have laid planks across barrels, and the women have covered them with oilcloths. The boxes are there among them, Annie's chiffon cake and Mary Ann's pound cake. The women have carried in food as well: smoked ham, dried pumpkin, cornbread, apple butter, watermelon and tomatoes from their gardens. After everyone has eaten, the bidding on the boxes will begin. Then the couples, the young boys and girls, will sit together and enjoy the cakes and pies.

Annie's box is tied shut with a bright pink ribbon that Mary Ann imagines her mother bought from a pack peddler. No one's supposed to know which box is whose except the preacher, who will run the bidding, but Annie has made a point of showing hers to Mary Ann, fussing over the pink ribbon, and to Henry, who is standing now with Benton and Alfred over by the horses, talking, no doubt, about the war. What else do they pay any mind to these days, even here on Sunday when everything is so lovely—the sunlight and the boxes so prettily made up with ribbons and lace. Even the horses' soft nickering fills Mary Ann with joy. Across the road a field of timothy grass, still uncut, stirs in the breeze. She remembers how only a few days before she ran through the cut hay to Henry. She recalls how she put the blackberry in his mouth, touched his lips, his tongue. She wants to go to him now and do the same thing, wants to stop him from talking about rifles and cannons and bayonets, wants to take his hand, hold it in hers until he's calm, until what he feels coming from the heat of her skin is stronger than anything he can imagine about the war.

But just then her mother takes her by both hands and dances her around in a circle while the other women, startled, watch their happy jig. "Oh, Mary Ann," Clarissa says. "Isn't it the most wonderful day?"

Clarissa has done her hair in soft, loopy curls, so different from the other women—from Sally and Grandma Ridgley and Henry's mother, Elizabeth, all of whom have their hair parted down the middle and pinned up in knots at the napes of their necks. Mary Ann loves the way her mother's curls bounce as she dances. "It is," she says. "Oh, Mother. It really is."

Then they stop, and they squeeze each other's hands, and something about that moment—perhaps it's the fact that they realize that they've just made a sight of themselves, two little fools bursting into dance, or perhaps it's nothing they can identify at all—makes them see, without having to admit it, how very much alike they are.

"You're hoping Henry buys your cake, aren't you?" Clarissa leans forward until her forehead touches Mary Ann's. Mary Ann nods, pleased to bask in her mother's warmth, to feel a curl brush ever so lightly against her face. "Have you told him which one it is?" Clarissa says.

"No," says Mary Ann. "Annie told him about hers."

"Annie's older." They're talking in whispers now, telling secrets. "She's brazen. Tell me which box is yours."

"It's the one with the dried asters on it."

"From Grandma's garden," Clarissa says. "All right. You leave everything to me."

Mary Ann must be happy to let her mother think that, when it comes to boys, she's shy. She doesn't dare tell her about the day in the hayfield when she put the blackberry into Henry's mouth. But she's frightened, too. What if Henry doesn't bid on her box? What if he chooses Annie's instead? Oh, she knows there might be other boys. There might be years and years of boys. It isn't even about that, and she may or may not understand this. Perhaps she only feels it—this thin shiver somewhere in her heart, this tremble that tells her she will be, like her mother, forever afraid of being lonely.

Sometimes, even after twenty-six years, either Deb or I, at some ordinary moment—washing dishes, straightening closets, sweeping floors—will find ourselves overwhelmed with emotion, a rush of thanksgiving for all the time we've had together. One of us will rush to the other, and we'll wrap ourselves up in a fierce embrace. "One of those times," we call such moments, flashes of gratitude that rush into the heart and nearly knock us over with their force.

I'm sure that we feel these moments with such intensity because there was a time some years back when we almost walked away from each other, called an end to what before that time we had named "love." I'm convinced that what kept us from making the final break was the fact that, despite the difficulties we were suffering, we were each other's best friend, and there was something about that fact that remained indestructible no matter the ugly words and hurtful actions that we tried to levy against it. When we finally came out the other side of our trouble, we knew love in a way that we hadn't in those early years. We knew it as something forbearing and patient, willing to wait for us until we were truly capable of it.

A true love story is never separate from the others that have preceded it and the ones that will follow, never detached from the collective yearning, the collective fear that is our blessing and our curse from the moment we first draw breath and reach with our cry for someone to hold us, to touch us with tenderness, to let us know we aren't alone.

I can imagine Deb and I both mulling over the story of Mary Ann, dreaming it as we move through our days. Perhaps on occasion we even dream it at the same time. Maybe, during the silence of an evening, when we glance up from our reading and catch each other's eye, we're imagining the moment I've yet to write, the one where Clarissa leans close to Henry and whispers in his ear, tells him that Mary Ann would be tickled if he would buy her cake. "Nothing fancy," she says. "It's just a pound cake. The box has dried asters on it. You sure would make her day. She's sweet on you."

Of course, he's always known it to be true—of course he has. And he'll buy that cake—that pound cake—choke it down, because on this day, his last day for some time on Lukin Prairie, he wants to be in the company of someone like Mary Ann, someone who knows what it is to lose a father. He sits with her on the grass, after the bidding is done, and thinks about how, come nightfall, he'll sneak away—his father be damned—and go off to fight the war. He knows this in his heart and can't say it to anyone, not to his mother or Clarissa or his sister Sally, not to Benton or Alfred or William Bell.

Then Mary Ann says, "You'd of done better with Annie's cake. It's chiffon. Just look at Uncle Benton over there. Ain't he a sight?"

Benton, who bid on Annie's cake when it was plain that Henry wouldn't, is sitting cross-legged on the ground, taking dainty bites. Annie is sitting beside him, looking glum. He spears each little piece of cake with his fork and holds it up to the sunlight, twirling it on the fork's tines, squinting at it, as if it were a precious gem. Let him stay here, Henry thinks. Let him stay at home and eat fancy cakes. Henry holds a wedge of pound cake in his hands. He bites off a mouthful, imagining already the taste and weight of hardtack.

"Pound cake suits me fine," he says, not caring that crumbs are tumbling from his mouth, sticking to his chin, falling to his shirt front.

Mary Ann takes the handkerchief she has folded into the pocket of her dress and gently wipes the cake crumbs from Henry's face. She's careful not to let the raised stitches of the embroidery scratch him. He sticks out his chin just the slightest bit so she can clean it. Suddenly she's overcome by how he gives himself over to her as if they've been married for years.

Something about this intimacy strikes Henry, too, and before he knows it, he's telling her his secret. "I'm going off tonight," he says. "Going off to Lancaster to join up."

Mary Ann's heart races. "Your daddy," she says.

"He won't know," says Henry. "Not 'til it's too late."

Mary Ann looks out across the grove to the couples who are lazing now. Some of the men have lain back on the grass, their hands behind their heads. The women sit demurely, their legs tucked under them, hidden beneath the swirls of their skirts. Henry's mother and father are there, and Alfred and Sally, and

Clarissa and William, and Grandpa and Grandma Ridgley. The wheat has been threshed, the hay is almost in. Everyone is alive and well and thankful for this splendid day. A lone crow calls from overhead, but not even that screech can disturb the men and women at rest in the grove. Even Annie has started to giggle. Something Benton has said has tickled her.

"I won't tell anyone," Mary Ann says.

And that's when Henry knows. He knows that whatever lies ahead of him, he'll play this moment over and over in his head: he and Mary Ann in the shade, sealing secrets, while the leaves shiver above them. He doesn't dare say, or even think, the word "love," nor does she. But that's what's blossoming inside them, unfolding as delicately as the pink-tinged petals of blackberry blooms, tickling their chests, their throats, their tongues.

They have no idea that over a hundred years later, I'll try to imagine their story—my great-grandparents—a story that begins the day Jonathan Inyart dies and leaves Clarissa a widow and Mary Ann to grow to be this girl who can promise herself to Henry Martin with that simple vow, "I won't tell."

The crow calls once more and then wheels off across the sky. Mary Ann closes her eyes and listens to the voices in the grove. How low they are, how far away they seem. She wonders how long it will be before she sees Henry again. She won't even allow herself to think that he might die in the war. He doesn't speak, but she knows he's there. She can hear his breathing, can feel ever so lightly against her arm the tickle of his shirt sleeve. She thinks of her father's fiddle and how, if he were still alive, he would play it at her wedding. She remembers the chant from the hayfield: "One I love, two I love, three I love, I say." She'll count to four, and there he'll be—Henry Martin—hers now, at least for this afternoon, for this glorious, glorious day.

I have seen only that one photograph of them, the one taken late in their lives, sitting side by side in chairs on a wooden walkway outside their house. They look so old, it seems impossible that they could have once been young, but they were.

Imagine them in the grove, content to let the afternoon lengthen, and the sun dip below the tree line, and the light dim until they must rise, as do the others, everyone moving now toward home, toward the night of rest and dream and, if God wills, the morrow. Another day, and all it brings.

Leave them to whatever secrets of the heart they protected through the years. Leave them, moving through the dark, not speaking, enchanted and terrified, staring into what has just become the rest of their lives.

SONYA HUBER

Excerpt from
"The Promise of Power"

Opa Nobody

see Heina as a boy-man caught in a swirling torrent. War's burdens pushed many Germans to raise their voices and their weapons against the government. Putting myself in Heina's shoes, I hear voices from above, the confusing tumult of men and women making plans as a deafening backdrop to the daily challenge of finding food for three meals.

Heina clutched a small sack of potatoes. Men and women passing on the street corner prodded him with their shoulders and elbows. Where was Papa? He'd been here just a moment ago, haggling over the price of potatoes at a black-market stand. These hard-bargain potatoes looked like shriveled dead people's toes, but they were potatoes, after all. For four weeks that April it's quite possible the Buschmann family had eaten nothing but turnips, as the "Turnip Winter" of 1916–17 forced the inventiveness of fried turnip cutlets. There—from the direction of the tobacco shop came Papa's embarrassing Buschmann laugh-howl. Papa stood on the steps next to Guido Heiland, the charismatic miner who'd come to Marl in 1912 to organize the SPD.

"Hamburg and Bremen have formed Workers' and Soldiers' Councils!" Heiland yelled, cupping his hands against his mouth to broadcast the news. "Comrades, join us tonight at the hall, 8:00. We must plan, or the revolution will start without us!"

The shouts of response and assent rose up like a wave. Heina strained on tiptoe to see. He leaned forward and his paper sack ripped. Potatoes tumbled onto the cobblestones, and he squatted down to scoop them into his jacket pockets. One rolled off into the gutter. He angled through the crowd and crept toward the tobacco shop, locating Papa in the crowd.

"When the revolution gets here, we'll finally get the miners' issues settled—and we'll win!" boomed Papa.

Heina squeezed next to Papa and lifted the flap of Papa's jacket pocket, thinking to deposit the rest of the potatoes without interrupting Papa's conversations. Quick as a shot Papa's strong hand snapped down and caught Heina's wrist in a vice grip.

"Heina!" he hissed. "You don't sneak up on a war veteran like that. I thought you were a pickpocket or a cop."

Heina held out a potato. "I've got to put these somewhere, Papa. That sack busted."

As the shouting rang on around him, Papa looked quickly to the left and right and nudged a blond man with a handlebar mustache. "Comrade Franks," he said, "let my son use your handkerchief." Franks flourished his wrinkled red hankie. Papa tied the potatoes in a bundle.

"Go give these to your mother. Tell her . . ." Papa stopped and considered. "Tell her it looks like revolution is about to break. Ask her to come to the hall with some supper."

Three days later, November 9, 1918, the German Revolution exploded. Papa announced over dinner that the Kaiser, embattled in Berlin and unable to control the strikes and protests in every corner of the country, had abdicated.

"Who's in power, then?" Jupp asked. He leaned over his soup, his curly hair falling in front of his eyes. There was no school, no work. Everyone was on holiday.

"We are," said Papa, "so finish your food, because this is history. We'll see the end of war before the week is through." Papa leaned back and laughed, his eyes bright as stars. "The munitions workers in Kiel decided they've had enough. Boom, a strike!" He smacked the table hard, and the plates rang like bells. "The soldiers coming back from the front are sick of war, hungry and armed: good people to have on our side."

Would Papa and Mama never get done with their soup? Finish

up and let's go! Heina had wanted to leave the house last night, but Papa said it was too dangerous after dark. Instead Heina had stood at the open window, listening to the street noises of yelling and chanting, the cracking of a fire, rifle shots of warning, and late at night a crowd running down the street singing a revolutionary song in laughing voices.

In one lifetime Heina saw three German governments crumble into dust. In 1990 the Berlin Wall disintegrated piece by piece, and two cocoons ripped open as living creatures mingled and touched each other's faces after what seemed an eternal separation. Each subway train in Berlin stopped at every station, a prosaic sea change. No more would western trains zoom past a bleak fluorescent blur of communism, no more would eastern trains halt in midtrack and reverse. I rode the Berlin trains that fall as a student, grateful to live this history.

Even the most jaded Berlin cynic in a black turtleneck stood at the spontaneous gatherings and mumbled in time to the chants: "Unser Deutschland," our Germany. To an outsider, this might have seemed a frightening refrain of German nationalism, but at the time it sounded only a long-buried hope from Heina's era that Germany might forge a path determined by direct democracy. At that moment in the fall of 1990 all questions could be asked. Some wondered if the fall of the wall meant West Germany could also remake itself, if the conservative government led by Chancellor Kohl would crumble in the face of the people's desire to form a completely new country out of east and west.

Returning one night from an evening at a German pub, we rode an old East German train that rose on elevated tracks from an underground station. Flames leapt from the street below. A house on fire or a chemical explosion? The old East German subway car had no safety controls on its doors, so my classmate Lewis heaved on the brass handle to force open the door as we sped above the fire.

"Look!" he screamed against the wind, the light of the flames reflecting in his glasses. "It's the Autonomen. Holy shit!" The Autonomen, or the Autonomous, was a long-standing and loosely organized band of anarchists in Berlin. To take direct action against the housing shortage in West Berlin, the anarchists had transformed vacant buildings into vast squatter communities, often refurbishing walls, pirating electricity, and performing wild and fanciful decorating schemes. They would soon spread eastward, reclaiming the empty spaces of the other Berlin.

"The street at Kreuzberger Platz is dug up . . . They're dropping huge pieces of pavement on the cop cars!" Lewis yelled. "Get up! You've got to see this!"

I grabbed a brass pole near the door as the wind blew my hair over my eyes. Fire exploded below at a barricade near a police car. The street was furrowed like a plowed field. Orange fire streaked down from a balcony against the blue night. Lewis braced himself against the open doors, filling the car with cold and the light of fire. As we rolled away I had to repeat to myself what I had seen to make sure I had not imagined it. In three months I would see the flaming Dumpsters of the antiwar protests in Minneapolis. On both nights I stood stunned at these acts that were simply not allowed and therefore technically invisible, unseeable. I realized how much momentum and anger it would take for someone like me to propel myself beyond the realm of normal expectations.

Standing at that window, Heina felt his old personality dissolve. His lungs expanded, and even the flesh that helped him breathe seemed to be infused with freedom. People like Papa had seized the country for themselves, which meant no one was Kaiser and yet everyone was Kaiser. The spd's plans on paper would sketch themselves on the earth: the unions would run the factories and mines, and no one would ever stomp on Heina's toes or scream in his face at work again. Maybe bosses at work would be elected, there would be potatoes to eat, and workers would get vacation time for hiking. Maybe it meant an end forever to that taken-hostage feeling of knowing the bigwigs and industrialists could wage war for as long as they wanted. It meant that the warm feeling in his Worker Youth meetings would spread out and flow through the streets.

The Buschmann family walked toward the old town center, and Mama Lina pulled at the boys' collars to keep them near. Miners and factory workers stood at street corners with their arms crossed, some cradling rifles. They looked like rambunctious children as they beamed with smiles and nodded at everyone who passed. Heina saw an unaccustomed splash of red from the newsstand. Overnight, the *Daily Spectator* had become the *Red Flag*, and the headline read, "German Republic Declared!"

They stood for hours, the whole day, shoulder to shoulder in the town square behind the church. The crowd listened to speeches beneath the red banner, and Heina tucked his hands in his armpits to keep warm in the early evening chill. Men and women ran around the edges of the crowd to pull each other into urgent conversations in the city hall, now occupied by the Workers' and Soldiers' Council of Marl. Sandwiches and rolls were handed through the crowd as the sun glared behind the city building. Party leaders rushed into a meeting. An hour later a line of men and women strode out onto the stage, some with determined gazes and others unable to hold back broad smiles.

A woman called out, "Comrades! I present to you the newly appointed Workers' and Soldiers' Council of Marl-Hüls!" Heina scanned the faces and recognized many from SPD functions and from meetings around his parents' kitchen table. Impressive—about half the group came from the new Independent Social Democratic Party. Heina applauded with the crowd until his palms were sore, but a small feeling of disappointment curled in his chest.

Trying to make a joke of it, he leaned over to his mother, who was scowling intently. "Mama," Heina said. "I'd have voted for Papa, wouldn't you?"

"Papa has a position," she said. "He's one of the new local administrators. He helped the committee get organized." I'd come across this fact—that Heinrich had been a key administrator in the revolutionary government—in a slim paperback volume on the history of Marl, and I might have missed its significance entirely had I not known what upheaval gripped Germany in these months. I imagine that Lina started her analyzing and murmuring, explaining the factions represented by each person on the committee. Heina nodded and pretended to follow Mama's detailed analysis, but squatted down to reach quickly for a pebble near his shoe. He tucked it into his pocket, thinking that some day he would show his children this stone and tell them about the moment it stood for.

Papa pushed through the crowd to reach them. "Heina—listen, we need a favor from you."

"*Schatz*, sweetheart, it's getting late," Mama said to Papa. "There's a curfew, and Heina's not yet seventeen."

Papa ruffled his moustache with his lip, his gaze firm. "This is man's work. Don't worry, I'll have a soldier bring him home in an hour."

"Man's work," his mother scoffed. "If you'd read August Bebel at all, you'd know it's 'Comrade' now."

Heina clutched the stone in his pocket and tried to assemble his face into a serious, manly look. With a nudge on the shoulder Papa propelled Heina through the crowd on the city hall steps. The city shield above the doorway had been draped in red cloth, and a man with a rifle yelled for people to get back. Maybe the council wanted him to have a role in a decision-making session, maybe even vote as one of the youth leaders! Then someday soon he'd be up on that stage, and Mama would have to nod and give a grudging, quiet smile.

Instead of turning toward the meeting room, Papa led the way toward another door. "Son," he said, "I need you to take one of the bicycles in the courtyard there and go to Meier's Print Shop across town—by the old church and the bridge, *ja*? There will be a bundle of posters. Say you're from the Marl Council. Bring them back here. Okay?"

Heina pushed open the door and wheeled a bicycle toward the road. Papa reappeared with a slip of paper. "In case any of the patrols stops you," he said. "It's got Guido's signature." Papa stood for a second, looking around the courtyard. "You'll remember this day, won't you?" he asked, his eyes misting and shining bright blue in the half-light. Heina's throat tightened.

Love and admiration for his father, for the confusion and excitement, took away his breath. He nodded.

Heina rode from the printers with the flat package of posters balanced against the handlebars, almost hoping a patrol of men with red armbands would stop him so he could show them the paper to prove his official business. He stopped to adjust the load and peeled back the wrapping to look inside the package. "All Citizens of Marl," the text began in large letters. Below the headline ran a list of crimes now punishable by death or imprisonment during this period of upheaval: looting, carrying a gun without permission, and hoarding groceries.

Within weeks the surge of energy in the Workers' and Soldiers' Councils across Germany gave way in some cities to furious infighting as socialist activists laid out their goals for the new republic and saw just how far each would dare move toward revolution. I have no idea where Papa Heinrich stood in these battles. Because he was a miner, I will guess that he continued to take the miners' position, usually more left-wing than that held by many SPD functionaries. I can only imagine the long hours of trying to establish a working Soviet-modeled committee and the heartbreak in watching it deadlock. And I have to imagine him bringing that heartbreak home and transforming it into a silent ache that hung over the family.

"Go and ask your father if he wants a sandwich," Mama said to Jupp, who rolled his eyes with dread.

"Why do I have to be the one to do it?" Jupp pulled himself off the kitchen bench, sighing, then hurried back in. "Papa's coming," he whispered.

Papa leaned into the kitchen, bracing himself against the doorframe. Over the last month he had lost weight and collected new wrinkles under his eyes, exhausted with running back and forth between the miners' co-op, union meetings, and the Workers' Council.

"We asked the council today to formally support the miners' strike," he said. Then in a roar, "They said NO!" His eyes reddened with sadness and rage.

Triumphant red flags still hung from the lampposts, but each day's newspaper brought bad news. The Congress of Workers' and Soldiers' Councils, elected in Berlin, had seated 2 women out of 496 delegates. Mama shook her head grimly, tracing her finger down the newspaper column of names. "Rosa Luxemburg isn't on this list. I'm no Bolshevik, but only an idiot would say she isn't one of the smartest people in the country, man or woman."

Were these the birth pangs of the new republic or the premature death throes? During the last two weeks of 1918 the country seemed poised to plunge into chaos. Two days before Christmas naval officers in Berlin went on strike because they hadn't been paid in weeks. Noske, the new SPD head of police, called in the Kaiser's conservative troops to brutally crush the strike. The SPD press avoided the story, and the far-left papers hurled condemnation and news of a massacre. Moderates flinched in fear as far-left militias began arming against further attacks, and street fighting exploded in Berlin.

Christmas passed with barely a celebration. Three days later the independents, including Rosa Luxemburg, pulled out of the new socialist government to establish the German Communist Party. Local independent socialist groups debated in worried and muted tones whether to move left and declare themselves communists.

Papa sucked on his pipe, leaning over the newspaper-strewn kitchen table. "You can't set this kind of thing—a new country!— in motion and then decide you've had enough. *Nicht wahr*? Is it not true?" He looked up to get confirmation from Lina, who carefully poured bacon grease from the frying pan into the grease canister.

She sighed in annoyance. "Papa, *es reicht schon*. Enough already." He'd been expressing his shock at the communists for two days straight, expecting someone in the house to give him a decent and rational explanation for the split.

Heina didn't know what to think. Depending on which party newspaper you read, each perspective sounded so logical. He began to look forward to the distraction of mindless work, the copying and the ink on his fingers, the rattling of the windows in the drafty Recklinghausen administration building. The Congress in Berlin had decided to keep the old administrative structures in place for now, so Heina still had a job. The banner hanging above the Recklinghausen City Hall still proclaimed the victory of the Workers' Council. Heina wanted to take down the piece of embroidered silk, either to save it as a memento or to shield it, like a hopeful, wide-eyed child, from the reality of the unreliable world.

We rounded a corner on one of Leipzig's cobblestone streets, absorbing the last night in East Germany before the official 1990 German Reunion celebration. Our student group passed a church where a cluster of lit candles sputtered on the curved stone threshold of a doorway. I had seen a similar memorial in Prague: a massive ring of colored candles in a city square, an anonymous memorial to the students in the crushed Prague Spring revolution of 1968–69. The candles in Prague had been set and lit for years, accumulating a multicolored geology of wax rivulets like a foot-tall Bundt cake. The white candles in Leipzig looked naked and new, hard-edged and tall. We stopped to ask what it meant.

"That's for the dead revolution," an older woman said in English, her eyes searching our American faces to gauge whether we might understand. "The people who started the democracy movement didn't want capitalism, but now it's what we'll get. No one wants to celebrate tonight."

In Leipzig's medieval town square a sparse crowd huddled in a light rain. A mostly drunk rock band mouthed a slurred welcome into the microphones and played cover tunes, including "Back in the USSR," like a Disney version of the soundtrack of freedom. The noise echoed against the old pocked and crumbling stone.

My friends and I sported the scruffy hippie look, but we stood out in the crowd in our American-style windbreakers and jeans, every zipper pull and pants pocket screaming a logo. We shouted to each other over the noise of the band, rolled our eyes, debating whether to leave and where to find a bar.

A young guy with bad skin leaned toward us and asked in a shout if we were Americans. One of our group smiled and instinctively lied. "Canadian," he said.

The kid must not have believed him. Pale hands flew toward us, and a few shoves sent one of our group stumbling. We ran, ducked, and shielded our heads as chunks of terra cotta—either broken flower pots or roof tiles—rained around us and smashed on the slick cobblestones. I remember sprinting through the dark down a side street as orange-red shards ricocheted.

They chased us, screaming, "Ausländer raus!"—the skinhead battle cry, Foreigners out. In Germany my complexion was taken to be Turkish and had earned me growled threats and the occasional refusal of service at the rougher sort of bar, but this skirmish attacked our money, our Americanness. We dashed into the train station, arms windmilling, soles slapping concrete as we scanned the lit boards of clacking letters for any train headed west.

Then the roof seemed to cave in: a blast of sound exploded, shaking the ancient glass windows in their casings—like doomsday. Simultaneously the soot-blackened trains all sounded their horns in the shell of the station, a deafening salute to the last midnight in the former East Germany. The sound waves receded, leaving a thick, clogged silence.

An engine huffed. We found a train and slammed our bodies into seats, panting. Get me out of this dark, sooty country, get me out of the past, I wanted to yell, urging the train to move.

I did not know how to navigate a world without the oasis of 7-Elevens and credit cards to save me from whatever midnight trouble might find me. I still don't know what those kids might have done to us because I don't know who they were. Maybe skinheads. Or maybe they just wanted us out of their country so they could have it, briefly, for themselves.

Heina might have told me then that revolutions of every stripe, like people, live and breathe. Like any other living thing, they hold the capacity to mutate, to turn mangy and mean, to take side alleys and lose their way. And I imagine I would have cut my eyes at him, the way a real nineteen-year-old granddaughter might get sarcastic and impatient and then regret it. Heina, I wouldn't have bothered to look for you if I had wanted to watch a marionette show ending with a lesson for children, the homily that making revolution is inherently dangerous and flawed. He would open his mouth, looking for an entry point to reply, frustrated to tell me what I had misunderstood. We both know power is grasped and overthrown, grasped and overthrown. What I want to know is how to live through the pounding of that surf.

Tell me, Opa, which scenario frightened you more in your teenage years: a bloody revolution from the Left, or an orderly and respectable progression of tyranny from the Right? Which of those poor old puppets, worn but still eminently serviceable, cast the more ominous shadow?

In early January 1919 I know only that Heina must have paid close attention to this puppet show as revolutionary charges parried with reaction. A huge street battle raged in Berlin, and the SPD police arrested Rosa Luxemburg and Karl Liebknecht. The communists occupied a newspaper building in protest. In Heina's neighborhood and throughout the county, the right wing reorganized. As Heina walked home from work one evening he may have passed two unfamiliar men with rifles. He nodded in greeting, and they glared back.

"Get on home, son," a man said.

"Why, Comrade?" Heina asked. "What's going on?"

The man abruptly lunged and swung his rifle butt at Heina's thigh. Heina turned and sprinted, the man yelling behind him, "Don't you give me that 'Comrade' shit, you Red!"

Panting, Heina opened the apartment door and ran inside, slamming it behind him. Mama rushed out from the kitchen, forehead knotted at the racket. "Who are those men?" Heina asked.

Papa stood in the kitchen doorway, coughing and wheezing.

"You've met the right-wing militia, the Freikorps. They're patrolling the miners' neighborhoods to keep us in line. Our so-called Revolutionary Council is doing everything it can to appease those thugs."

The next morning before work Heina became mired in a thick crowd gathered around the newspaper stand. The news flew from mouth to ear: Luxemburg and Liebknecht had been shot in Berlin "while attempting to escape."

"How could a person attempt to bust out of the most highly guarded cell in the Berlin jail?" asked a woman clutching a crumpled paper.

The SPD paper offered no clues. Heina opened the independent paper and read, "The prisoners' bodies were found, mutilated, in a drainage ditch."

"The SPD has blood on its hands!" said a boy.

"No, it was the right-wing idiots on the police payroll. Hire the last administration's lackeys, and look what you get," a gruff voice replied.

Heina must have closed his eyes to imagine in that hollow moment the last seconds of Rosa Luxemburg, just a woman named Rosa, who cowered as a man in uniform struck her. Or maybe she was stoic to the end, having prepared herself for this. Who was the man who took the air from the lungs of Germany's Lenin? Did he choke back a retch as the blood of a woman pooled on the stone? Or maybe he felt fully and feverishly alive, a flutter of personal triumph as if he with his own weapon had saved the Fatherland.

With a revolution crumbing and the knife-edge of extremism glinting, a young man of sixteen must have felt the responsibility to act. If my guess is correct and Heina chose this time to rebel against the SPD, there must have been a moment of decision, a first step. Maybe a flyer on the cluttered message board near the door caught his eye: "Young People, the Government, and the War: A lecture and discussion at the Miners' Hall . . ." The meeting was Saturday—tonight—sponsored by the Independent Social Democratic youth group.

That evening Heina made a sandwich for dinner and waved to his mother on his way out. She didn't look up from her newspaper as he passed. Outside the night wind peppered his skin with tiny ice crystals, but he inhaled deeply as he walked. It was good to get his legs moving, to work out some of this energy. Was he nervous that he might see that dark-haired girl from the rally a few months ago? Or maybe he feared the desire and anger in his own heart. Heina had somehow forgotten to mention to Papa that he was headed to this meeting.

Rows of chairs lined the hall's rough wood floor, and the space bustled with warmth and light. Heina shook hands with kids he knew from the SPD youth group and other former SPD activists who'd joined the independents or the Ruhr's first communist groups. They sprawled on the floor and straddled chairs, talking loudly. Heina ran his hand through his hair and laughed over some cynical joke about the SPD government. This scenario, or something like it, was likely, as young people moved left of their parents and toward both the socialists and the communists.

"So, my father—he just can't imagine anything besides the SPD," a guy named Fritz complained. "It's like he's married to it!"

"I think it's our duty to make up our own minds," a girl added.

The conversation turned serious and loud as the young people nodded and confessed their feelings of disillusionment and betrayal. Heina took off his jacket. As he listened to a friend's point about the local SPD, he felt the gentle brush of goose bumps, the realization that this hall was home. Honesty lived here, and so did hope, in the eyes of these young people willing to come out on a Saturday night to talk politics.

The speaker climbed toward the podium, but the din in the hall refused to abate. Squinting through tiny glasses, the speaker began his lecture. Conversations faded reluctantly, and the kids around Heina began to nod in agreement with the speaker, who first laid out what they already knew about the SPD and then analyzed the reasons why the country needed an independent push from the Left.

The question-and-answer session after the lecture threatened to disintegrate. Kids from the new communist youth group stood and invited everyone to join their organization, and someone from the SPD group protested, saying they needed to devise a German and not a Soviet solution. Altogether there were five organizations in attendance vying for membership, with tensions among them barely controlled. The speaker pounded on the podium with a gavel twice, three times, the wood sounding as if it would split.

As the lecture dissolved into clumps of conversation, Heina pulled on his jacket and realized he'd forgotten to eat his sandwich. He unwrapped it and was about to take a bite when he saw the dark-haired girl walking toward him, holding the arm of another young woman. Heina stuffed his sandwich in his pocket.

"Comrade, hello there!" he called out.

She smiled and blushed. "Good evening, Comrade," she said.

They introduced all around, and Heina learned the dark-haired girl was named Elfriede Klejdzinski, but everyone called her Friedchen. I have no idea where my grandparents met—it might well have been earlier in the SPD youth group—but part of me loves the romance of Heina's youthful rebellion twined with infatuation. So I'll leave this moment be.

"What did you think of the lecture?" she asked. The bold raucousness of the meeting seemed to charge the air in the emptying hall, and it made Heina reckless.

"There's lots to discuss, *nicht*? I could walk you home so we can talk about it. If you wouldn't mind." Friedchen's friend grinned and pushed her on the elbow toward Heina.

Near the hall exit, two long tables were scattered with membership forms. A group of kids leaned on their elbows and scratched their names in the blanks, joining the independents. His heart filled with the evening, Heina looked at Friedchen with a daring smile, grabbed a membership card, and printed his name.

Heina, I know that delicious sense of falling in love with the hope of a new family. I dove into the storm surge, though I didn't realize as I approached the surf of radicalism that the first place I'd land was the hospital.

The upheavals for me were not as massive as a German revolution, but maybe the seismic echoes of the Berlin Wall crashing down had started it all. By the time I returned from studying in Germany in late 1990, plans for the first Gulf War had been launched. Back in the United States I threw myself into campus antiwar organizations, working every night to help plan rallies, to edit an antiwar poetry collection, to raise money for a bus trip to Washington DC. The snow and the springtime of 1991 presented a never-ending palindrome of a year that still makes my shoulders knit with remembered worry and overwhelming sadness. Something had to be done. How did one change the course of one's own country?

I spent the next summer in a crowded attic apartment near campus, talking politics and itching with the sadness of a broken dream. Drawing strategy charts and planning timelines for logical campus campaigns had not stopped a war or made a dent on the evening news. Unlike the students who raged on campus in the sixties, our groups with their careful media strategies had remained strangely invisible. We drew thousands to rallies, but then we seemed not to exist. And that stoked my hunger to be heard at any cost.

During the day I traveled the back roads of southeastern Minnesota to interview farmers as part of an internship in environmentally sustainable farming with the Minnesota Department of Agriculture. At night I had sex with my long-haired boyfriend from New York. I subsisted on dense vegan homemade bread, cereal with apple juice instead of milk, and too much coffee. I was hungry and jittery all the time.

One quiet afternoon that summer my boyfriend and I lugged

our bags of dirty clothes into the basement laundry room of a campus dorm. Maybe we joked and tickled each other. I remember that I laughed as I pulled laundry from a dryer. I stood up quickly to put quarters in the machine. I saw spots and sat down, thinking I'd had a simple rush of blood to my head. Somehow I ended up in the hallway outside the laundry room. I must have walked in a swerving line to clear my head. I slid down the wall and found myself pressed to the cool cement floor, eyes closed, unable to catch my breath.

My mind shrank to a small point inside a body that felt as massive and empty as space. The muscles of my chest and throat clenched in a choke, so I gave in and sipped air in thimblefuls. The voices of my boyfriend and someone else shouted to call 911. Those sounds announced an irrelevant crisis, almost funny because it spooled out on the other side of the world. I couldn't seem to open my heavy eyes. Admit it: I didn't want to. The deep black pool beneath my closed eyelids invited me to stay and rest. I remember cold on my skin as a bit of spit trickled down my chin. I imagine that shallow breathing and a lack of oxygen had worked together to shut down my whirring brain.

Depression and exhaustion, those vague words, draw a crayon circle around the symptoms that triggered this moment. The words with their state-of-being *ion* endings present an illusory comfort, describe a problem without providing an answer. On that basement floor I had no experience with depression or admitting I might be "sad," so those forces grabbed me bodily to demand my attention.

In the box of the ambulance with its metallic echo of clambering and chopped words, a knuckling of hard plastic dug into my sternum. The EMTs rubbed this sensitive area as a pain stimulus to shock me awake. It seemed to take too much energy to respond. Maybe they wondered as they yelled my name if I was an overdose case. My boyfriend might have told them herbal tea was the strongest thing I'd consumed that afternoon. In the ER they cut my black Earth First T-shirt down the middle to get to my chest, maybe for CPR. I fought to maintain my safe, dark bubble.

Then a nurse in the ER said softly: "Sonya." I opened my eyes to the sweet kindness in her voice.

I know I spent a few days and nights in the hospital. After the electrodes and monitors and tests, the doctors declared me free of heart problems and epilepsy. They sent me home. That night and the next day I blacked out again and again. My roommates, nineteen and twenty and as mystified as I was, watched helplessly and then had to cart me back to the hospital, where more tests produced no more answers. I quit my job because I was afraid to drive. Mom drove up from Chicago to take me to the Mayo Clinic an hour away, where a short-tempered emergency room resident examined me and dryly commented that this might be "in my head" without providing suggestions for what to do next. I tell myself this was fifteen years ago, that such a strange mind-body split would not happen today, that a woman who could not breathe would at least be handed a pamphlet on panic attacks.

As we drove away from the clinic I repeated two fantasy solutions. Either I had to get in my car, drive somewhere far out west like Wyoming, and get a waitressing job. Or I had to shoot myself. "In My Head" was a seemingly insoluble problem. I didn't know a thing about panic or therapy. Mom next took me to a neurologist in Chicago who did tests and declared me biologically healthy. Mom demanded I see a counselor, which I adamantly refused. I imagined the counselor would tell me to stop being dramatic and to shape up.

That fall I drove back to Minnesota and registered for classes, thinking I would show this humiliating "In My Head" thing who was boss. Before my first class started, I sat on the floor near a bank of payphones in the student center, counting the black blotches fogging my vision and trying to decide whom of my tapped-out friends to call for yet another crisis. I couldn't bother anyone, I was too much of a bother already. My pocket calendar contained a long list of political meetings that made my windpipe fold like origami. Was my to-do list the problem or the solution? Maybe the concrete, real world could reclaim the territory invaded by this problem In My Head.

Crying and scattered, I waited for the blotches to disappear. In these weeks I wrote in my journals only sporadically, so I am not sure what led me to the bold and blind decision to quit school and move alone to Minneapolis. I must have talked this plan over with friends, laid out the steps, but looking back, I am amazed that my escape from My Head was to move sixty miles away where I knew no one and had no job. I assume it was the closest I could imagine then to my Wyoming fantasy.

After I'd made my plans I walked to the college treasurer's office in the first floor of an ornate red brick building off the campus quad.

"I need to see the tuition check from my mom. She needs the check number," I said to the receptionist. She directed me to a bookkeeper, who located the check with surprising speed and handed it over with a smile and a slightly baffled look.

I took the check with my mother's careful slanting signature and turned away. I pushed open the heavy wooden doors, bursting into the crisp blue of a Minnesota fall morning, and I ripped the check into tiny pieces.

Those tuition checks had delivered me from small-town Illinois into a kind of Disneyland of trust, a place where young adults had free rein, could learn the skills and boldness necessary to seize their parents' checks. Sending me to that fancy hothouse of academia and activism equipped me with the skills I needed to leave it. But I was also a young woman aware of consequences and the bottom line, needing to rescue a check before it cleared, not a girl able to pack her car and leave school with hair flying and a foot pounding the gas pedal. If I quit school, I would take care of the details first.

Heina, this moment would probably have broken your heart in the same way it broke my mom's. She'd been lured to immigrate to the United States by a seedy relative's promise of a college education that never materialized. Instead she earned her GED after three kids were born. To thank her for her dream denied, I handed back my ticket to college so I could go hunt down my sanity in Minneapolis. And to top it off, I wanted her to understand, to be happy for me.

Your papa may have felt that betrayal, too, if it's true that you left the safety and respectability of the SPD he'd given his life to build. At the time, Heina, I imagine that the lure of finding your own life was irresistible. And I understand that necessity.

SOURCE ACKNOWLEDGMENTS

*All selections in this volume are reprinted by
permission of the University of Nebraska Press.*

"Winter 1997," from *Fault Line* by Laurie Alberts © 2004 by Laurie Alberts.

"The Boys of Summer," from *Pieces from Life's Crazy Quilt* by Marvin V.
Arnett © 2003 by Marvin V. Arnett.

"The Weight of Spoons," from *Songs from the Black Chair: A Memoir of
Mental Interiors* by Charles Barber © 2005 by the Board of Regents of
the University of Nebraska.

"Alternatives, 1979," from *Out of Joint: A Private and Public Story of Arthritis* by Mary Felstiner © 2005 by Mary Felstiner.

"Good, Alright, Fine," from *Falling Room* by Eli Hastings © 2006 by N. Eli
Hastings.

"The Promise of Power" (excerpt), from *Opa Nobody* by Sonya Huber ©
2008 by the Board of Regents of the University of Nebraska.

"The Second Trimester" (excerpt), from *Hannah and the Mountain: Notes
toward a Wilderness Fatherhood* by Jonathan Johnson © 2005 by the
Board of Regents of the University of Nebraska.

"Winter" (excerpt), from *Local Wonders: Seasons in the Bohemian Alps* by
Ted Kooser © 2002 by the University of Nebraska Press.

"Acting," from *Bigger than Life: A Murder, a Memoir* by Dinah Lenney ©
2007 by the Board of Regents of the University of Nebraska.

"Not Coming Out," from *What Becomes You* by Aaron Raz Link and Hilda
Raz © 2007 by Aaron Raz Link and Hilda Raz.

"One I Love, Two I Love," from *Turning Bones* by Lee Martin © 2003 by
Lee Martin.

"Son of Mr. Green Jeans," from *Between Panic and Desire* by Dinty W.
Moore © 2008 by Dinty W. Moore.

"The New Kitchen," from *Thoughts from a Queen-Sized Bed* by Mimi
Schwartz © 2002 by Mimi Schwartz.

"Fortuna," from *The Fortune Teller's Kiss* by Brenda Serotte © 2006 by the
Board of Regents of the University of Nebraska.

"'Long Live the Red Terror!'" from *Gang of One: Memoirs of a Red Guard* by Fan Shen © 2004 by Fan Shen.

"Moving Water, Tucson," from *Just Breathe Normally* by Peggy Shumaker © 2007 by the Board of Regents of the University of Nebraska.

"And There Fell a Great Star," from *Scraping By in the Big Eighties* by Natalia Rachel Singer © 2004 by the Board of Regents of the University of Nebraska.

"A Measure of Acceptance," from *In the Shadow of Memory* by Floyd Skloot © 2003 by Floyd Skloot.

"Hard Luck Suit," from *Secret Frequencies: A New York Education* by John Skoyles © 2003 by the Board of Regents of the University of Nebraska.

Untitled excerpt from *Phantom Limb* by Janet Sternburg © 2002 by Janet Sternburg.

LAURIE ALBERTS teaches fiction and creative nonfiction at Vermont College and is the author of three novels, *Lost Daughters*, *The Price of Land in Shelby*, and *Tempting Fate*, and a second memoir, *Between Revolutions: An American Romance with Russia*. Her work has won numerous prizes including a Michener Award for the Novel and an American Fiction award.

MARVIN V. ARNETT is a retired manager who worked in the federal service for more than twenty-five years and is a former vice president of the National Organization of Blacks in Government. Arnett is a member of the Society of Midland Authors and lives in Southfield, Michigan, where she lectures and tutors.

CHARLES BARBER is currently a senior executive at the Connection, an innovative social services agency, and a lecturer in psychiatry at the Yale University School of Medicine. He is the author of *Comfortably Numb: How Psychiatry is Medicating a Nation* and is a regular blogger on the Huffington Post.

MARY FELSTINER is a professor of history at San Francisco State University, the author of *To Paint Her Life: Charlotte Salomon in the Nazi Era*, and the recipient of the American Historical Association Joan Kelly Memorial Prize in Women's History.

ELI HASTINGS is a Seattle native who received an MFA in creative nonfiction from the University of North Carolina at Wilmington and has been published in numerous literary journals. He has worked in food service and retail sales, as a creative-writing teacher and a manual laborer, and as a Get-Out-the-Vote coordinator and a health care and utilities campaign coordinator.

SONYA HUBER is an assistant professor in the Department of Writing and Linguistics at Georgia Southern University. She is the author of many short stories, essays, and poems appearing in journals such as *Fourth Genre*, *Sub-Lit*, and *Kaleidoscope*.

JONATHAN JOHNSON is a poet and author whose work has appeared in various literary magazines and in *The Best American Poetry*. He is the author of *Mastodon, 80% Complete*, a book of poems.

TED KOOSER, Presidential Professor of the University of Nebraska, is a former U.S. poet laureate and winner of the Pulitzer Prize in Poetry. In addition to his many volumes of poetry, he is the author of *The Poetry Home Repair Manual: Practical Advice for Beginning Poets* and the coauthor (with Steve Cox) of *Writing Brave and Free: Encouraging Words for People Who Want to Start Writing*, both available in Bison Books editions.

DINAH LENNEY received her BA from Yale and a Certificate of Acting from the Neighborhood Playhouse School. She holds an MFA from the Bennington Writing Seminars, and her essays and reviews have appeared in national journals and papers including the *New York Times* and the *Los Angeles Times*. Continuing to work on stage and screen, Dinah played Nurse Shirley on NBC's critically acclaimed series *ER* for fourteen seasons. She teaches acting as well as writing at UCLA and at USC and is the coauthor of *Acting for Young Actors*. She lives in Los Angeles with her husband and their two children.

AARON RAZ LINK, a writer, performing artist, curator, and historian of science, is the director of the Museum of Nature in Portland, Oregon.

LEE MARTIN is director of the creative-writing program at the Ohio State University and the author of the Pulitzer Prize finalist *The Bright Forever*. He is also the author of *From Our House*, which is available in a Bison Books edition. He has won a fellowship from the National Endowment for the Arts, the Mary McCarthy Prize in Short Fiction, a Lawrence Foundation Award, and the Glenna Luschei Prize.

DINTY W. MOORE is a professor of English at Ohio University and the author of several books including *The Truth of the Matter: Art and Craft in Creative Nonfiction* and *The Accidental Buddhist: Mindfulness, Enlightenment, and Sitting Still*.

HILDA RAZ, a professor of English and women's and gender studies at the University of Nebraska–Lincoln, is the Glenna Luschei Endowed Editor of *Prairie Schooner* and the author of the poetry collections *Trans* and *What Happens*, both available in Bison Books editions.

MIMI SCHWARTZ is the author of five books including *Good Neighbors, Bad Times* (Nebraska, 2008) and *Writing True: The Art and Craft of Creative Nonfiction* (with Sondra Perl). Her essays are widely anthologized and five of them are Notables in *Best American Essays*. A professor emerita at Richard Stockton College in New Jersey, Schwartz teaches workshops in memoir and creative nonfiction nationwide and abroad.

BRENDA SEROTTE is a poet and an adjunct professor at Nova Southeastern University in Fort Lauderdale, Florida. Her poetry and prose have appeared in numerous publications such as *Atlanta Review*, *Kit-Kat Review*, *Quarter after Eight: A Journal of Prose and Commentary*, and *Fourth Genre*, from which her essay "Contagious" was nominated for a Pushcart Prize.

FAN SHEN, who hails from the People's Republic of China, is a professor at Rochester Community and Technical College in Minnesota. He has published three translated books and numerous articles in both Chinese and English.

PEGGY SHUMAKER is professor emerita of English at the University of Alaska–Fairbanks and the author of several books of poetry including *Blaze* and *Underground Rivers*. She teaches in the Rainier Writing Workshop at Pacific Lutheran University.

NATALIA RACHEL SINGER is a professor of English at St. Lawrence University and the coeditor of *Living North Country: Essays on Life and Landscapes in Northern New York*.

FLOYD SKLOOT is the author of four novels, most recently *Patient 002*; six collections of poetry, including *The End of Dreams*; a collection of essays; and three other memoirs. He is the winner of three Pushcart Prizes, the most recent for his essay "The Voice of the Past," which appears in *The Wink of the Zenith* (Nebraska, 2008). *In the Shadow of Memory* was named a Best of 2003 nonfiction title by the *Chicago Tribune* and was a 2003 Barnes & Noble Discover Great New Writers Award nonfiction finalist. His memoir *A World of Light* (Nebraska, 2005) was a *New York Times Book Review* Editor's Choice selection for 2005.

JOHN SKOYLES is the author of a collection of essays and four books of poetry, including *Definition of the Soul* and *The Situation*. He teaches at Emerson College in Boston and is the poetry editor for *Ploughshares*.

JANET STERNBURG is a widely published poet and essayist whose books include *The Writer on Her Work*. A faculty member of the California Institute for the Arts, she is also a photographer whose work appears in private and museum collections.

In the American Lives Series

Fault Line
by Laurie Alberts

Pieces from Life's Crazy Quilt
by Marvin V. Arnett

Songs from the Black Chair
A Memoir of Mental Illness
by Charles Barber

Driving with Dvořák
Essays on Memory and Identity
by Fleda Brown

Searching for Tamsen Donner
by Gabrielle Burton

American Lives
A Reader
edited by Alicia Christensen
introduced by Tobias Wolff

Out of Joint
A Private & Public Story of Arthritis
by Mary Felstiner

Falling Room
by Eli Hastings

Opa Nobody
by Sonya Huber

Hannah and the Mountain
Notes toward a Wilderness Fatherhood
by Jonathan Johnson

Local Wonders
Seasons in the Bohemian Alps
by Ted Kooser

Bigger than Life
A Murder, a Memoir
by Dinah Lenney

What Becomes You
by Aaron Raz Link and Hilda Raz

Turning Bones
by Lee Martin

In Rooms of Memory
Essays
by Hilary Masters

Between Panic and Desire
by Dinty W. Moore

Thoughts from a Queen-Sized Bed
by Mimi Schwartz

The Fortune Teller's Kiss
by Brenda Serotte

Gang of One
Memoirs of a Red Guard
by Fan Shen

Just Breathe Normally
by Peggy Shumaker

Scraping By in the Big Eighties
by Natalia Rachel Singer

In the Shadow of Memory
by Floyd Skloot

Secret Frequencies
A New York Education
by John Skoyles

Phantom Limb
by Janet Sternburg

Yellowstone Autumn
A Season of Discovery in a
Wondrous Land
by W. D. Wetherell

To order or obtain more
information on these
or other University of
Nebraska Press titles, visit
www.nebraskapress.unl.edu.